BAD MACHINERY

THE CASE OF THE TEAM SPIRIT

AN ONI PRESS PUBLICATION

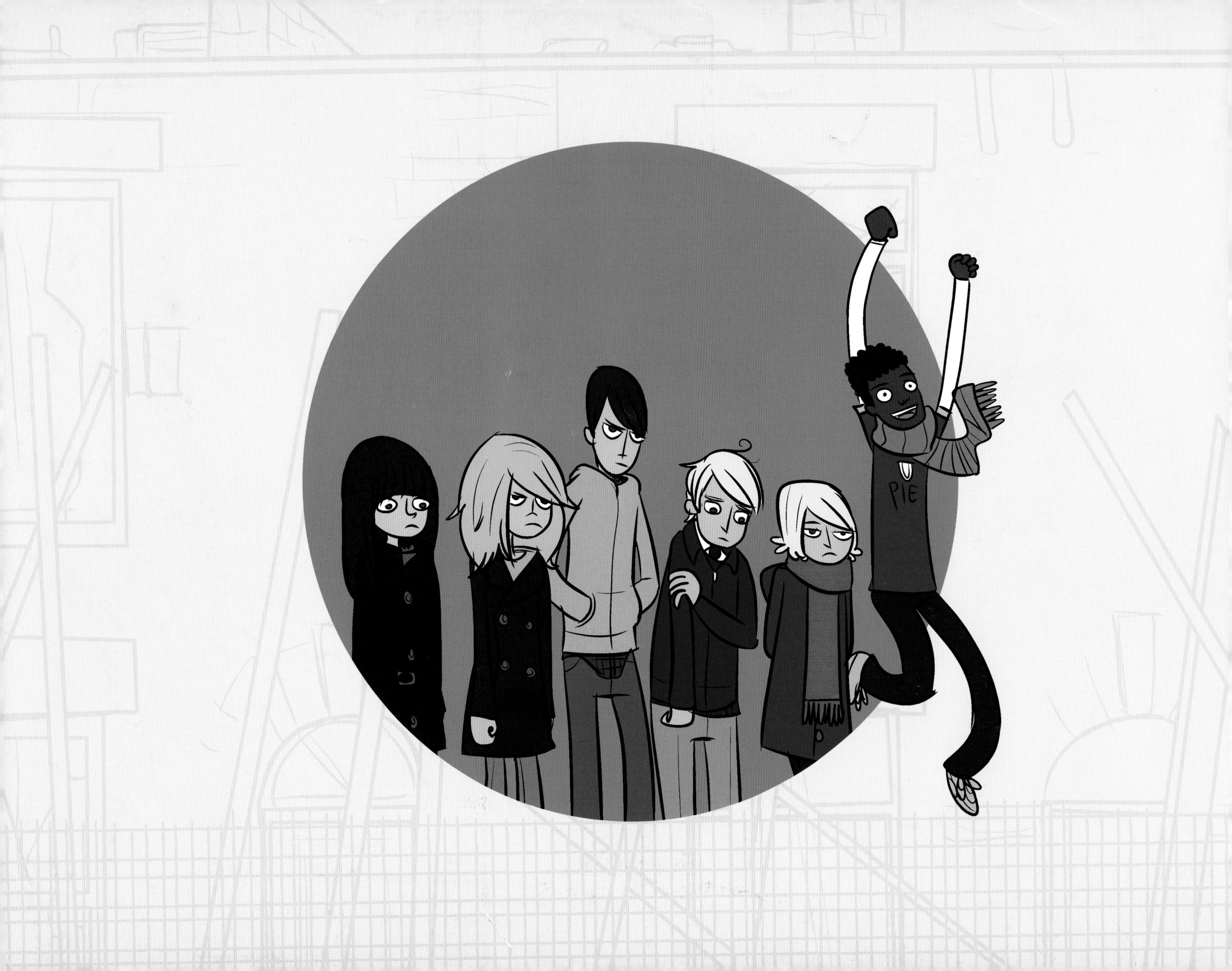
PIE

BAD MACHINERY

THE CASE OF THE TEAM SPIRIT

By
John Allison

Edited by
James Lucas Jones & Jill Beaton

Designed by
Keith Wood & Jason Storey

Oni Press, Inc.

publisher, Joe Nozemack
editor in chief, James Lucas Jones
art director, Keith Wood
director of marketing, Tom Shimmin
director of business development, George Rohac
editor, Jill Beaton
editor, Charlie Chu
digital prepress lead, Troy Look
graphic designer, Jason Storey
administrative assistant, Robin Herrera

Oni Press, Inc.
1305 SE Martin Luther King Jr. Blvd.
Suite A
Portland, OR 97214

onipress.com
badmachinery.com

Become our fan on Facebook: facebook.com/onipress
Follow us on Twitter: @onipress
onipress.tumblr.com

ISBN: 978-1-62010-084-4

Library of Congress Control Number: 2012953355

First Edition: March 2013

20 19 18 17 16 15 14 13 12 11 10 9 8 7 6 5 4 3 2 1

Printed in China.

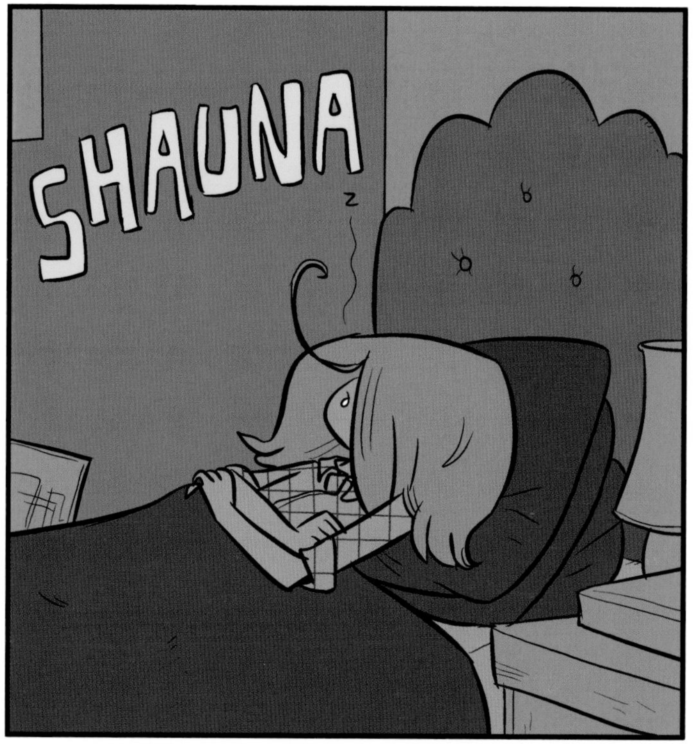
SHAUNA
z
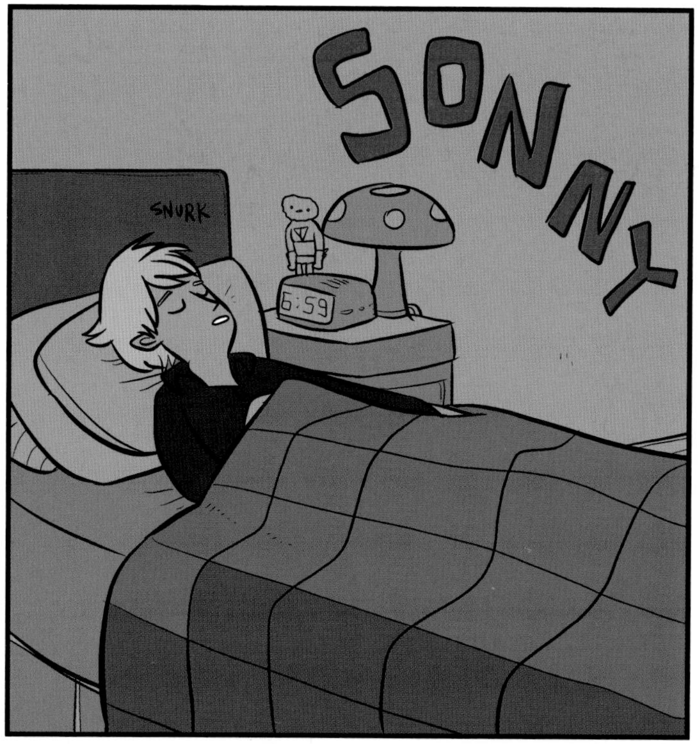
SONNY
SNURK
6:59
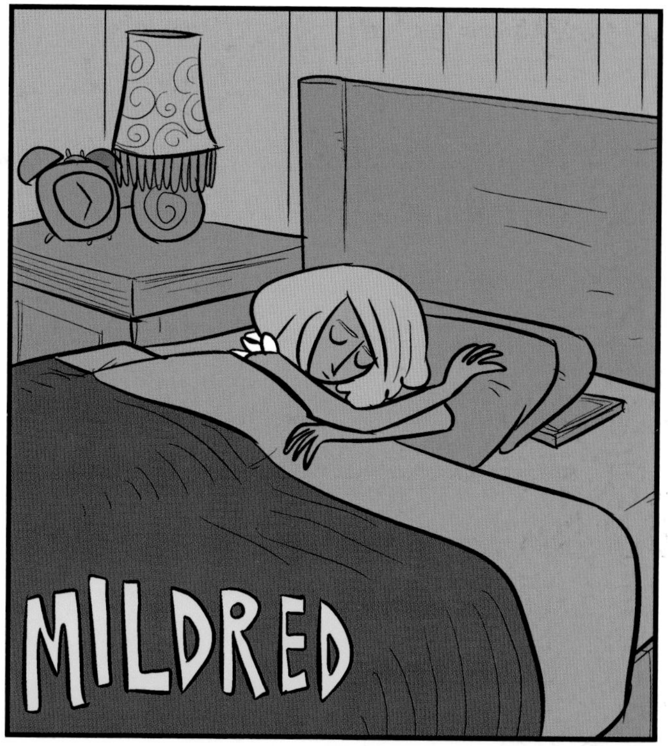
MILDRED
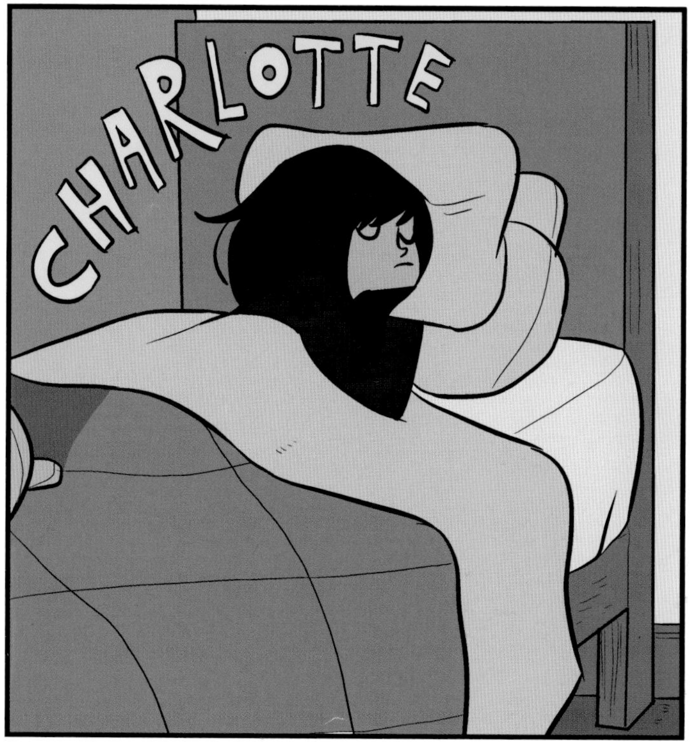
CHARLOTTE
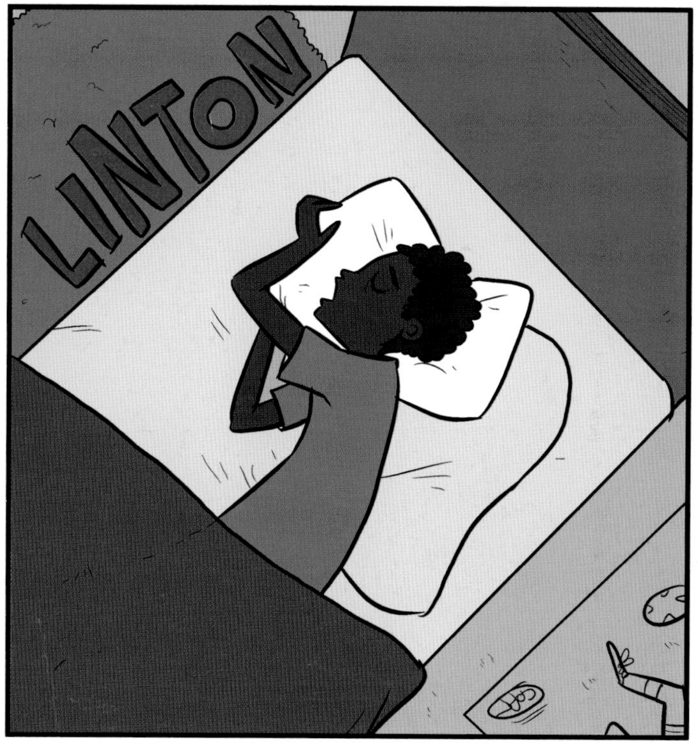
LINTON
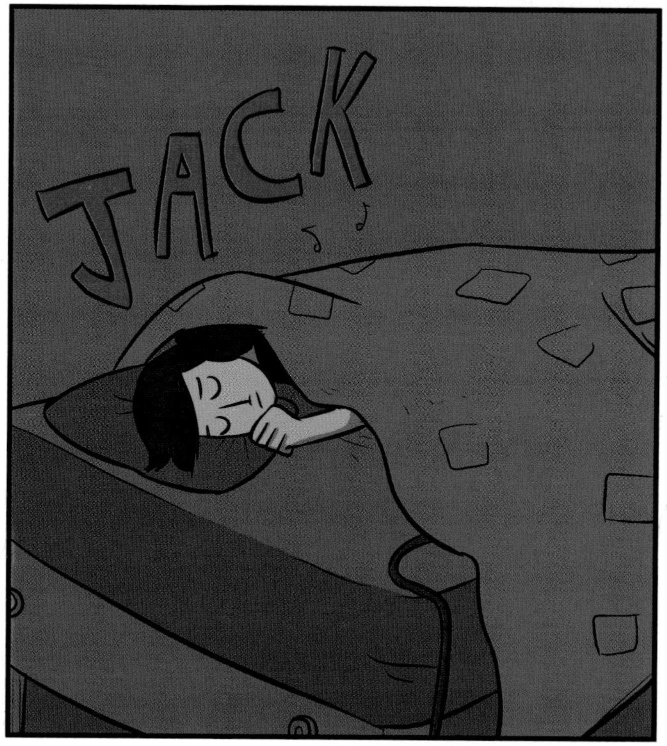
JACK

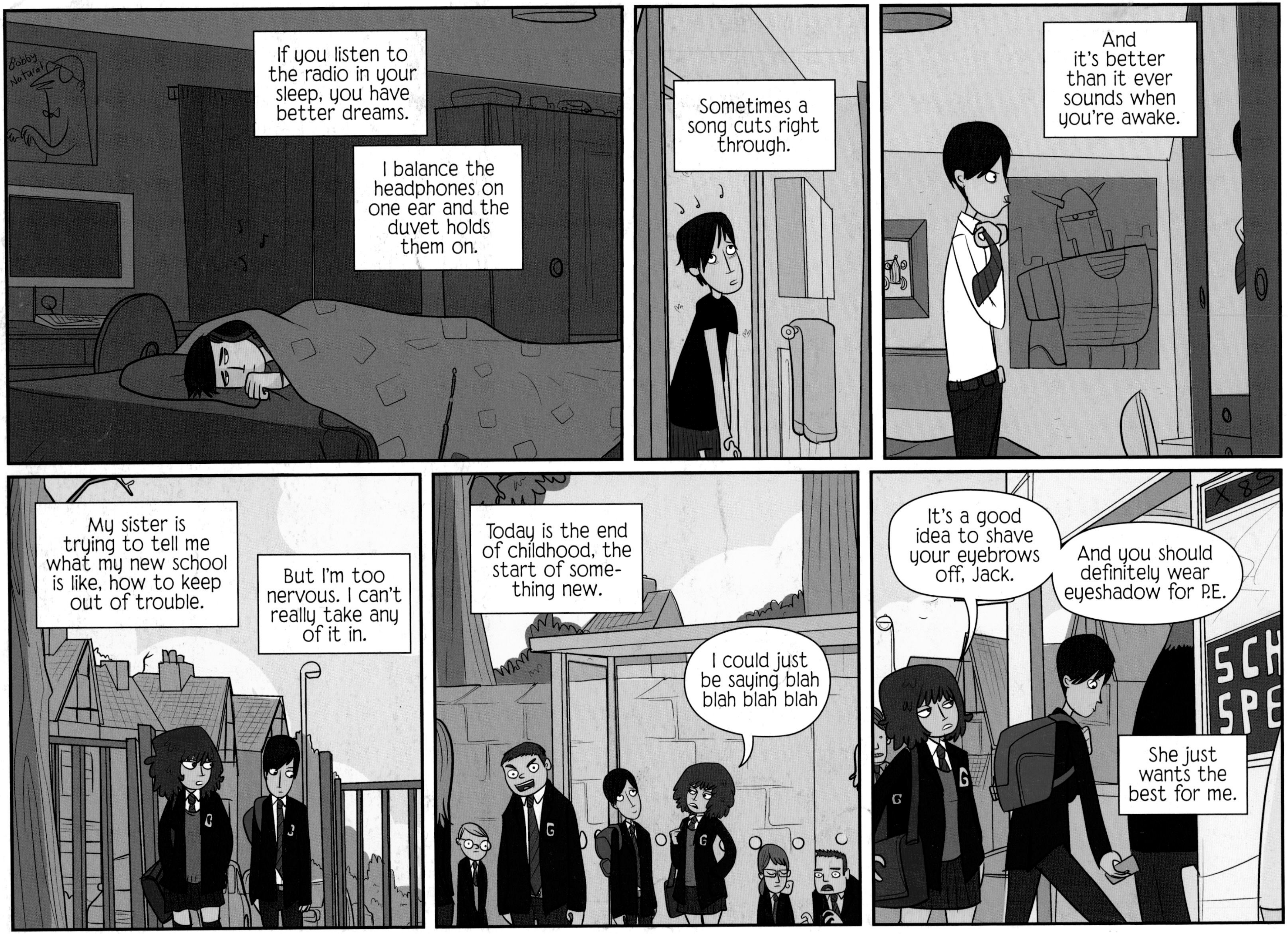
If you listen to the radio in your sleep, you have better dreams.
I balance the headphones on one ear and the duvet holds them on.
Sometimes a song cuts right through.
And it's better than it ever sounds when you're awake.
My sister is trying to tell me what my new school is like, how to keep out of trouble.
But I'm too nervous. I can't really take any of it in.
Today is the end of childhood, the start of something new.
I could just be saying blah blah blah blah
It's a good idea to shave your eyebrows off, Jack.
And you should definitely wear eyeshadow for P.E.
She just wants the best for me.

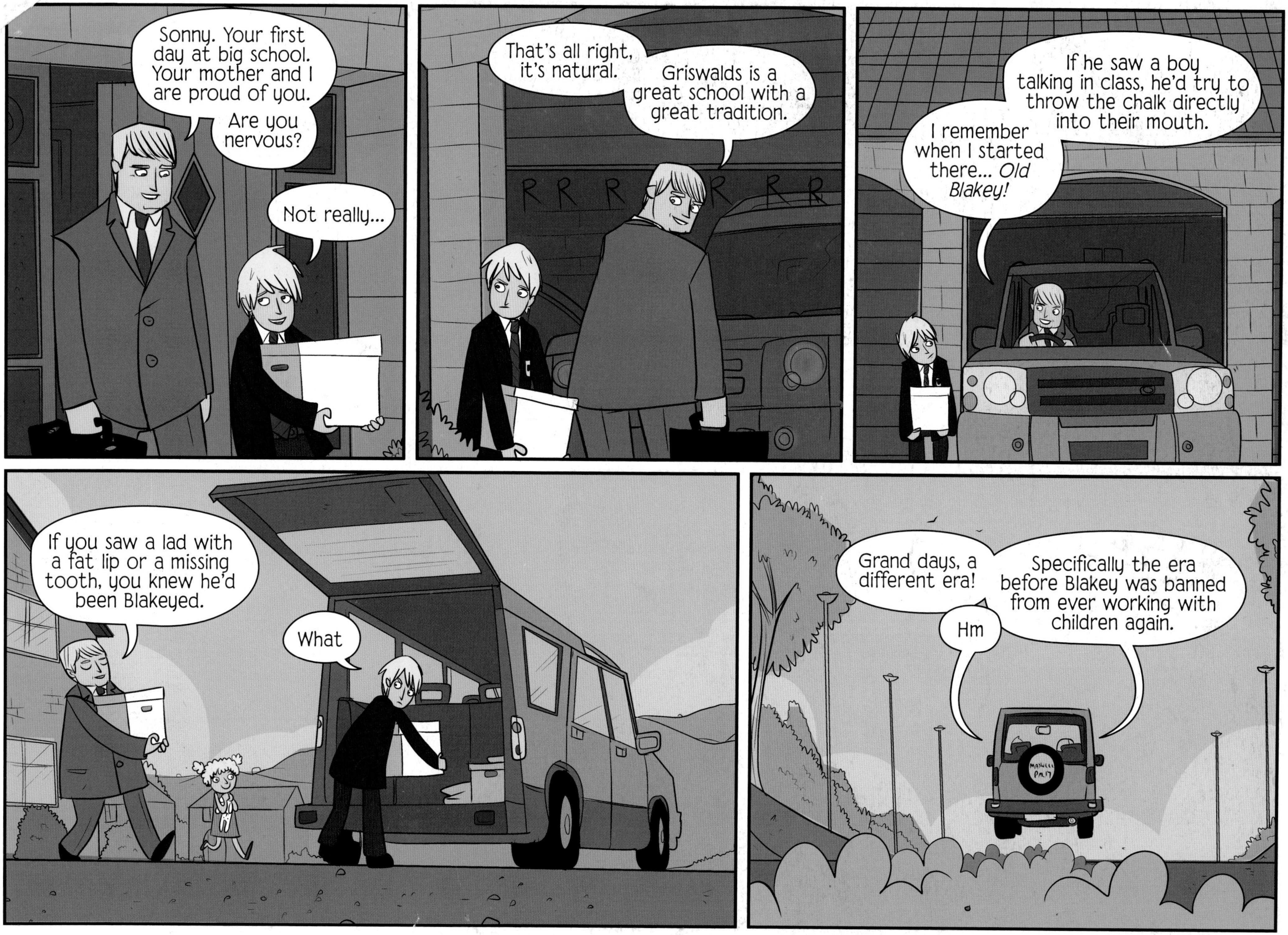
Sonny. Your first day at big school. Your mother and I are proud of you.
Are you nervous?
Not really...
That's all right, it's natural.
Griswalds is a great school with a great tradition.
RRRRRR
I remember when I started there... *Old Blakey!*
If he saw a boy talking in class, he'd try to throw the chalk directly into their mouth.
If you saw a lad with a fat lip or a missing tooth, you knew he'd been Blakeyed.
What
Grand days, a different era!
Hm
Specifically the era before Blakey was banned from ever working with children again.

Bad Machinery, Volume One

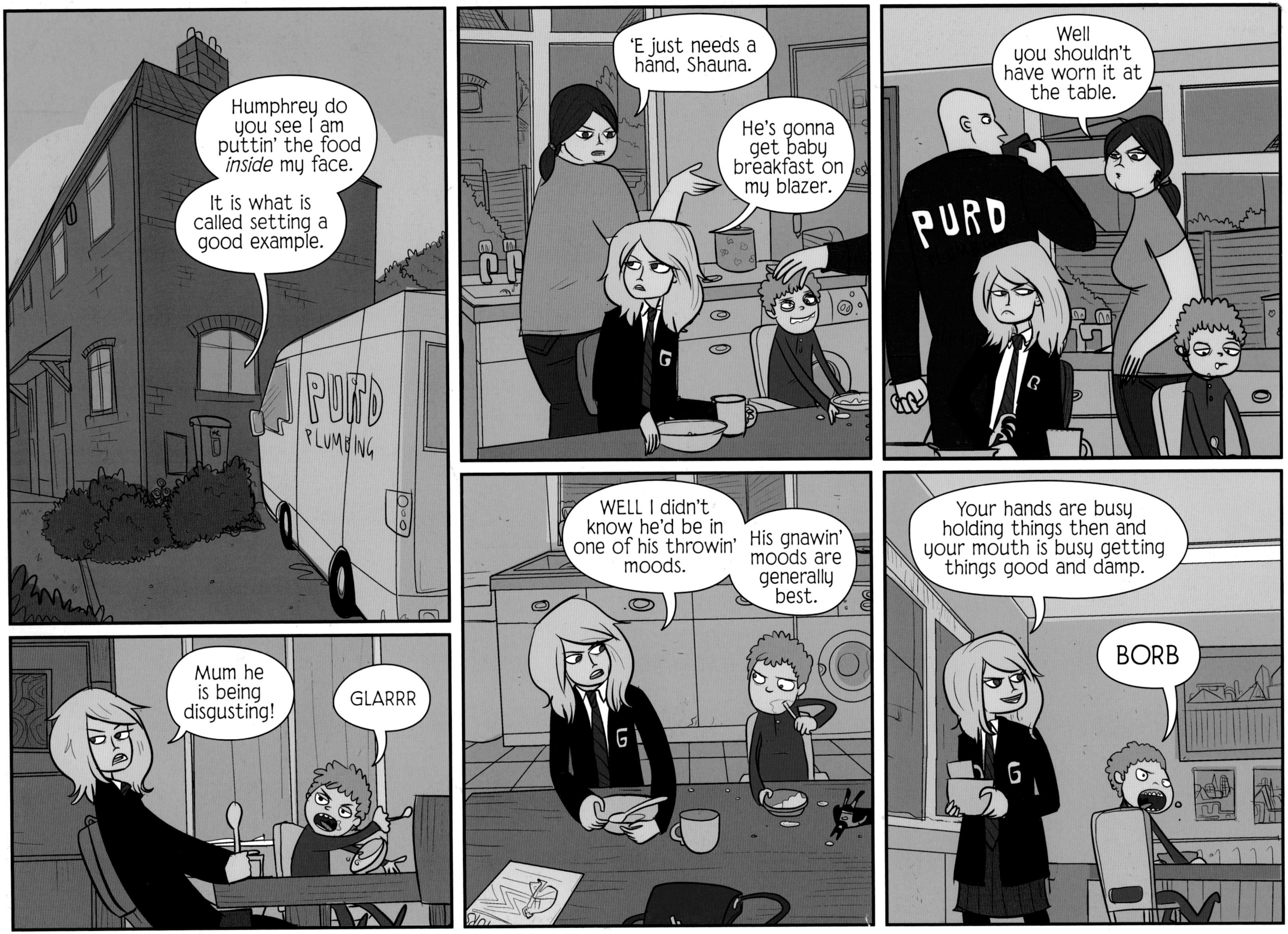
Humphrey do you see I am puttin' the food *inside* my face.
It is what is called setting a good example.
PURD PLUMBING
'E just needs a hand, Shauna.
He's gonna get baby breakfast on my blazer.
Well you shouldn't have worn it at the table.
PURD
Mum he is being disgusting!
GLARRR
WELL I didn't know he'd be in one of his throwin' moods.
His gnawin' moods are generally best.
Your hands are busy holding things then and your mouth is busy getting things good and damp.
BORB

The Case of The Team Spirit

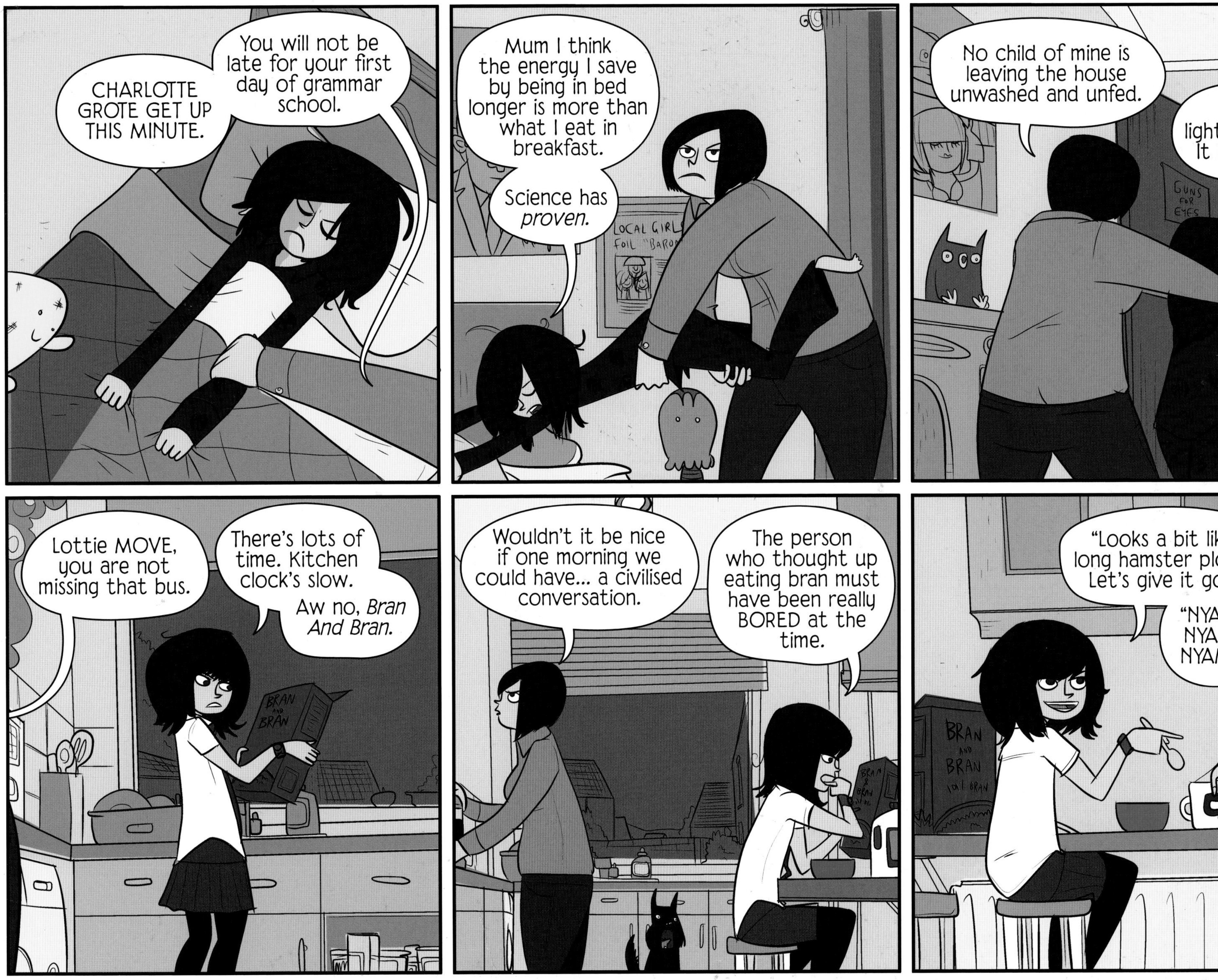
CHARLOTTE GROTE GET UP THIS MINUTE.
You will not be late for your first day of grammar school.
Mum I think the energy I save by being in bed longer is more than what I eat in breakfast.
Science has *proven.*
LOCAL GIRLS FOIL "BARON
No child of mine is leaving the house unwashed and unfed.
The light HURTS! It BURNS!
GUNS FOR EYES
Lottie MOVE, you are not missing that bus.
There's lots of time. Kitchen clock's slow.
Aw no, *Bran And Bran.*
BRAN AND BRAN
Wouldn't it be nice if one morning we could have... a civilised conversation.
The person who thought up eating bran must have been really BORED at the time.
"Looks a bit like long hamster plops. Let's give it go."
"NYAM NYAM NYAM"
BRAN AND BRAN

Bad Machinery, Volume One

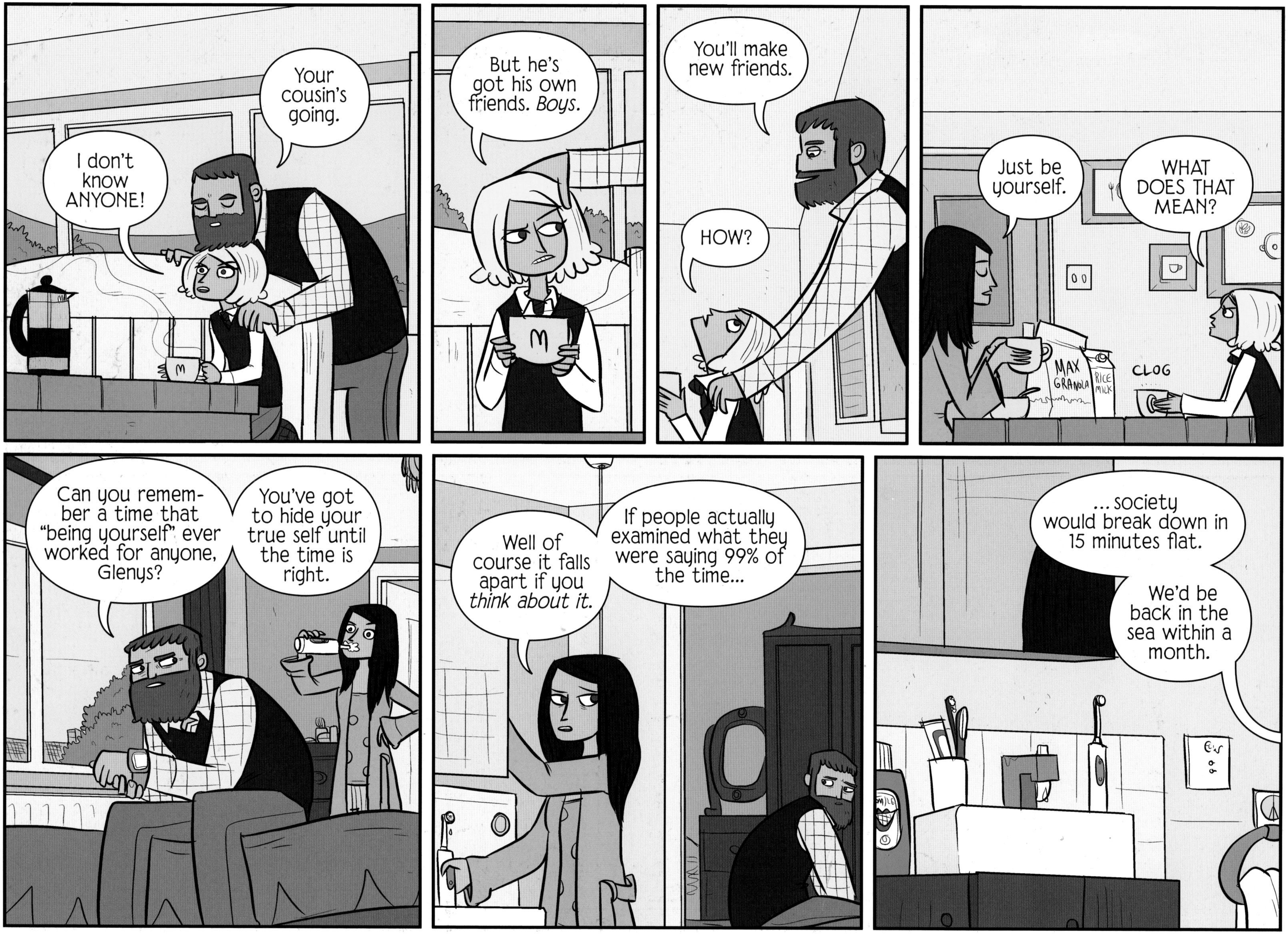
Your cousin's going.
I don't know ANYONE!
But he's got his own friends. *Boys.*
You'll make new friends.
HOW?
Just be yourself.
WHAT DOES THAT MEAN?
MAX GRANOLA
RICE MILK
CLOG
Can you remember a time that "being yourself" ever worked for anyone, Glenys?
You've got to hide your true self until the time is right.
Well of course it falls apart if you *think about it.*
If people actually examined what they were saying 99% of the time...
...society would break down in 15 minutes flat.
We'd be back in the sea within a month.

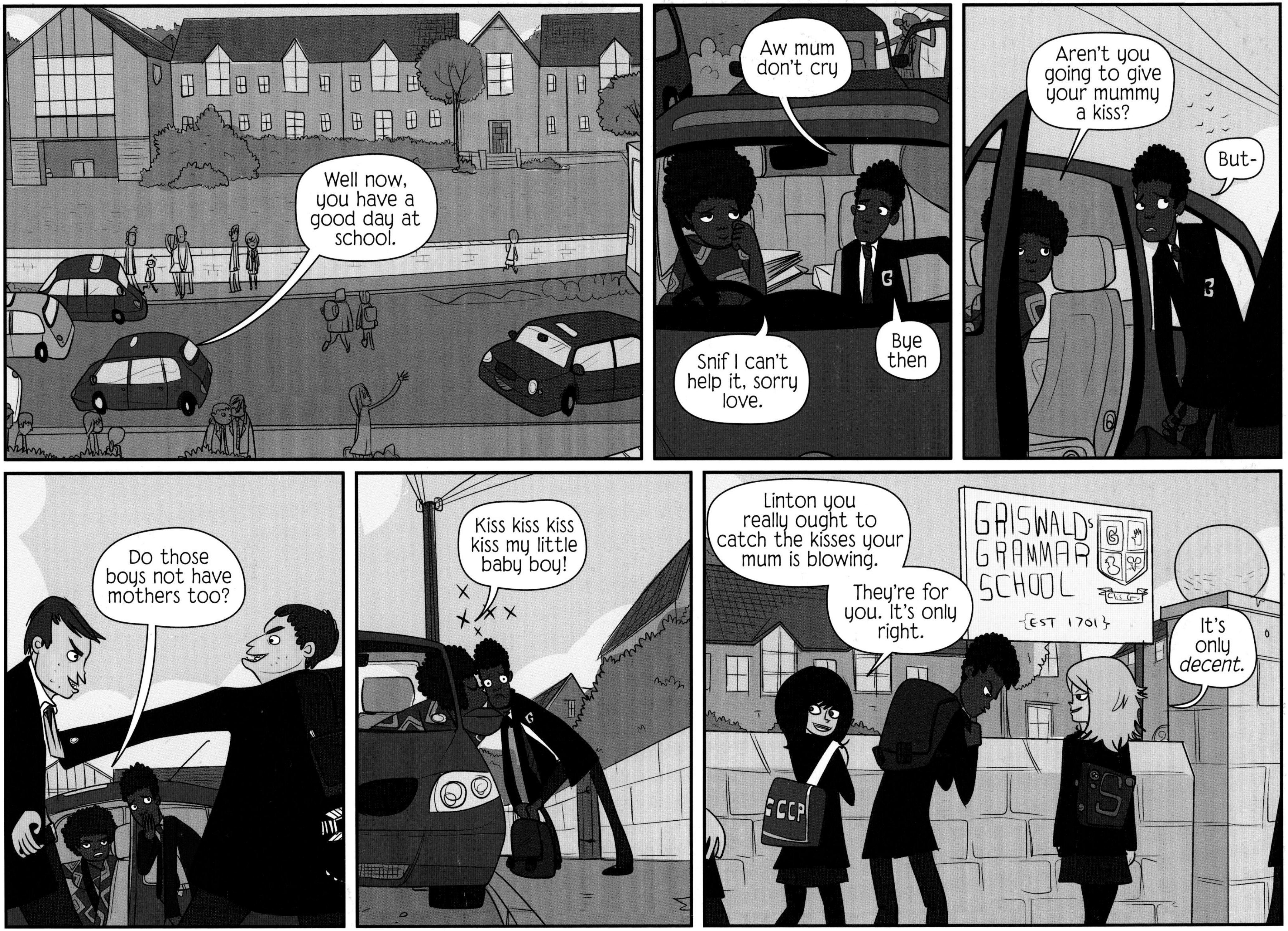
Well now, you have a good day at school.
Aw mum don't cry
Snif I can't help it, sorry love.
Bye then
Aren't you going to give your mummy a kiss?
But-
Do those boys not have mothers too?
Kiss kiss kiss kiss my little baby boy!
Linton you really ought to catch the kisses your mum is blowing.
GRISWALD's GRAMMAR SCHOOL
{EST 1701}
They're for you. It's only right.
It's only *decent*.

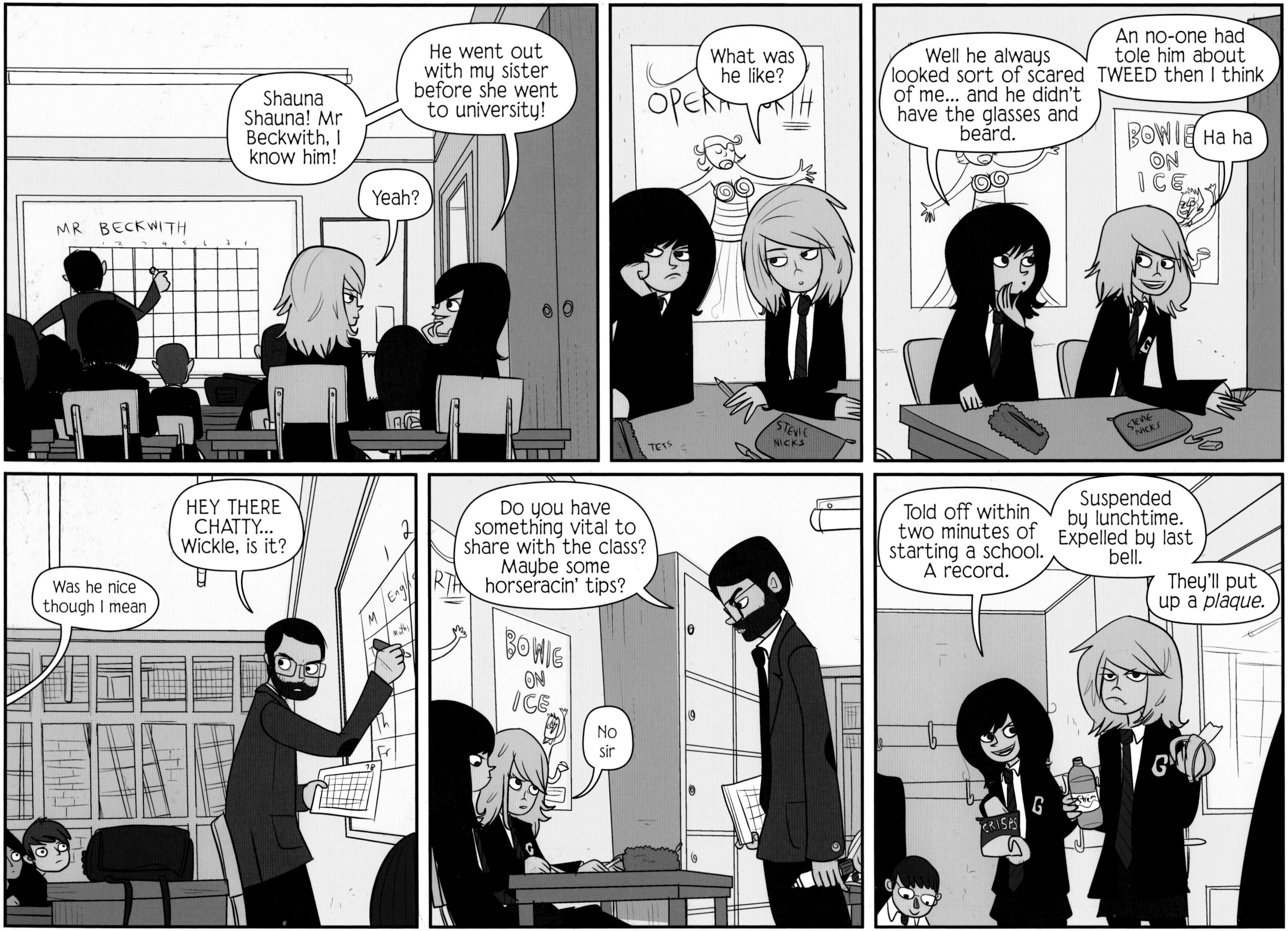
MR BECKWITH
Shauna Shauna! Mr Beckwith, I know him!
Yeah?
He went out with my sister before she went to university!
What was he like?
STEVIE NICKS
Well he always looked sort of scared of me... and he didn't have the glasses and beard.
An no-one had tole him about TWEED then I think
BOWIE ON ICE
Ha ha
STEVIE NICKS
Was he nice though I mean
HEY THERE CHATTY... Wickle, is it?
Do you have something vital to share with the class? Maybe some horseracin' tips?
BOWIE ON ICE
No sir
Told off within two minutes of starting a school. A record.
Suspended by lunchtime. Expelled by last bell.
They'll put up a *plaque*.
CRISPS

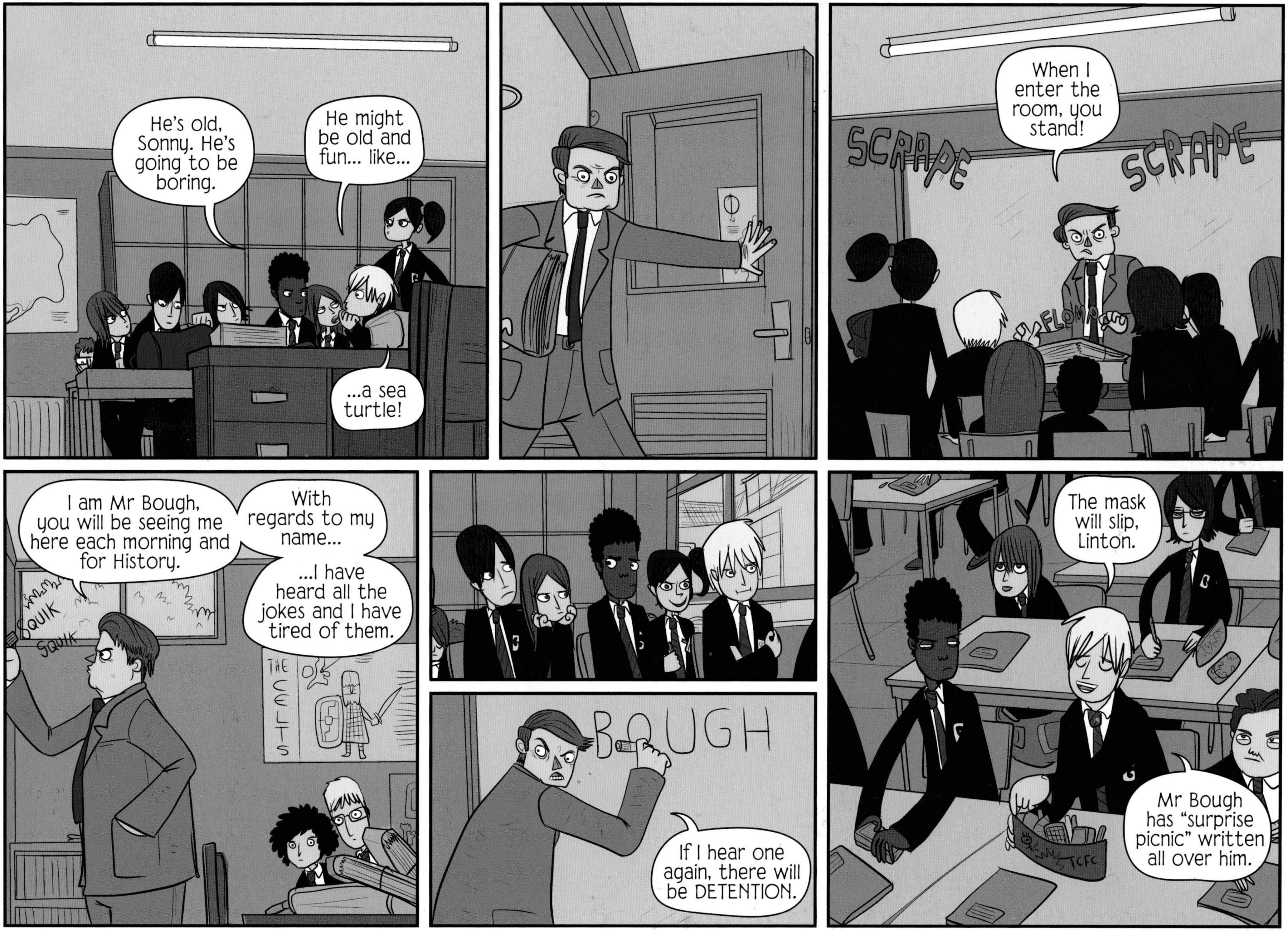
He's old, Sonny. He's going to be boring.
He might be old and fun... like...
...a sea turtle!
When I enter the room, you stand!
SCRAPE
SCRAPE
FLOMP
I am Mr Bough, you will be seeing me here each morning and for History.
With regards to my name...
...I have heard all the jokes and I have tired of them.
SQUIK
SQUIK
THE CELTS
BOUGH
If I hear one again, there will be DETENTION.
The mask will slip, Linton.
Mr Bough has "surprise picnic" written all over him.
TCFC

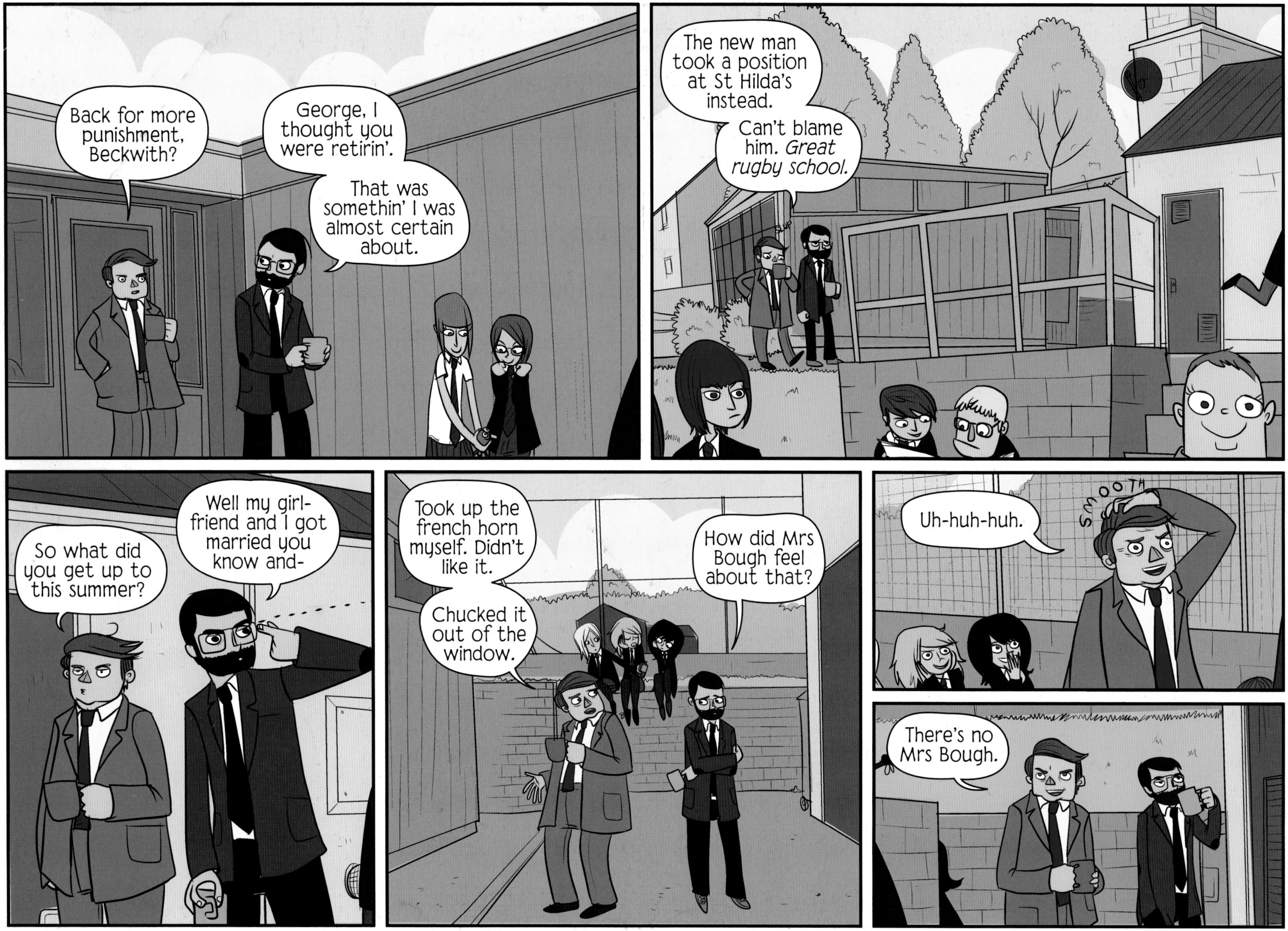

Back for more punishment, Beckwith?
George, I thought you were retirin'.
That was somethin' I was almost certain about.
The new man took a position at St Hilda's instead.
Can't blame him. *Great rugby school.*
So what did you get up to this summer?
Well my girl-friend and I got married you know and-
Took up the french horn myself. Didn't like it.
Chucked it out of the window.
How did Mrs Bough feel about that?
Uh-huh-huh.
SMOOTH
There's no Mrs Bough.

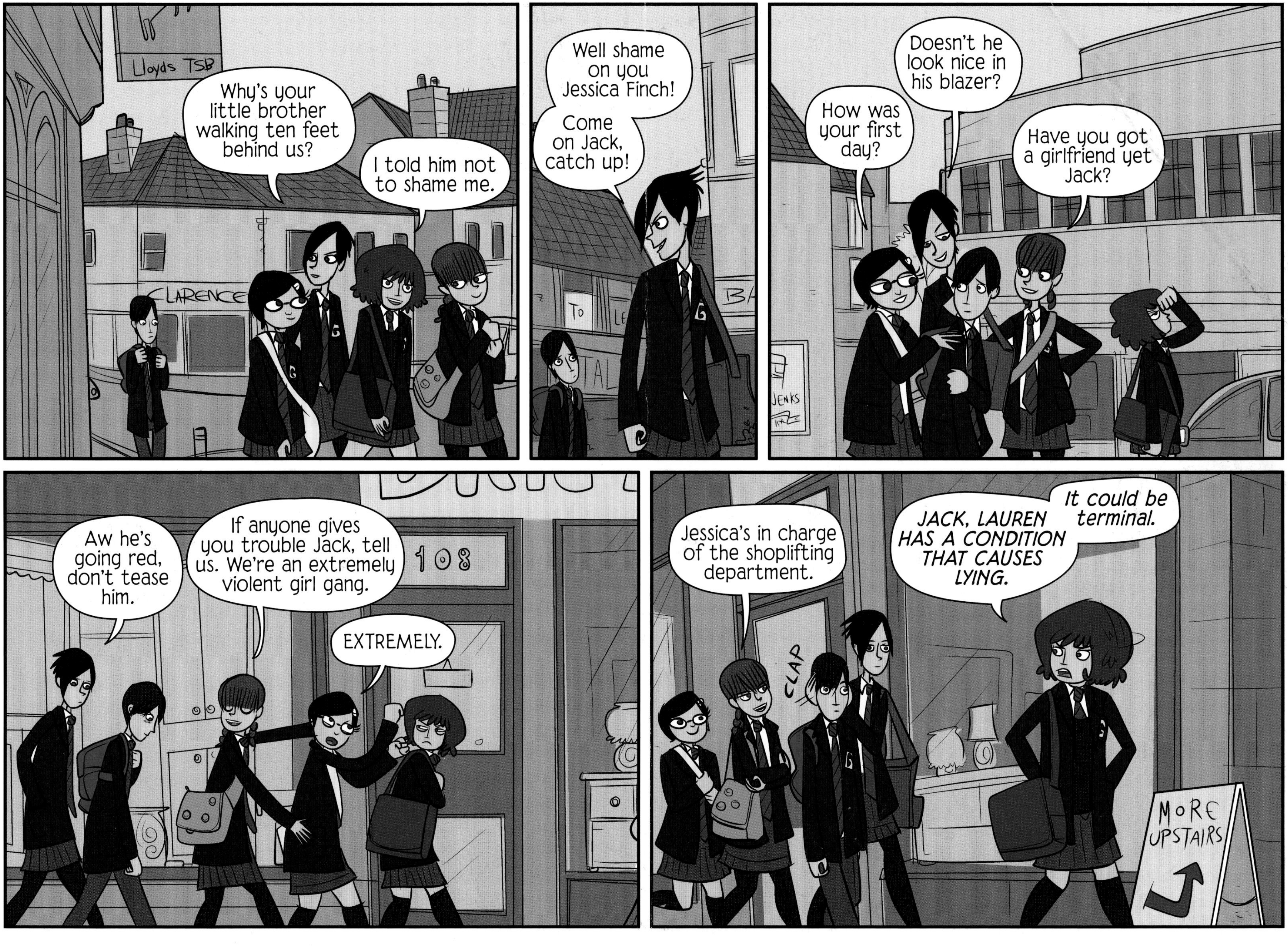
Lloyds TSB
Why's your little brother walking ten feet behind us?
I told him not to shame me.
CLARENCE
Well shame on you Jessica Finch!
Come on Jack, catch up!
How was your first day?
Doesn't he look nice in his blazer?
Have you got a girlfriend yet Jack?
JENKS
Aw he's going red, don't tease him.
If anyone gives you trouble Jack, tell us. We're an extremely violent girl gang.
108
EXTREMELY.
Jessica's in charge of the shoplifting department.
CLAP
JACK, LAUREN HAS A CONDITION THAT CAUSES LYING.
It could be terminal.
MORE UPSTAIRS

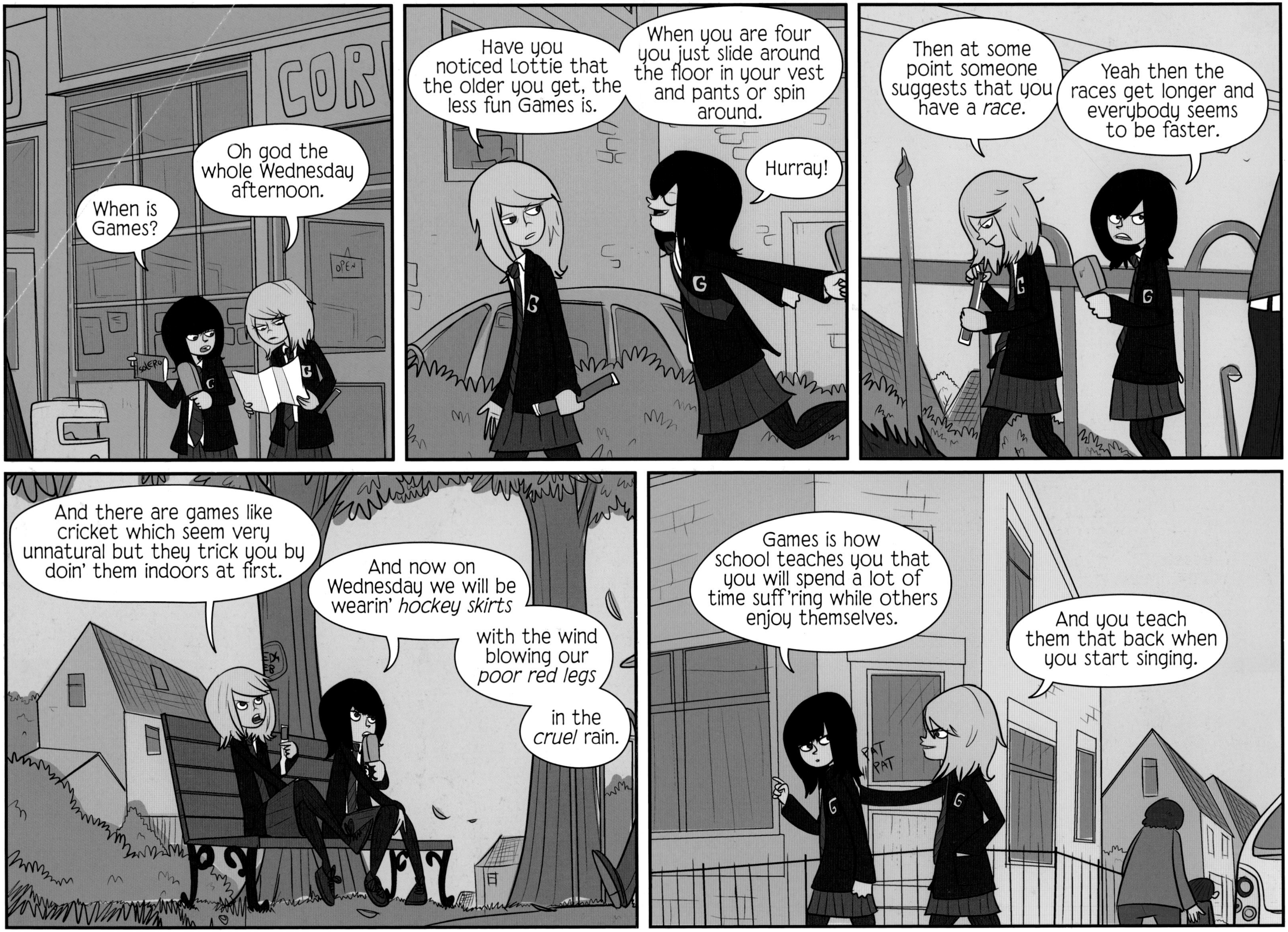
When is Games?
Oh god the whole Wednesday afternoon.
Have you noticed Lottie that the older you get, the less fun Games is.
When you are four you just slide around the floor in your vest and pants or spin around.
Hurray!
Then at some point someone suggests that you have a *race*.
Yeah then the races get longer and everybody seems to be faster.
And there are games like cricket which seem very unnatural but they trick you by doin' them indoors at first.
And now on Wednesday we will be wearin' *hockey skirts*
with the wind blowing our *poor red legs*
in the *cruel* rain.
Games is how school teaches you that you will spend a lot of time suff'ring while others enjoy themselves.
PAT PAT
And you teach them that back when you start singing.

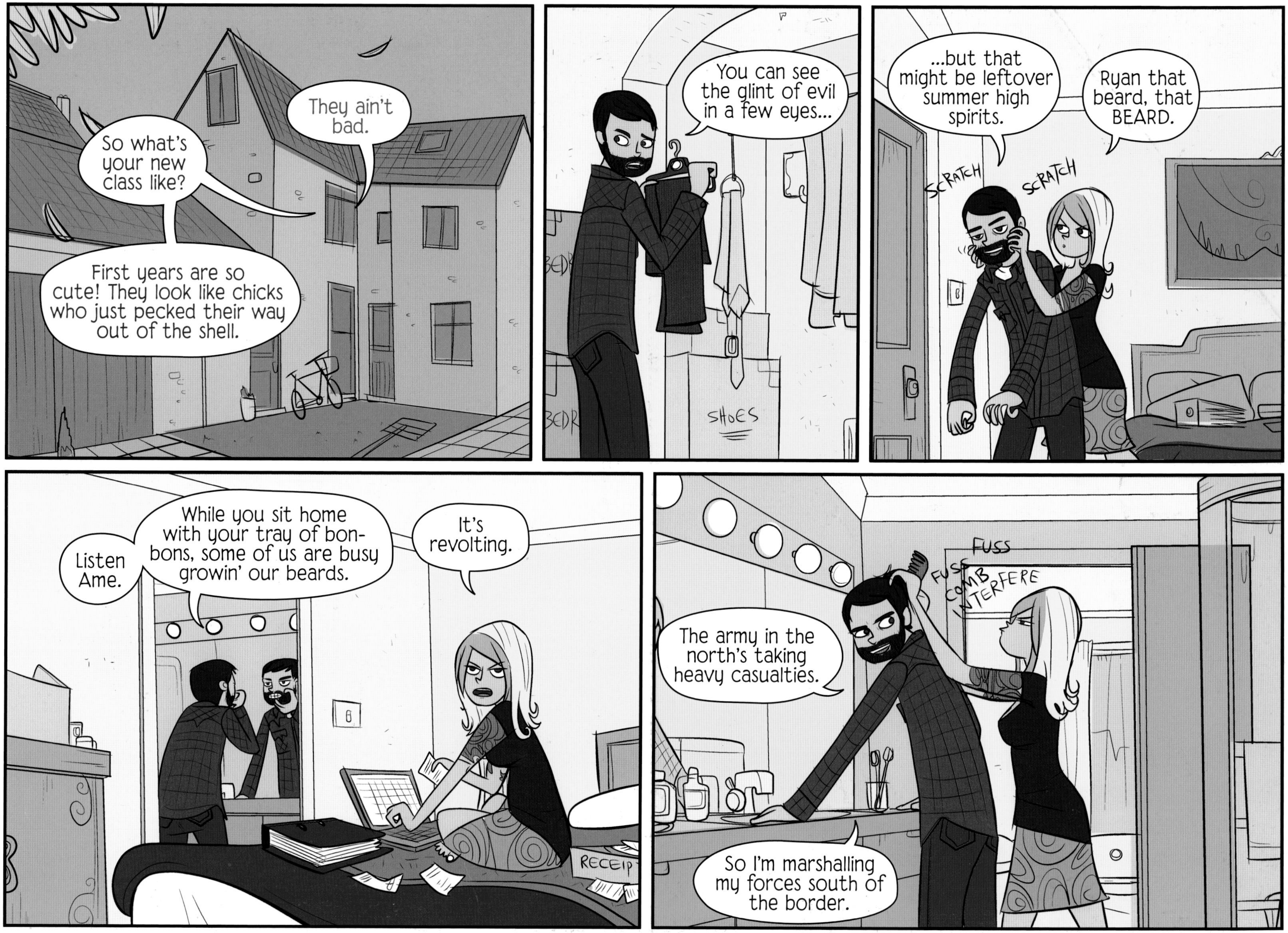
So what's your new class like?
They ain't bad.
First years are so cute! They look like chicks who just pecked their way out of the shell.
You can see the glint of evil in a few eyes...
SHOES
...but that might be leftover summer high spirits.
Ryan that beard, that BEARD.
SCRATCH
SCRATCH
Listen Ame.
While you sit home with your tray of bon-bons, some of us are busy growin' our beards.
It's revolting.
RECEIP
FUSS
FUSS
COMB
INTERFERE
The army in the north's taking heavy casualties.
So I'm marshalling my forces south of the border.

Bad Machinery, Volume One

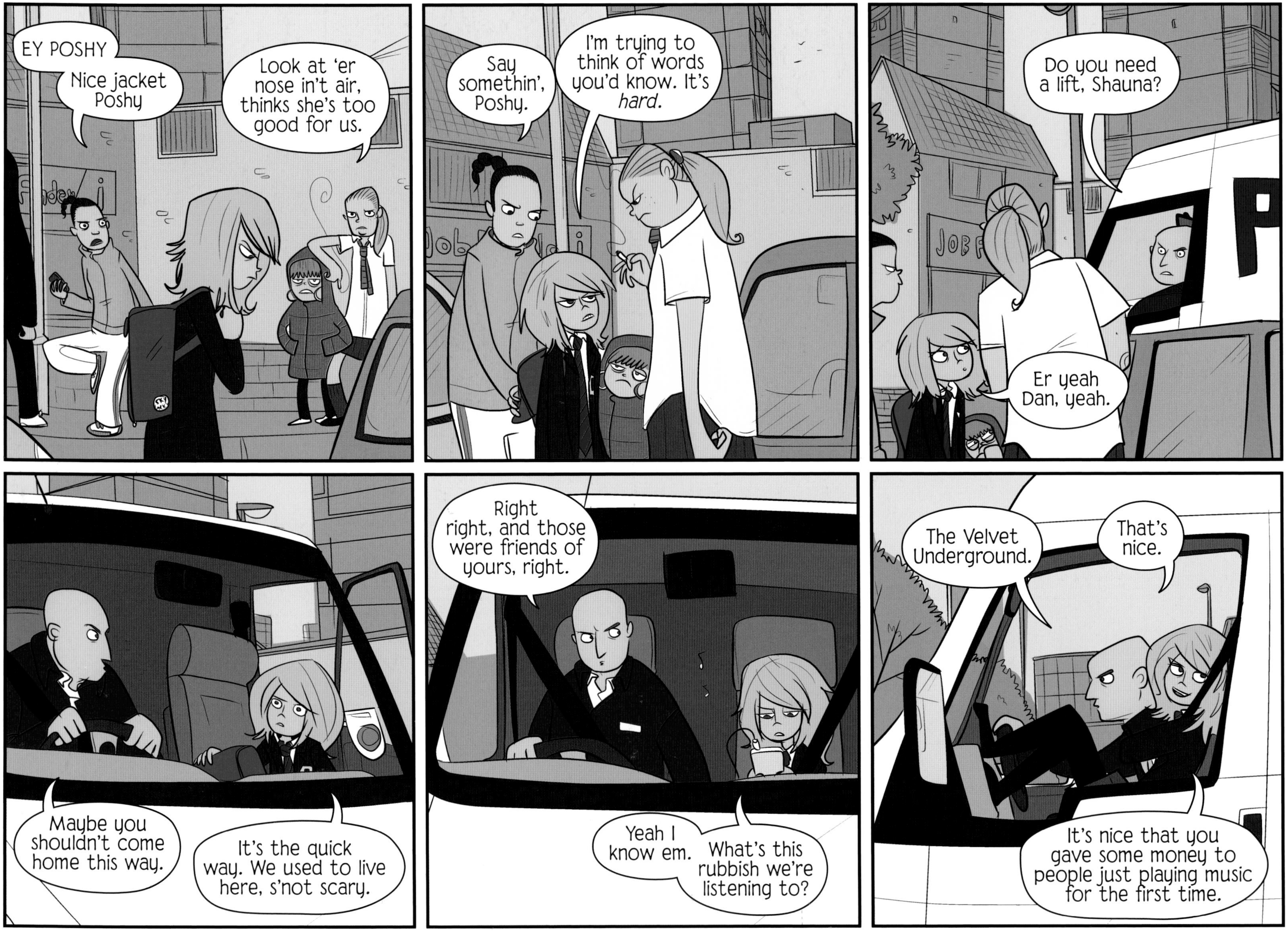
EY POSHY
Nice jacket Poshy
Look at 'er nose in't air, thinks she's too good for us.
Say somethin', Poshy.
I'm trying to think of words you'd know. It's *hard.*
Do you need a lift, Shauna?
Er yeah Dan, yeah.
Maybe you shouldn't come home this way.
It's the quick way. We used to live here, s'not scary.
Right right, and those were friends of yours, right.
Yeah I know em.
What's this rubbish we're listening to?
The Velvet Underground.
That's nice.
It's nice that you gave some money to people just playing music for the first time.

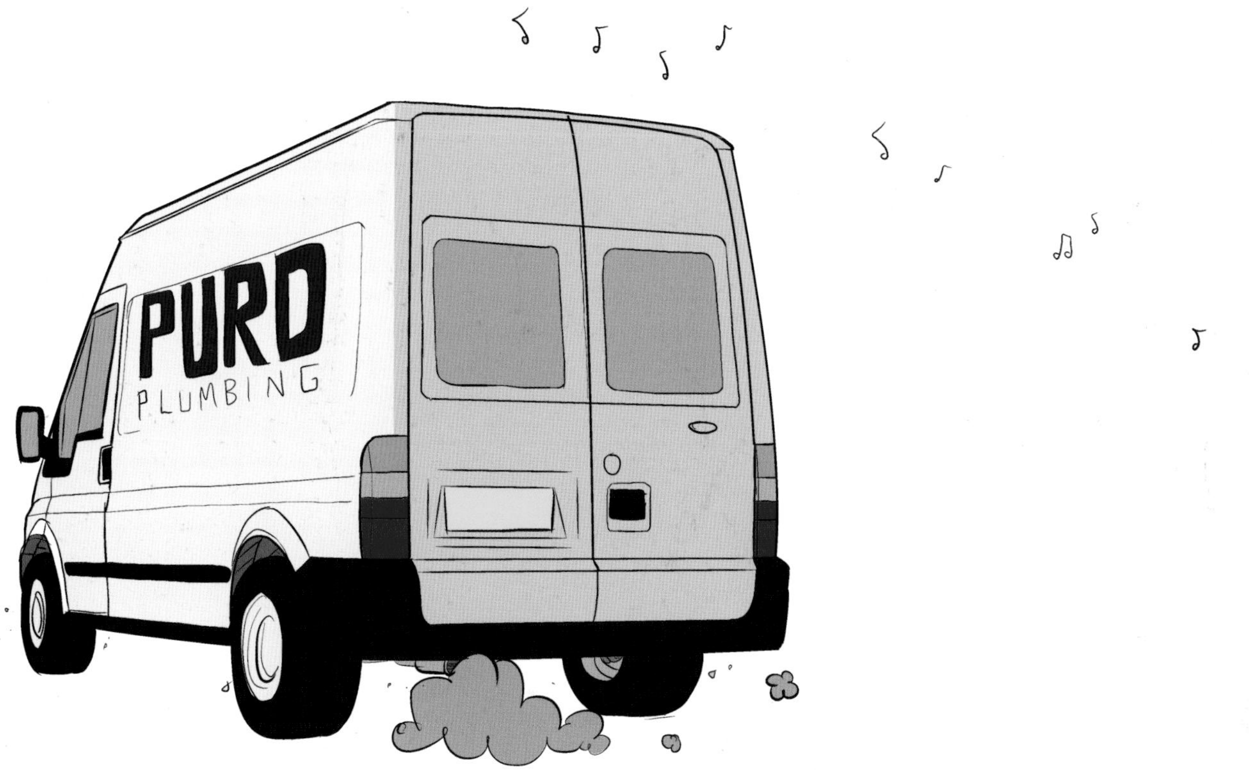
PURD
PLUMBING

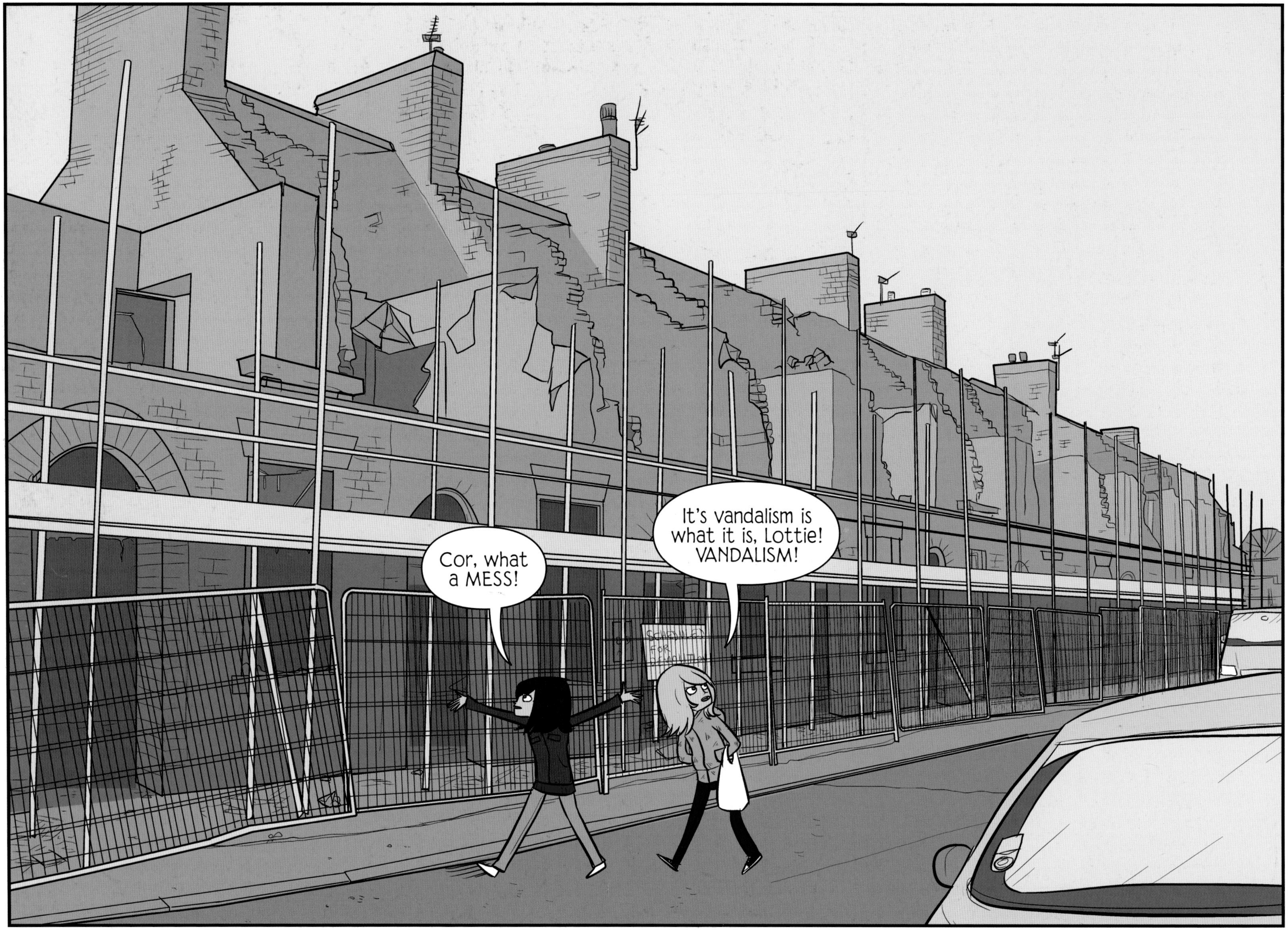
Cor, what a MESS!
It's vandalism is what it is, Lottie! VANDALISM!

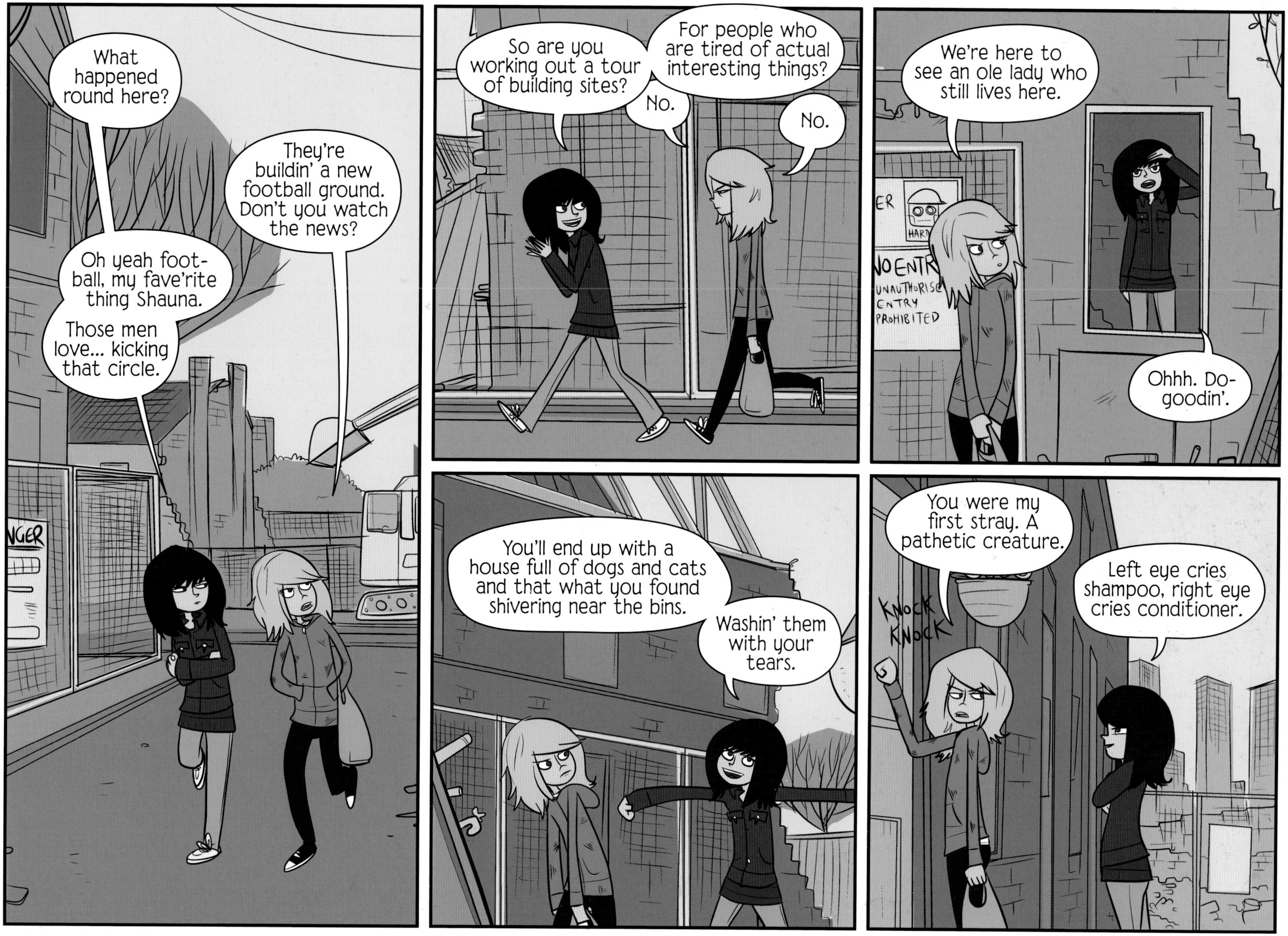
What happened round here?
They're buildin' a new football ground. Don't you watch the news?
Oh yeah foot-ball, my fave'rite thing Shauna.
Those men love... kicking that circle.
NGER
So are you working out a tour of building sites?
No.
For people who are tired of actual interesting things?
No.
We're here to see an ole lady who still lives here.
NO ENTR
UNAUTHORISE
ENTRY
PROHIBITED
Ohhh. Do-goodin'.
You'll end up with a house full of dogs and cats and that what you found shivering near the bins.
Washin' them with your tears.
KNOCK
KNOCK
You were my first stray. A pathetic creature.
Left eye cries shampoo, right eye cries conditioner.

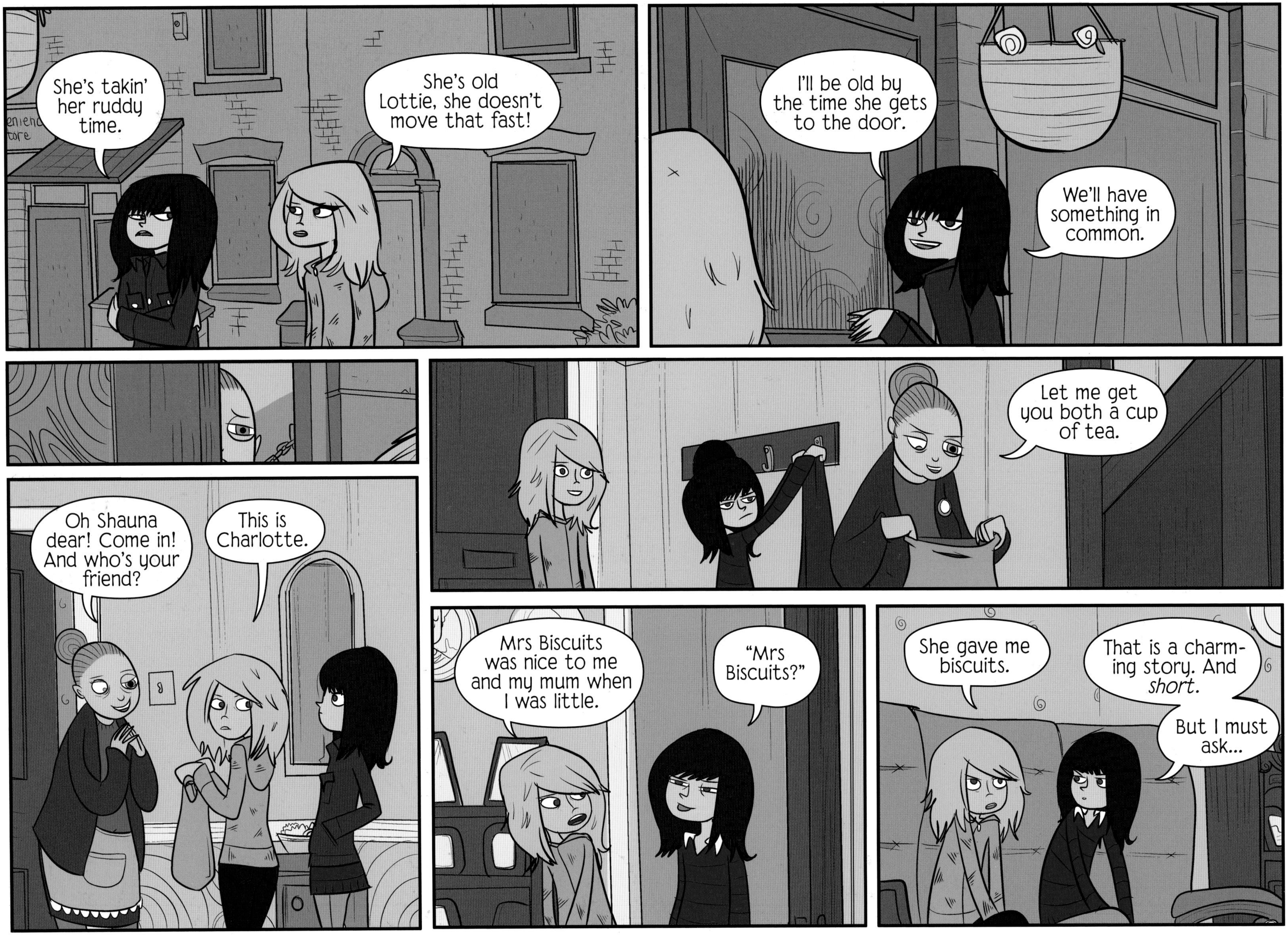
She's takin' her ruddy time.
She's old Lottie, she doesn't move that fast!
I'll be old by the time she gets to the door.
We'll have something in common.
Let me get you both a cup of tea.
Oh Shauna dear! Come in! And who's your friend?
This is Charlotte.
Mrs Biscuits was nice to me and my mum when I was little.
"Mrs Biscuits?"
She gave me biscuits.
That is a charming story. And *short*.
But I must ask...

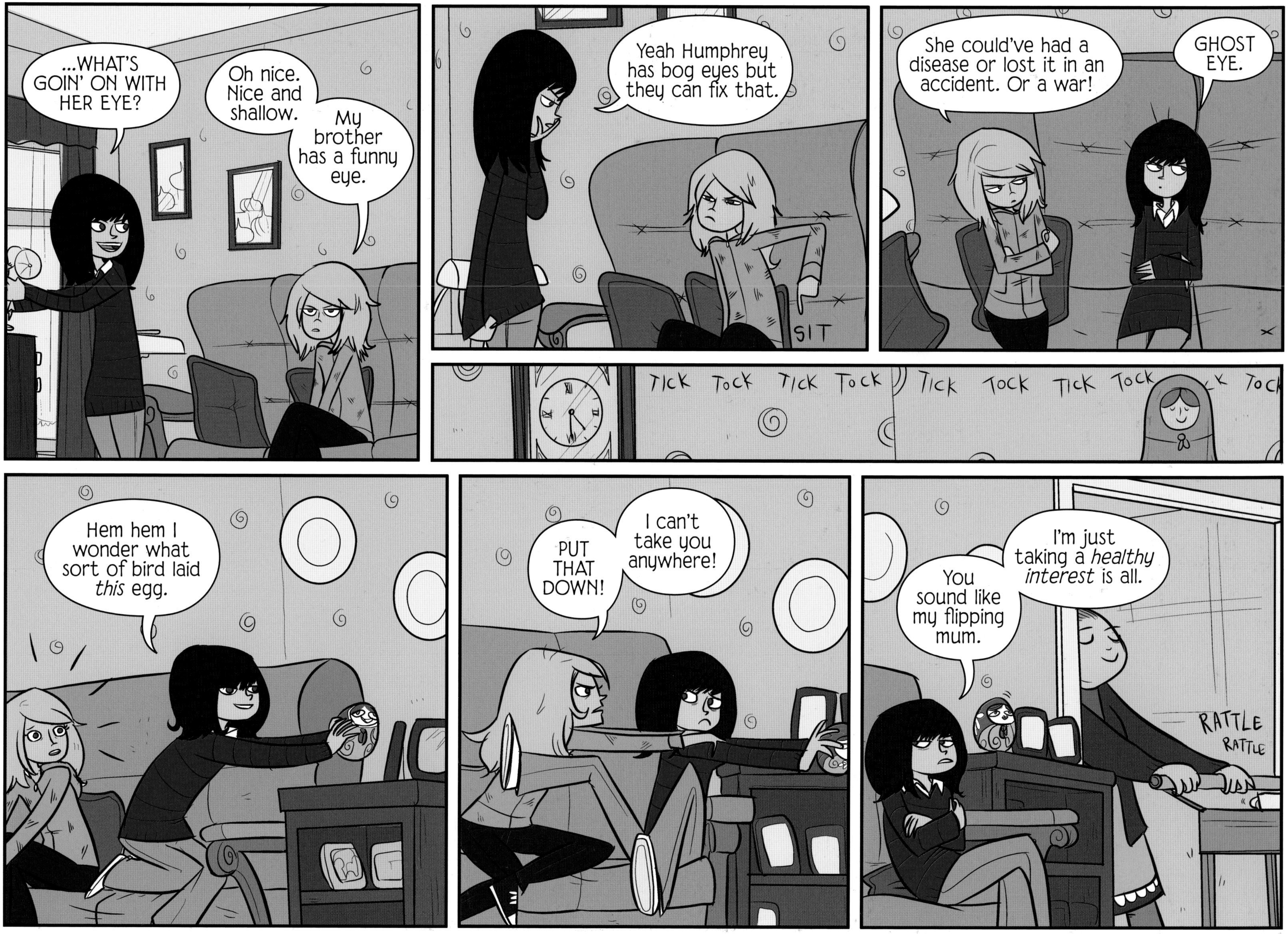
...WHAT'S GOIN' ON WITH HER EYE?
Oh nice. Nice and shallow.
My brother has a funny eye.
Yeah Humphrey has bog eyes but they can fix that.
SIT
She could've had a disease or lost it in an accident. Or a war!
GHOST EYE.
TICK TOCK TICK TOCK
TICK TOCK TICK TOCK
Hem hem I wonder what sort of bird laid *this* egg.
PUT THAT DOWN!
I can't take you anywhere!
I'm just taking a *healthy interest* is all.
You sound like my flipping mum.
RATTLE
RATTLE

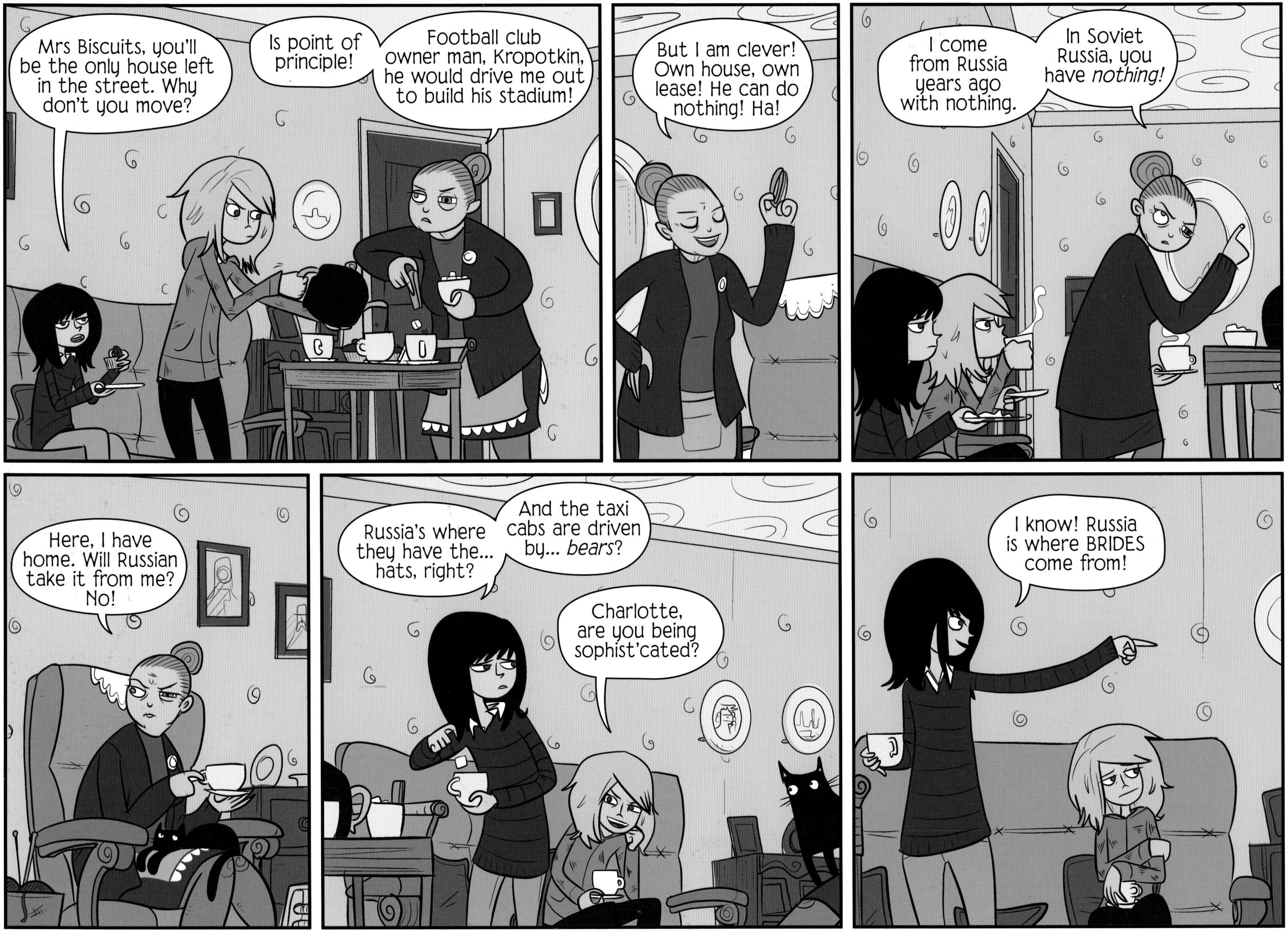
Mrs Biscuits, you'll be the only house left in the street. Why don't you move?
Is point of principle!
Football club owner man, Kropotkin, he would drive me out to build his stadium!
But I am clever! Own house, own lease! He can do nothing! Ha!
I come from Russia years ago with nothing.
In Soviet Russia, you have *nothing!*
Here, I have home. Will Russian take it from me? No!
Russia's where they have the... hats, right?
And the taxi cabs are driven by... *bears*?
Charlotte, are you being sophist'cated?
I know! Russia is where BRIDES come from!

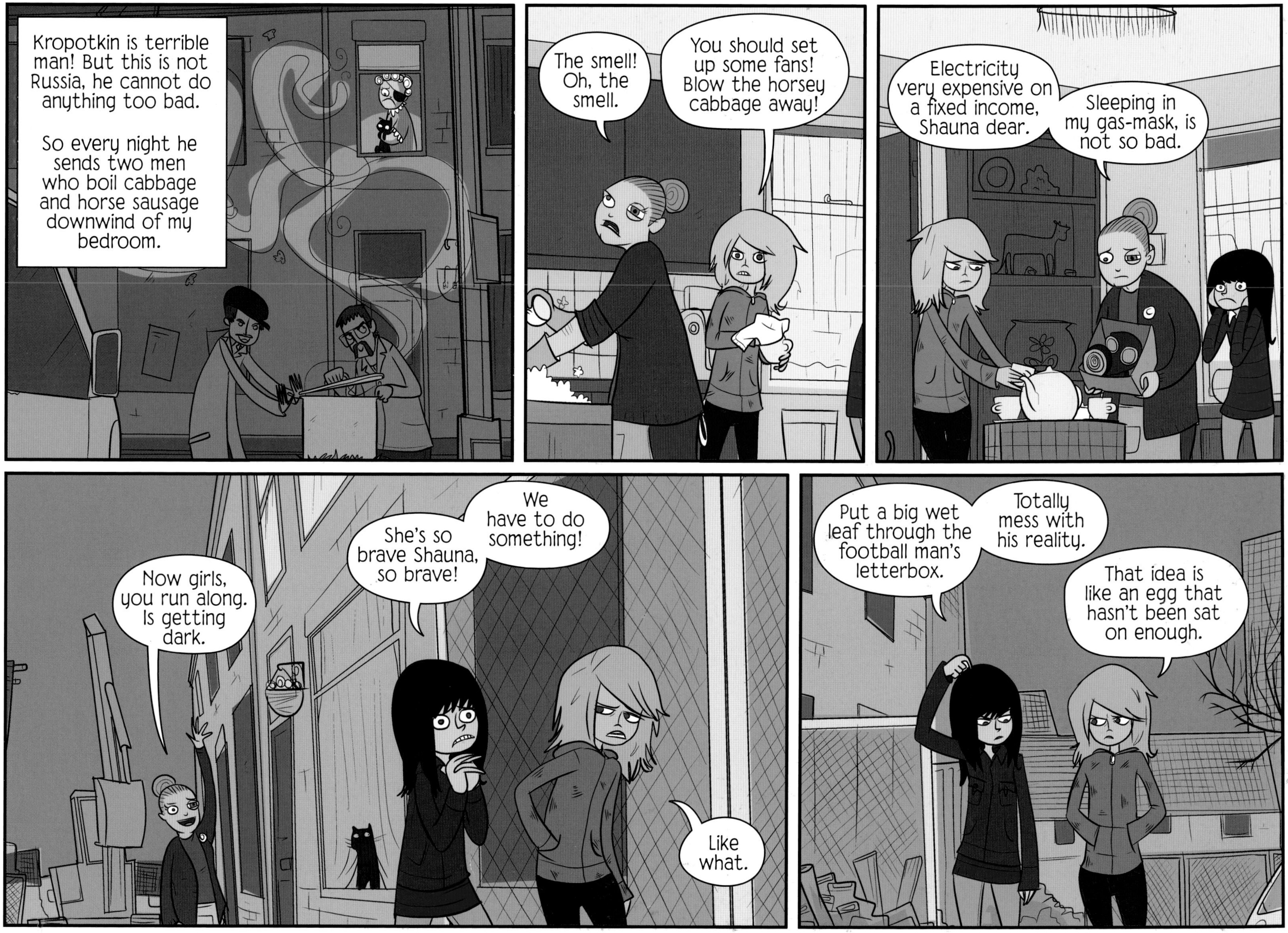
Kropotkin is terrible man! But this is not Russia, he cannot do anything too bad.
So every night he sends two men who boil cabbage and horse sausage downwind of my bedroom.
The smell! Oh, the smell.
You should set up some fans! Blow the horsey cabbage away!
Electricity very expensive on a fixed income, Shauna dear.
Sleeping in my gas-mask, is not so bad.
Now girls, you run along. Is getting dark.
She's so brave Shauna, so brave!
We have to do something!
Like what.
Put a big wet leaf through the football man's letterbox.
Totally mess with his reality.
That idea is like an egg that hasn't been sat on enough.

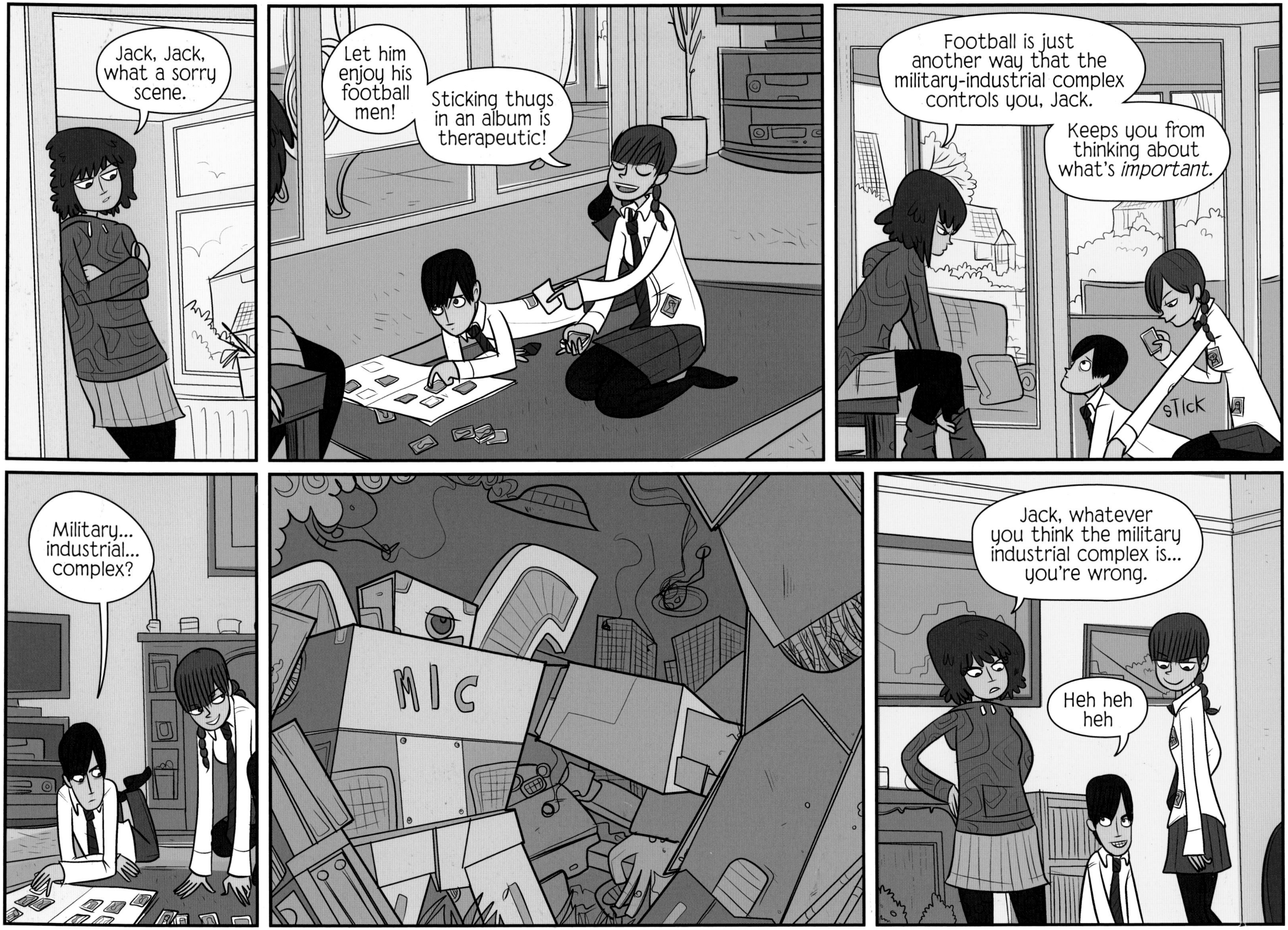
Jack, Jack, what a sorry scene.
Let him enjoy his football men!
Sticking thugs in an album is therapeutic!
Football is just another way that the military-industrial complex controls you, Jack.
Keeps you from thinking about what's *important*.
STICK
Military... industrial... complex?
MIC
Jack, whatever you think the military industrial complex is... you're wrong.
Heh heh heh

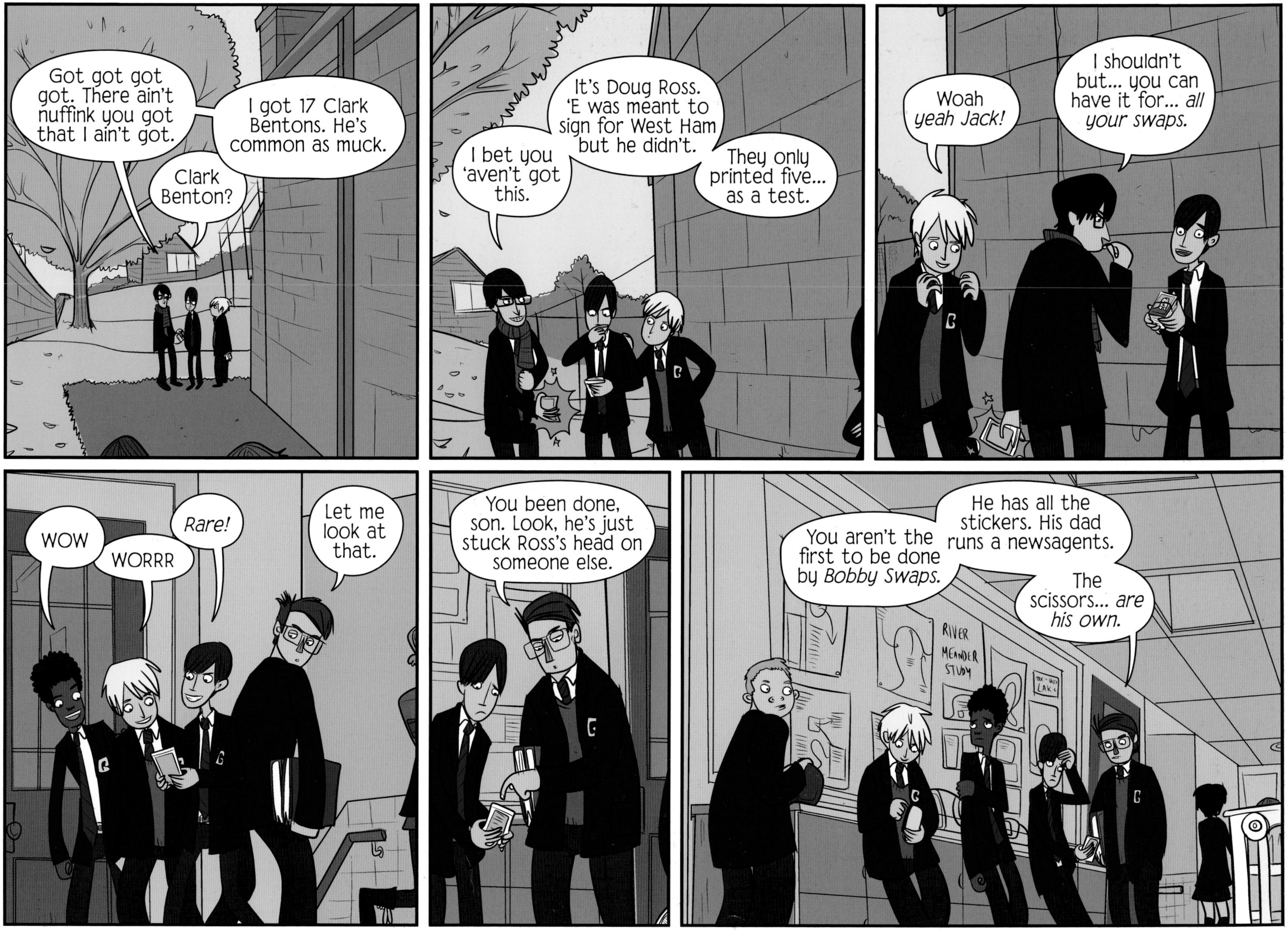
Got got got got. There ain't nuffink you got that I ain't got.
I got 17 Clark Bentons. He's common as muck.
Clark Benton?
I bet you 'aven't got this.
It's Doug Ross. 'E was meant to sign for West Ham but he didn't.
They only printed five... as a test.
Woah *yeah Jack!*
I shouldn't but... you can have it for... *all your swaps.*
WOW
WORRR
Rare!
Let me look at that.
You been done, son. Look, he's just stuck Ross's head on someone else.
You aren't the first to be done by *Bobby Swaps.*
He has all the stickers. His dad runs a newsagents.
The scissors... *are his own.*
RIVER MEANDER STUDY

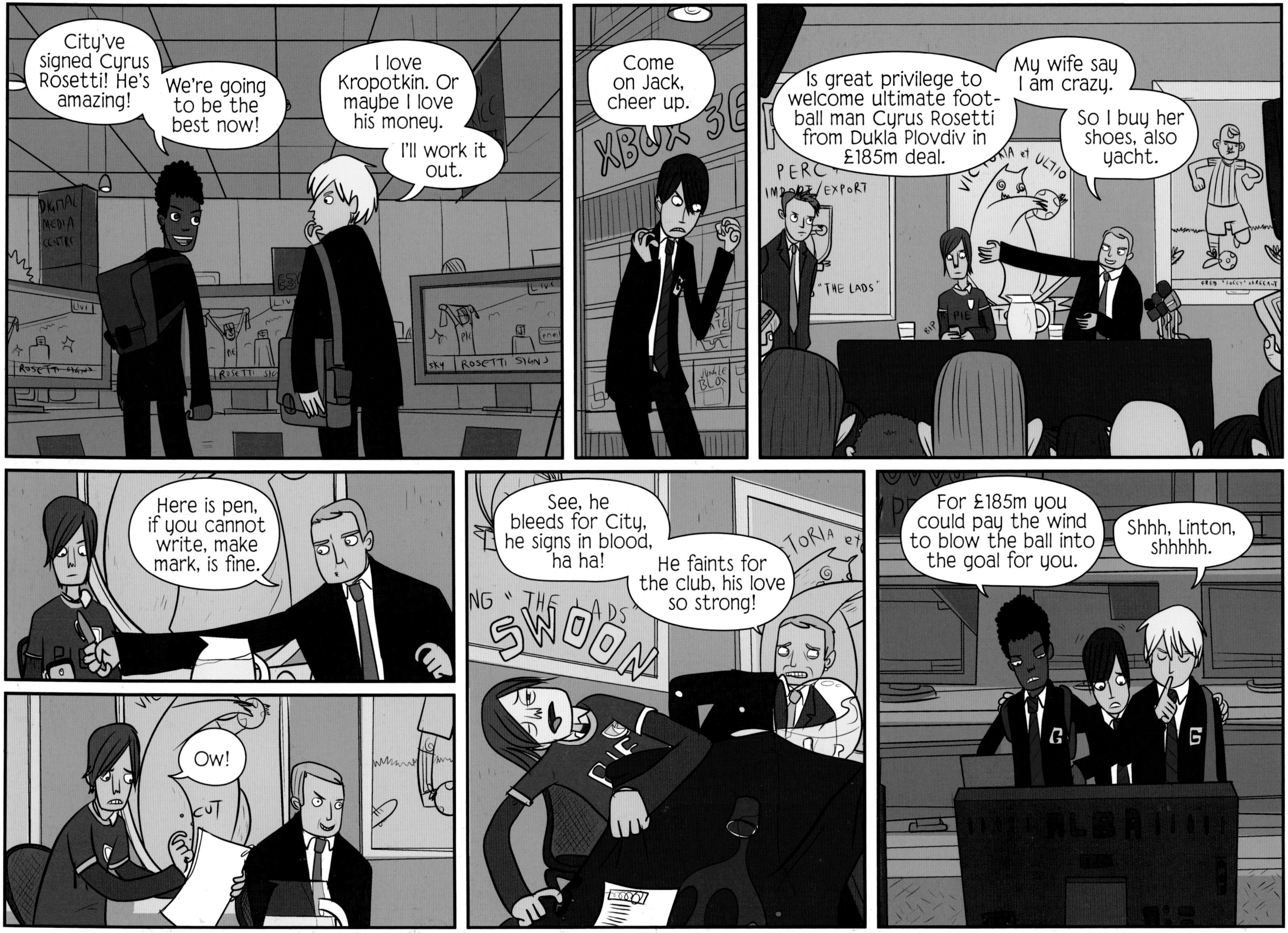
City've signed Cyrus Rosetti! He's amazing!
We're going to be the best now!
I love Kropotkin. Or maybe I love his money.
I'll work it out.
Come on Jack, cheer up.
XBOX 36
Is great privilege to welcome ultimate football man Cyrus Rosetti from Dukla Plovdiv in £185m deal.
My wife say I am crazy.
So I buy her shoes, also yacht.
VICTORIA et ULTIO
"THE LADS"
Here is pen, if you cannot write, make mark, is fine.
Ow!
CUT
See, he bleeds for City, he signs in blood, ha ha!
He faints for the club, his love so strong!
SWOON
For £185m you could pay the wind to blow the ball into the goal for you.
Shhh, Linton, shhhhh.

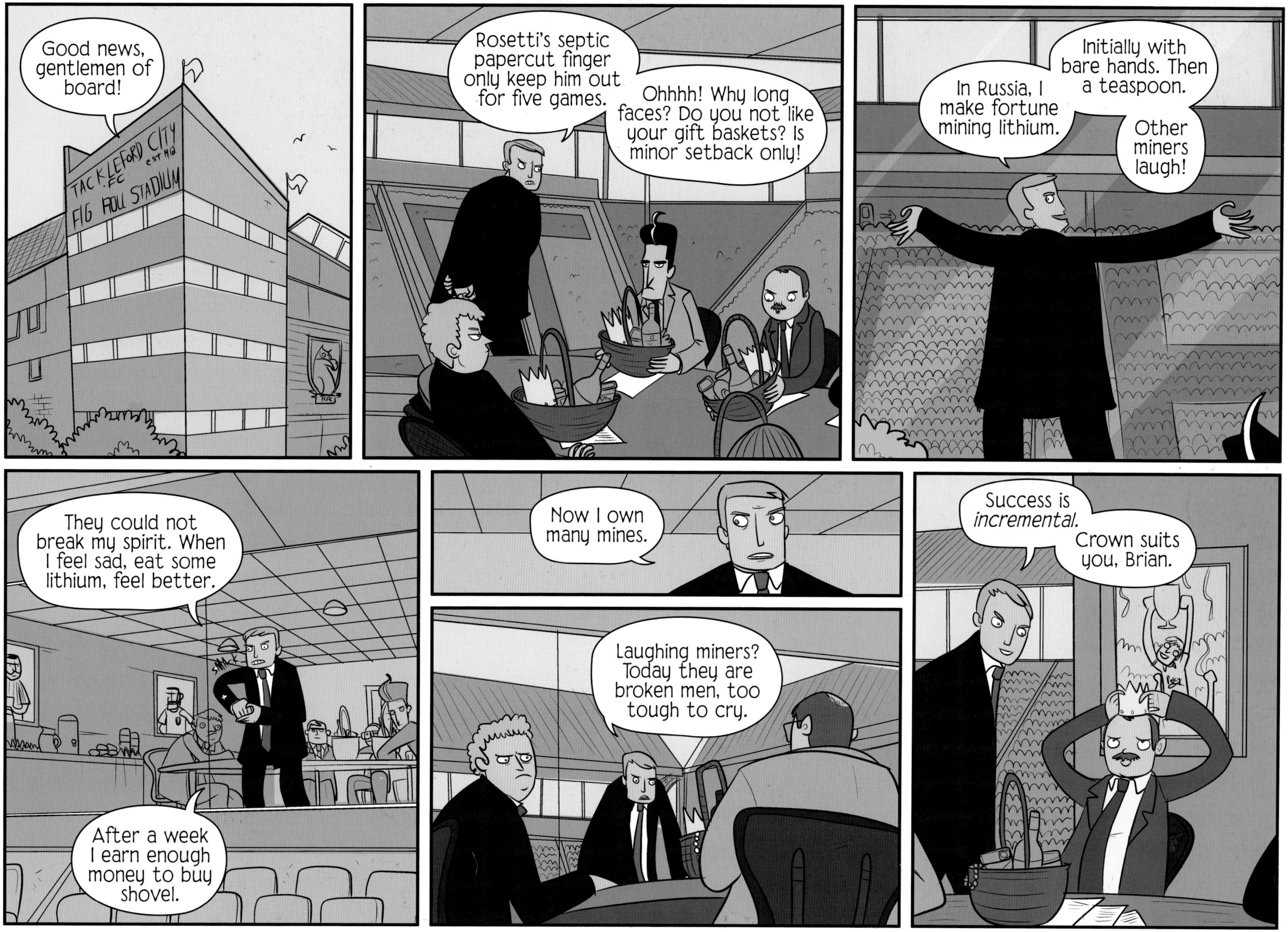
Good news, gentlemen of board!
TACKLEFORD CITY FC EST 1912
FIG ROLL STADIUM
Rosetti's septic papercut finger only keep him out for five games.
Ohhhh! Why long faces? Do you not like your gift baskets? Is minor setback only!
In Russia, I make fortune mining lithium.
Initially with bare hands. Then a teaspoon.
Other miners laugh!
They could not break my spirit. When I feel sad, eat some lithium, feel better.
SMACK
After a week I earn enough money to buy shovel.
Now I own many mines.
Laughing miners? Today they are broken men, too tough to cry.
Success is *incremental.*
Crown suits you, Brian.

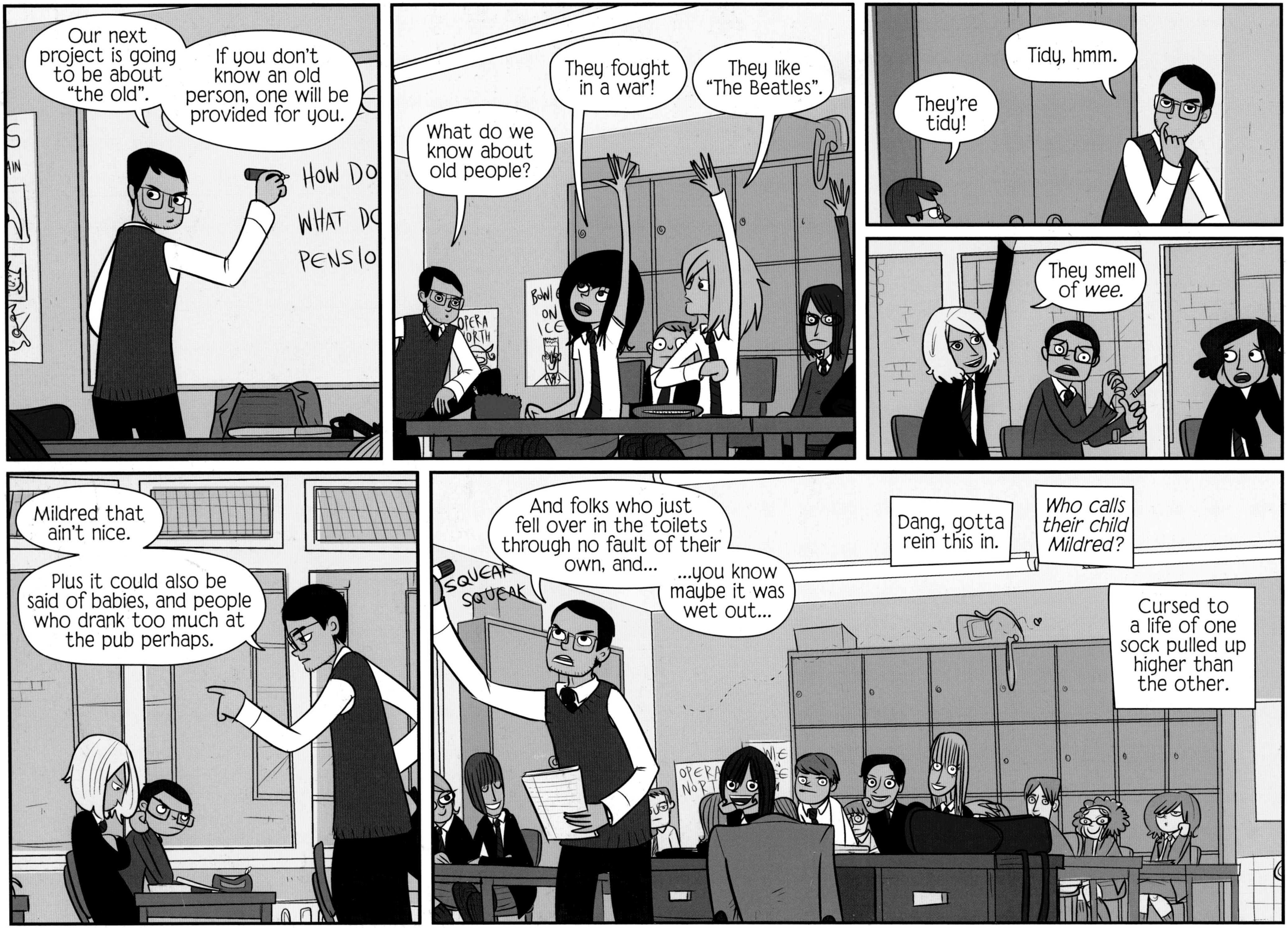
Our next project is going to be about "the old".
If you don't know an old person, one will be provided for you.
HOW DO
WHAT DO
PENSIO
What do we know about old people?
They fought in a war!
They like "The Beatles".
They're tidy!
Tidy, hmm.
They smell of *wee.*
Mildred that ain't nice.
Plus it could also be said of babies, and people who drank too much at the pub perhaps.
SQUEAK SQUEAK
And folks who just fell over in the toilets through no fault of their own, and...
...you know maybe it was wet out...
Dang, gotta rein this in.
Who calls their child Mildred?
Cursed to a life of one sock pulled up higher than the other.

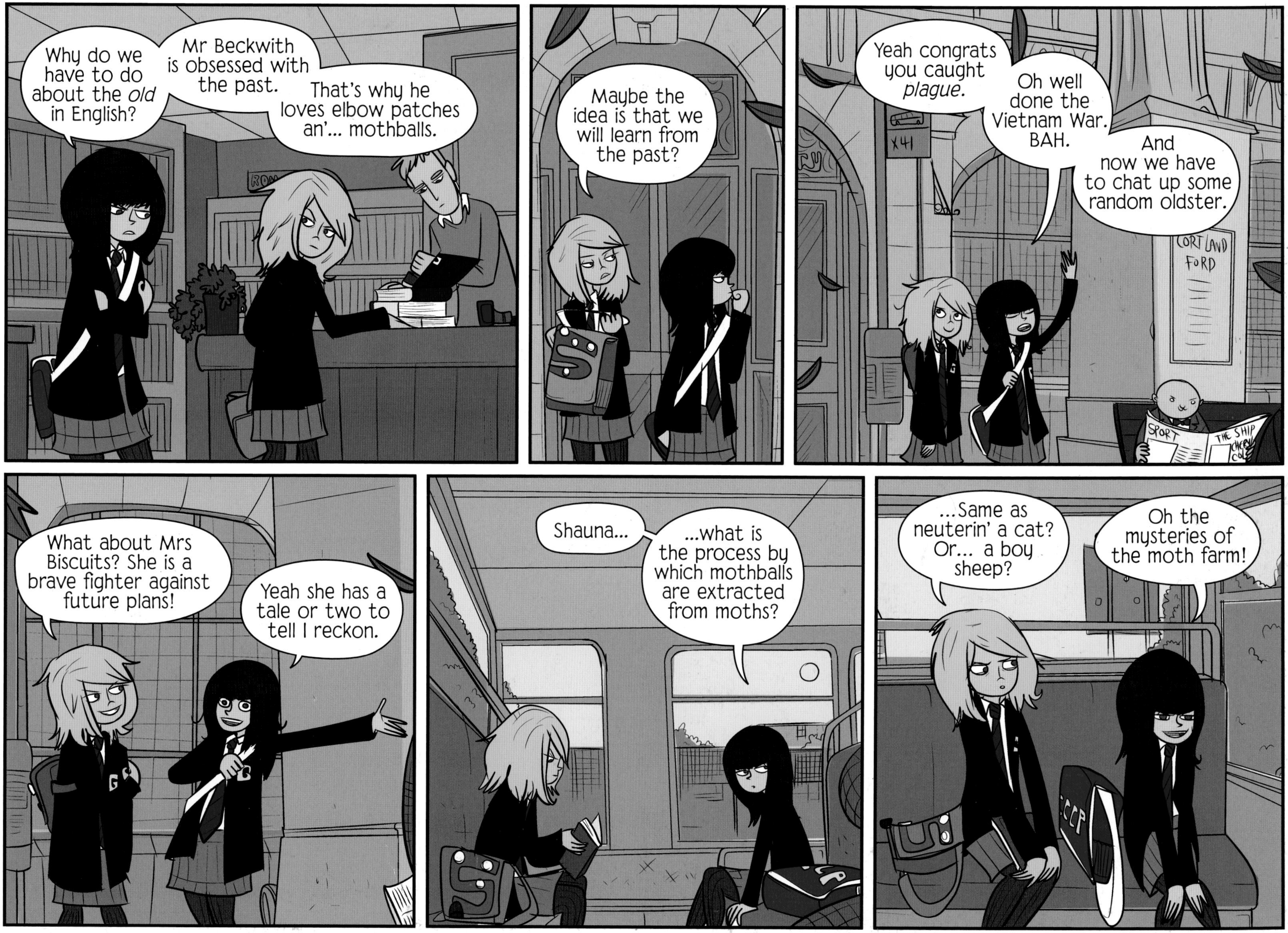
Why do we have to do about the *old* in English?
Mr Beckwith is obsessed with the past.
That's why he loves elbow patches an'... mothballs.
Maybe the idea is that we will learn from the past?
Yeah congrats you caught *plague*.
Oh well done the Vietnam War. BAH.
And now we have to chat up some random oldster.
X41
CORTLAND FORD
SPORT
THE SHIP
What about Mrs Biscuits? She is a brave fighter against future plans!
Yeah she has a tale or two to tell I reckon.
Shauna...
...what is the process by which mothballs are extracted from moths?
...Same as neuterin' a cat? Or... a boy sheep?
Oh the mysteries of the moth farm!

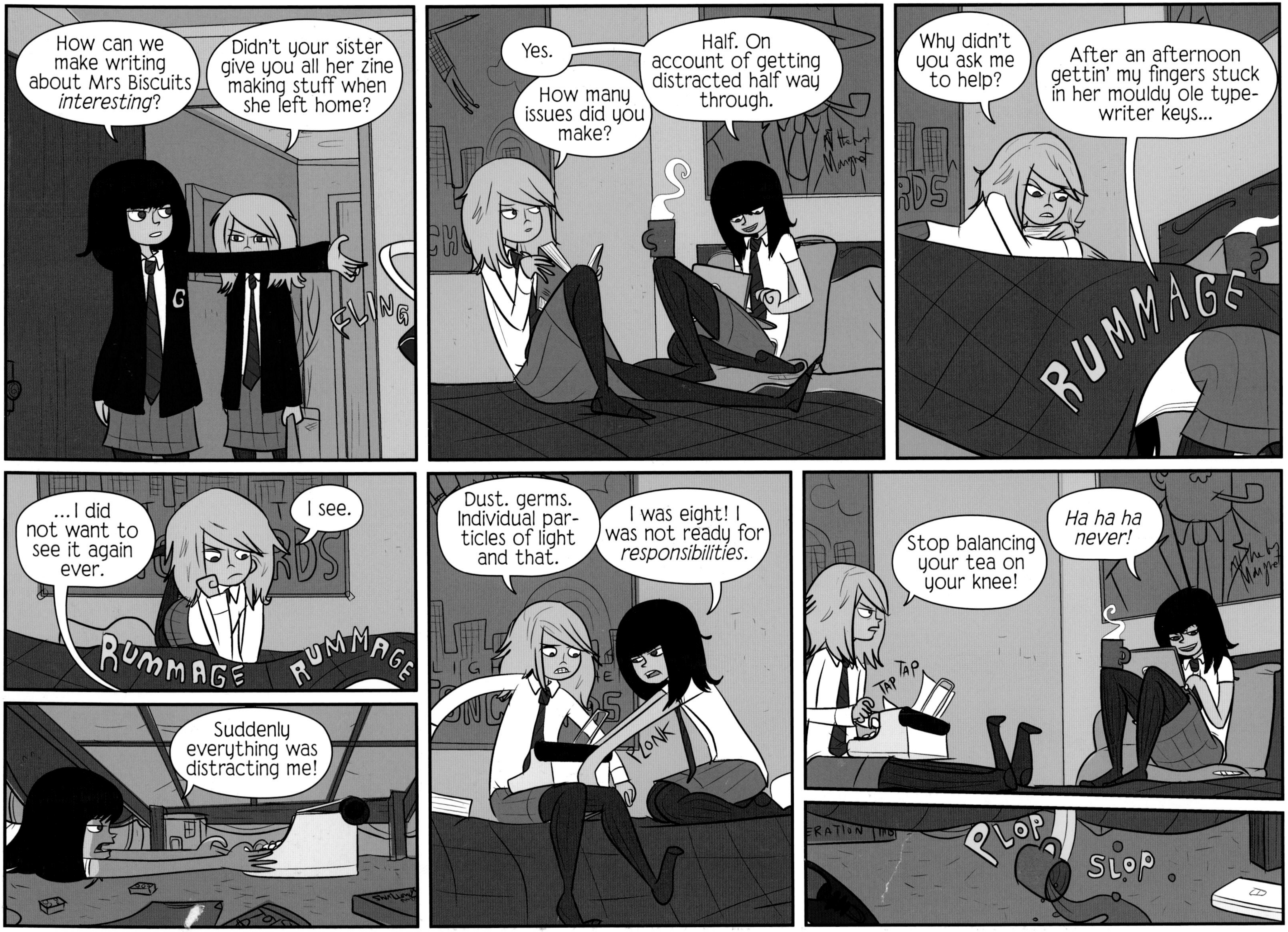
How can we make writing about Mrs Biscuits *interesting*?
Didn't your sister give you all her zine making stuff when she left home?
FLING
Yes.
How many issues did you make?
Half. On account of getting distracted half way through.
Why didn't you ask me to help?
After an afternoon gettin' my fingers stuck in her mouldy ole type-writer keys...
RUMMAGE
...I did not want to see it again ever.
I see.
RUMMAGE RUMMAGE
Suddenly everything was distracting me!
Dust. germs. Individual par-ticles of light and that.
I was eight! I was not ready for *responsibilities*.
PLONK
Stop balancing your tea on your knee!
Ha ha ha never!
TAP TAP
PLOP
SLOP

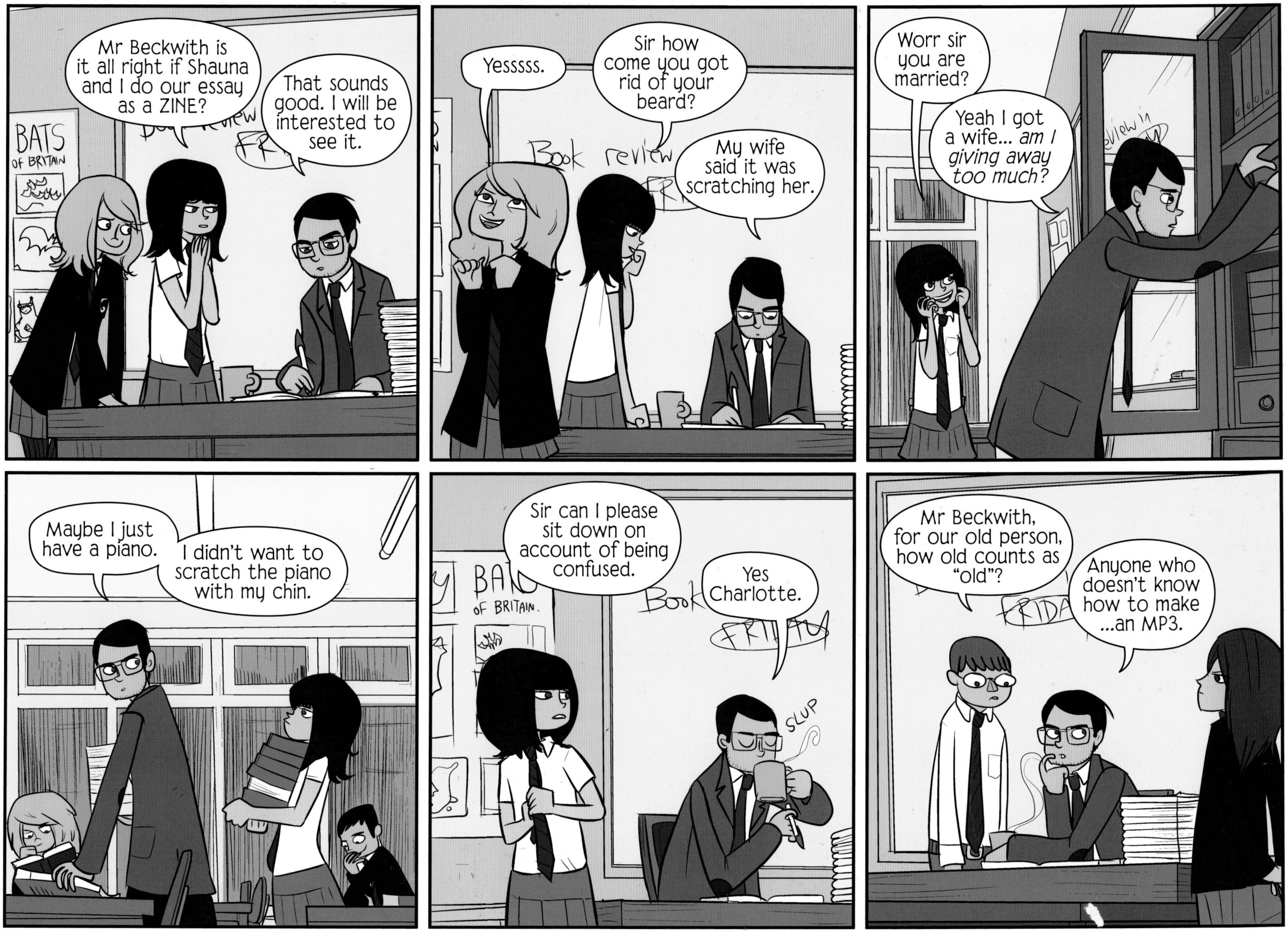
Mr Beckwith is it all right if Shauna and I do our essay as a ZINE?
That sounds good. I will be interested to see it.
BATS OF BRITAIN
Yesssss.
Sir how come you got rid of your beard?
Book review
My wife said it was scratching her.
Worr sir you are married?
Yeah I got a wife... *am I giving away too much?*
Maybe I just have a piano.
I didn't want to scratch the piano with my chin.
Sir can I please sit down on account of being confused.
Yes Charlotte.
SLUP
Mr Beckwith, for our old person, how old counts as "old"?
Anyone who doesn't know how to make ...an MP3.

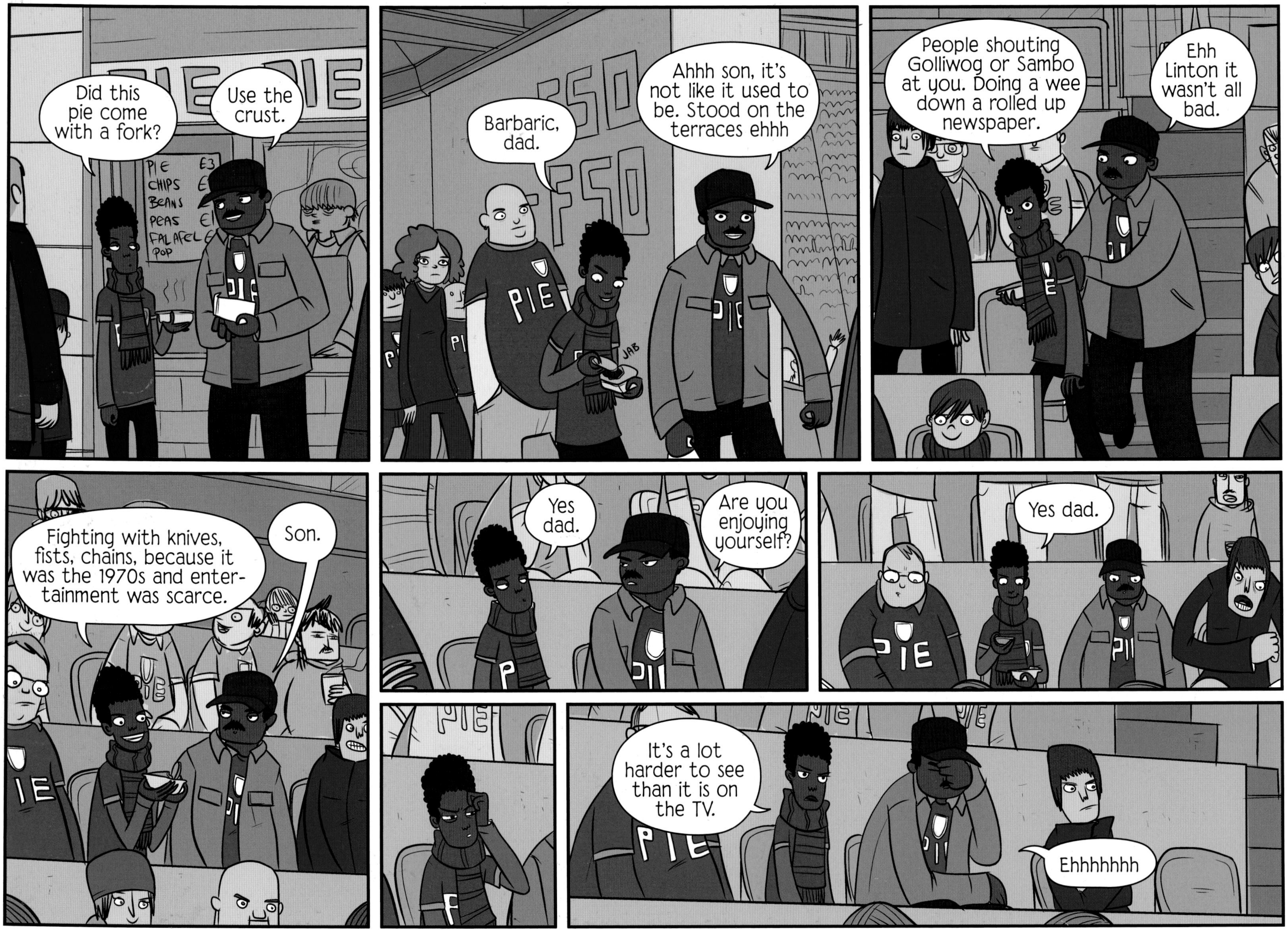
Did this pie come with a fork?
Use the crust.
Barbaric, dad.
Ahhh son, it's not like it used to be. Stood on the terraces ehhh
JAB
People shouting Golliwog or Sambo at you. Doing a wee down a rolled up newspaper.
Ehh Linton it wasn't all bad.
Fighting with knives, fists, chains, because it was the 1970s and entertainment was scarce.
Son.
Yes dad.
Are you enjoying yourself?
Yes dad.
It's a lot harder to see than it is on the TV.
Ehhhhhhh

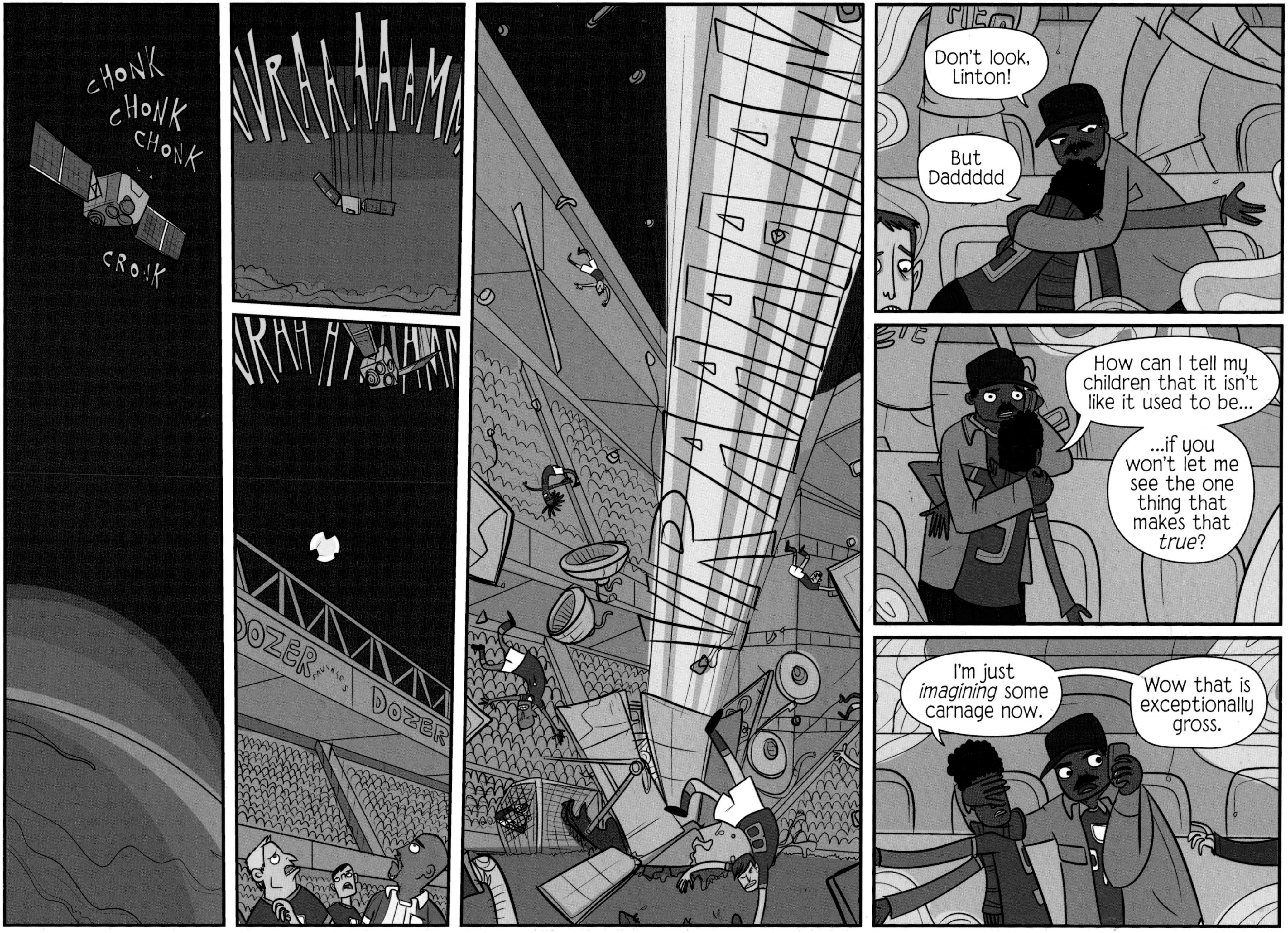
CHONK
CHONK
CHONK
CRONK
DOZER
DOZER
DOZER
Don't look, Linton!
But Dadddddd
How can I tell my children that it isn't like it used to be...
...if you won't let me see the one thing that makes that *true*?
I'm just *imagining* some carnage now.
Wow that is exceptionally gross.

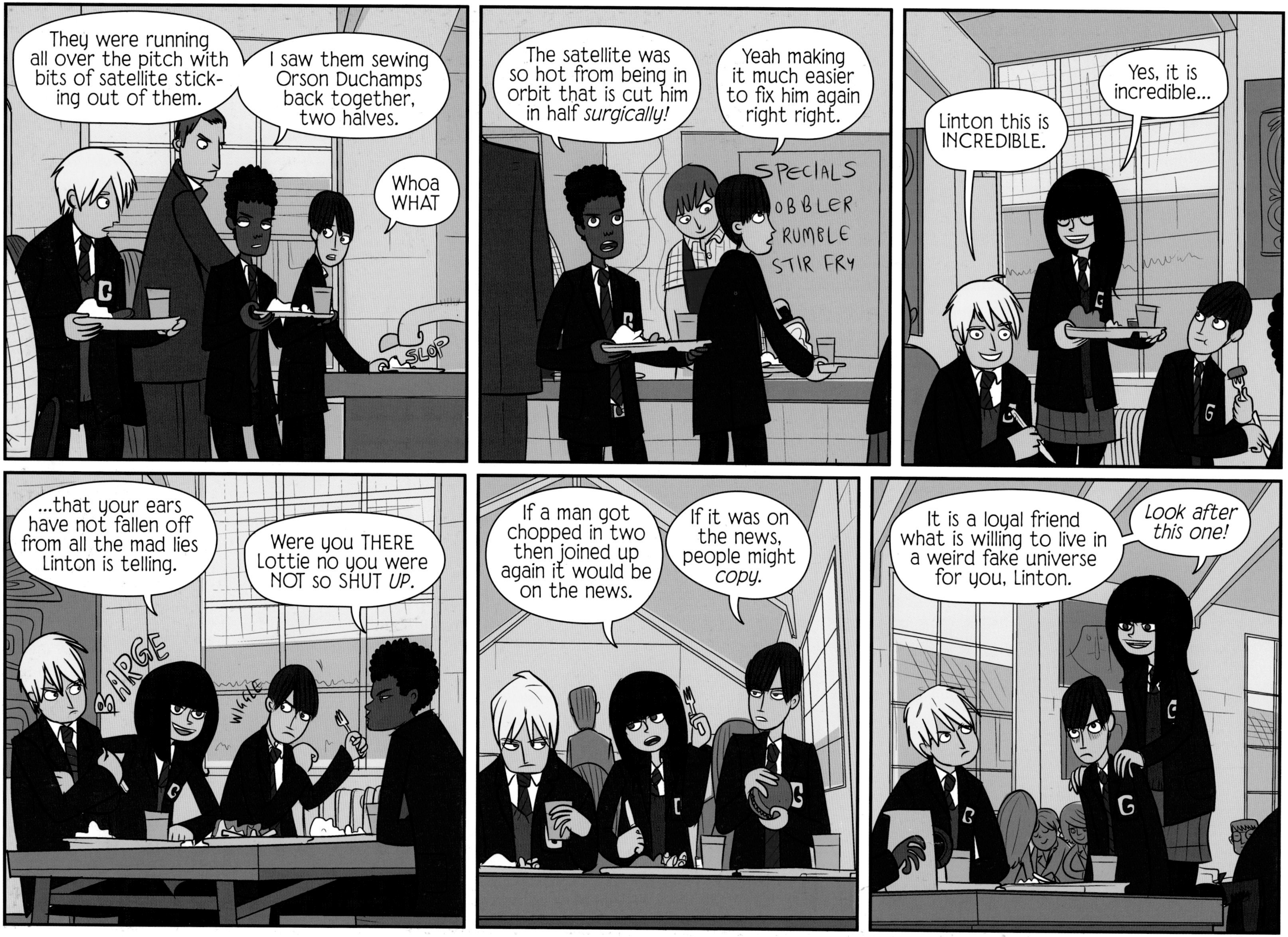
They were running all over the pitch with bits of satellite stick-ing out of them.
I saw them sewing Orson Duchamps back together, two halves.
Whoa WHAT
SLOP
The satellite was so hot from being in orbit that is cut him in half *surgically!*
Yeah making it much easier to fix him again right right.
SPECIALS
OBBLER
RUMBLE
STIR FRY
Linton this is INCREDIBLE.
Yes, it is incredible...
...that your ears have not fallen off from all the mad lies Linton is telling.
Were you THERE Lottie no you were NOT so SHUT *UP*.
BARGE
WIGGLE
If a man got chopped in two then joined up again it would be on the news.
If it was on the news, people might *copy.*
It is a loyal friend what is willing to live in a weird fake universe for you, Linton.
Look after this one!

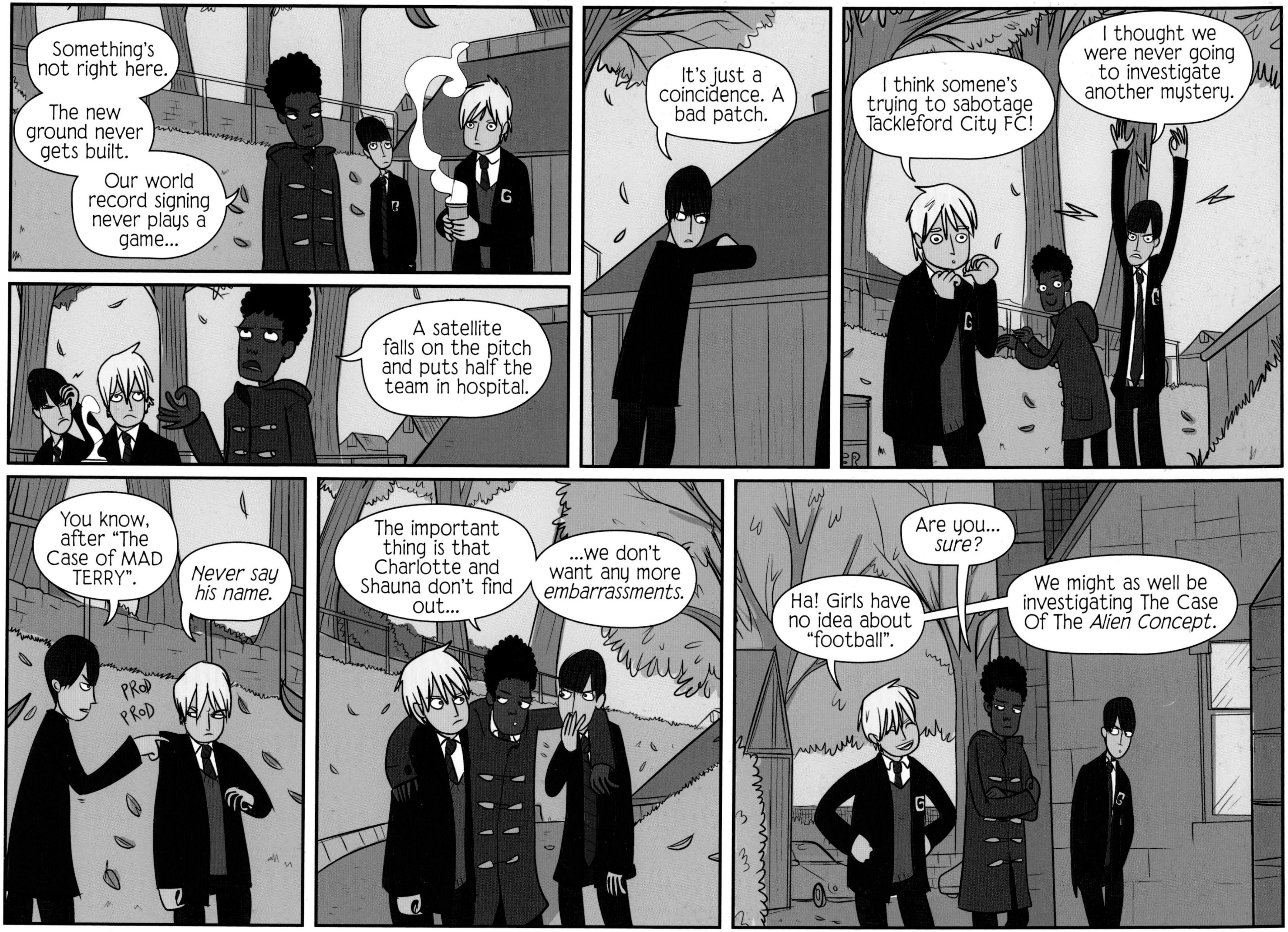
Something's not right here.
The new ground never gets built.
Our world record signing never plays a game...
A satellite falls on the pitch and puts half the team in hospital.
It's just a coincidence. A bad patch.
I think somene's trying to sabotage Tackleford City FC!
I thought we were never going to investigate another mystery.
You know, after "The Case of MAD TERRY".
Never say his name.
PROD
PROD
The important thing is that Charlotte and Shauna don't find out...
...we don't want any more embarrassments.
Ha! Girls have no idea about "football".
Are you... sure?
We might as well be investigating The Case Of The Alien Concept.

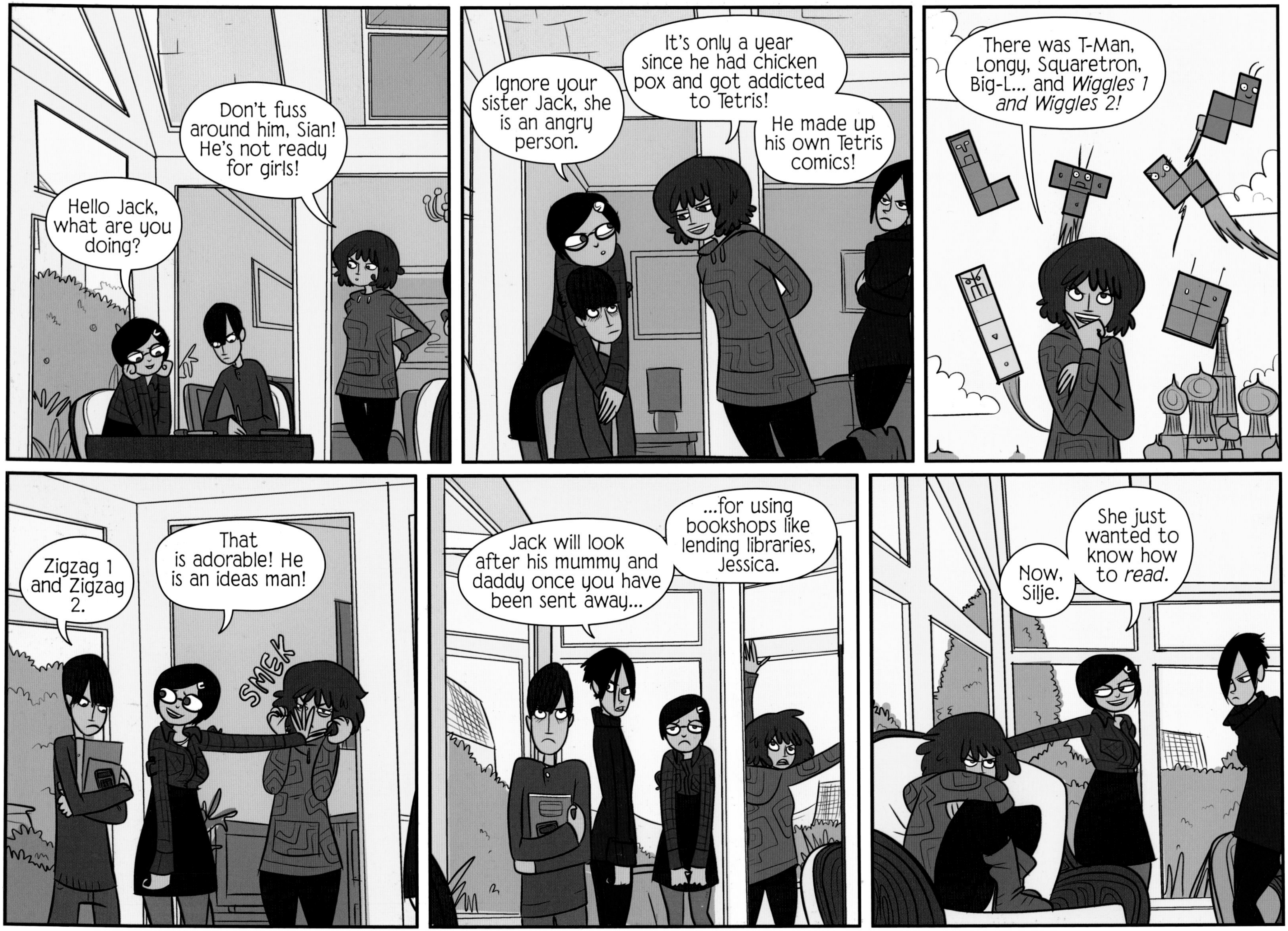
Hello Jack, what are you doing?
Don't fuss around him, Sian! He's not ready for girls!
Ignore your sister Jack, she is an angry person.
It's only a year since he had chicken pox and got addicted to Tetris!
He made up his own Tetris comics!
There was T-Man, Longy, Squaretron, Big-L... and *Wiggles 1 and Wiggles 2!*
Zigzag 1 and Zigzag 2.
That is adorable! He is an ideas man!
SMEK
Jack will look after his mummy and daddy once you have been sent away...
...for using bookshops like lending libraries, Jessica.
Now, Silje.
She just wanted to know how to *read*.

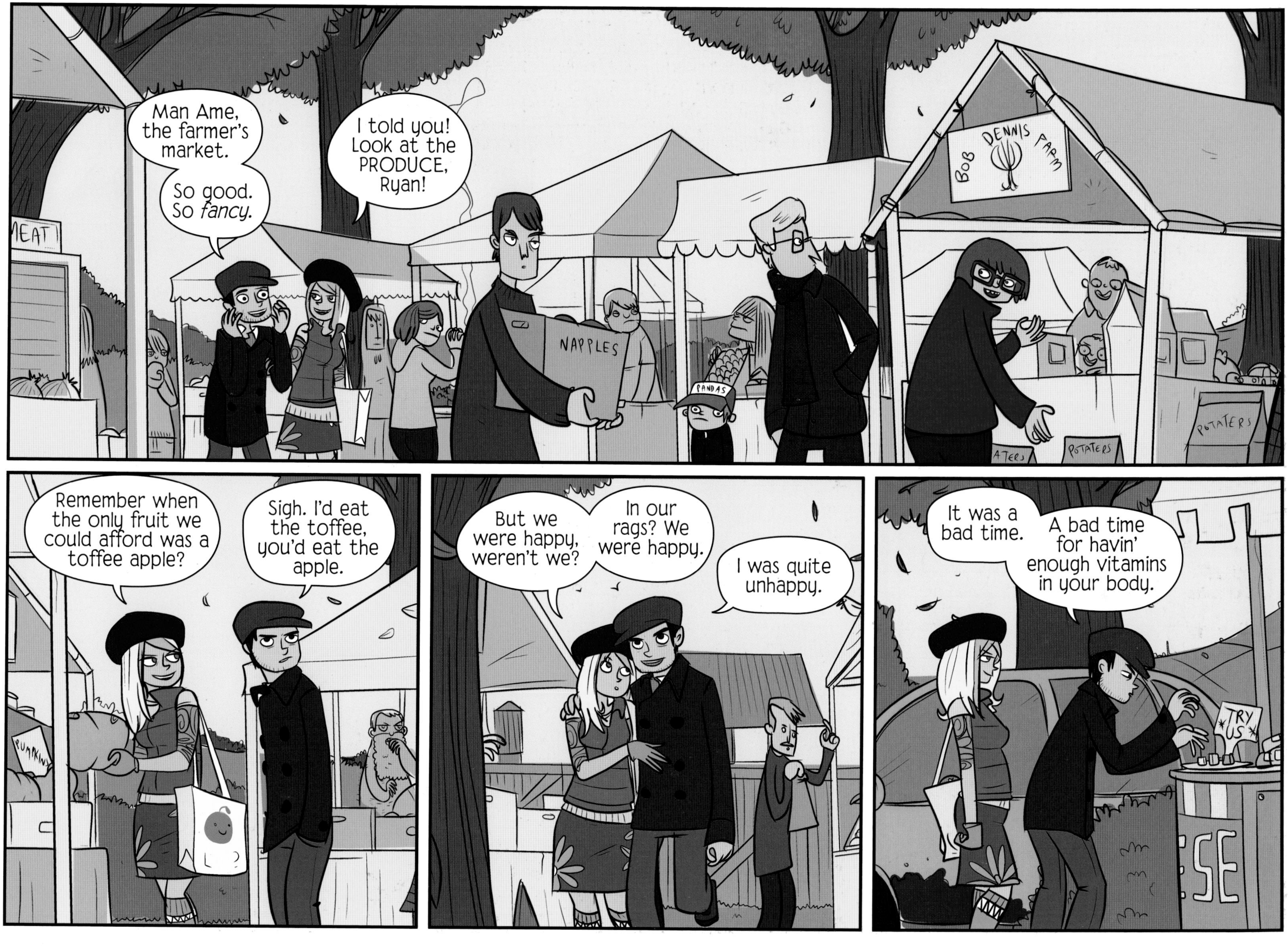
Man Ame, the farmer's market.
So good. So *fancy.*
I told you! Look at the PRODUCE, Ryan!
MEAT
NAPPLES
PANDAS
BOB DENNIS FARM
POTATERS
POTATERS
Remember when the only fruit we could afford was a toffee apple?
Sigh. I'd eat the toffee, you'd eat the apple.
PUMPKINS
But we were happy, weren't we?
In our rags? We were happy.
I was quite unhappy.
It was a bad time.
A bad time for havin' enough vitamins in your body.
TRY US

Bad Machinery, Volume One

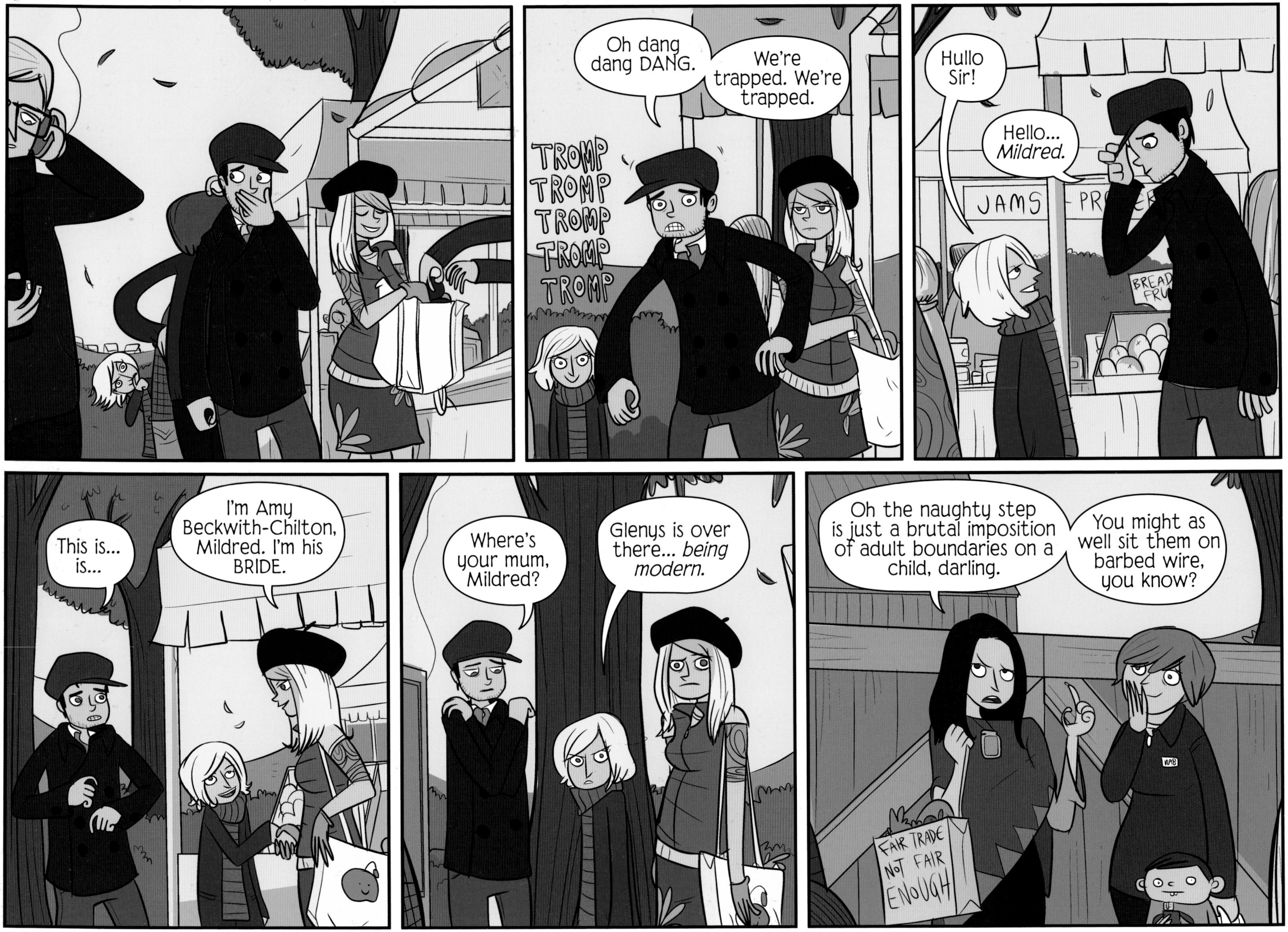
Oh dang dang DANG.
We're trapped. We're trapped.
TROMP TROMP TROMP TROMP TROMP TROMP
Hullo Sir!
Hello... *Mildred.*
JAMS
BREAD
This is... is...
I'm Amy Beckwith-Chilton, Mildred. I'm his BRIDE.
Where's your mum, Mildred?
Glenys is over there... *being modern.*
Oh the naughty step is just a brutal imposition of adult boundaries on a child, darling.
You might as well sit them on barbed wire, you know?
FAIR TRADE NOT FAIR ENOUGH

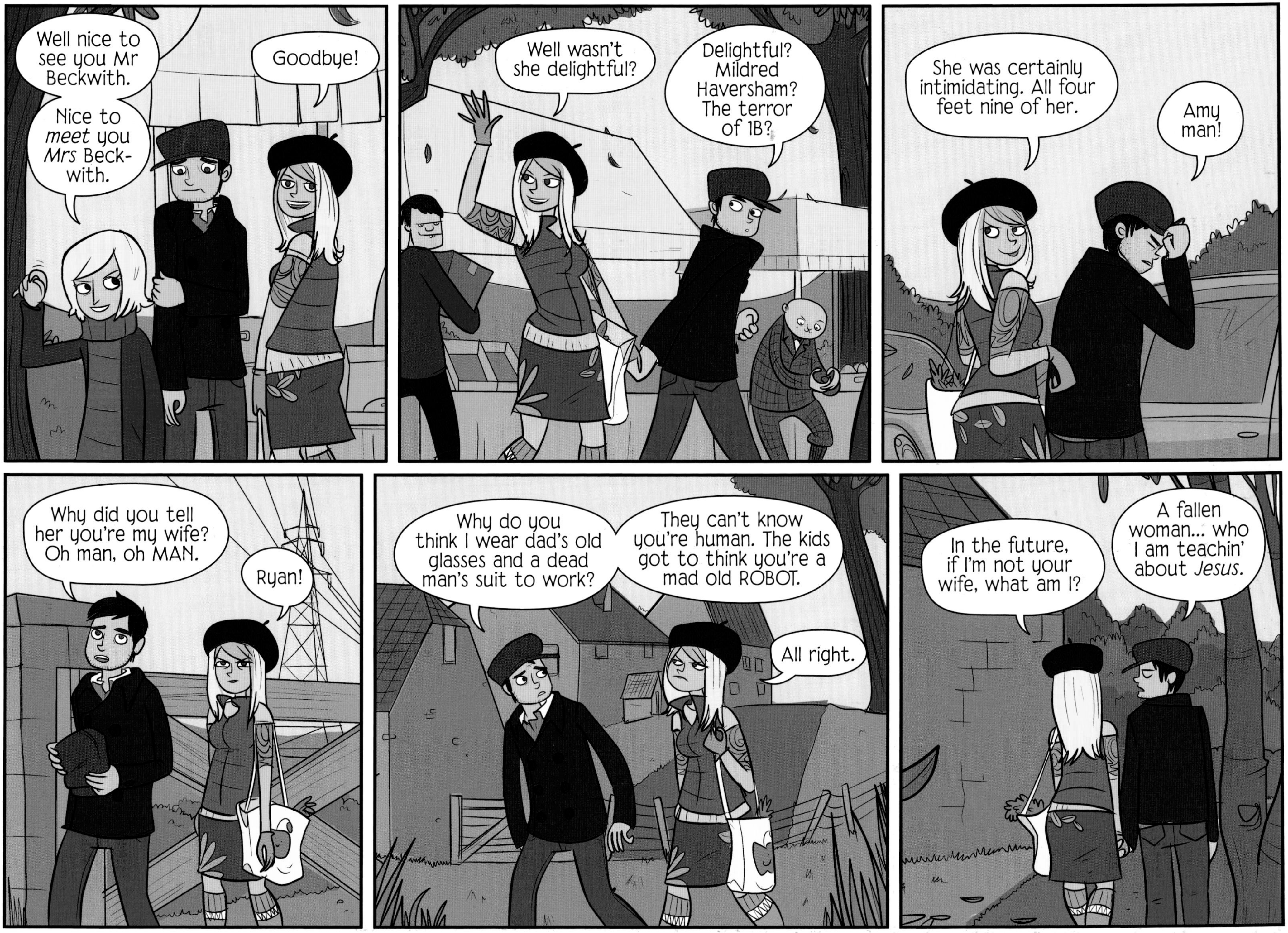
Well nice to see you Mr Beckwith.
Nice to *meet* you *Mrs* Beck-with.
Goodbye!
Well wasn't she delightful?
Delightful? Mildred Haversham? The terror of 1B?
She was certainly intimidating. All four feet nine of her.
Amy man!
Why did you tell her you're my wife? Oh man, oh MAN.
Ryan!
Why do you think I wear dad's old glasses and a dead man's suit to work?
They can't know you're human. The kids got to think you're a mad old ROBOT.
All right.
In the future, if I'm not your wife, what am I?
A fallen woman... who I am teachin' about *Jesus*.

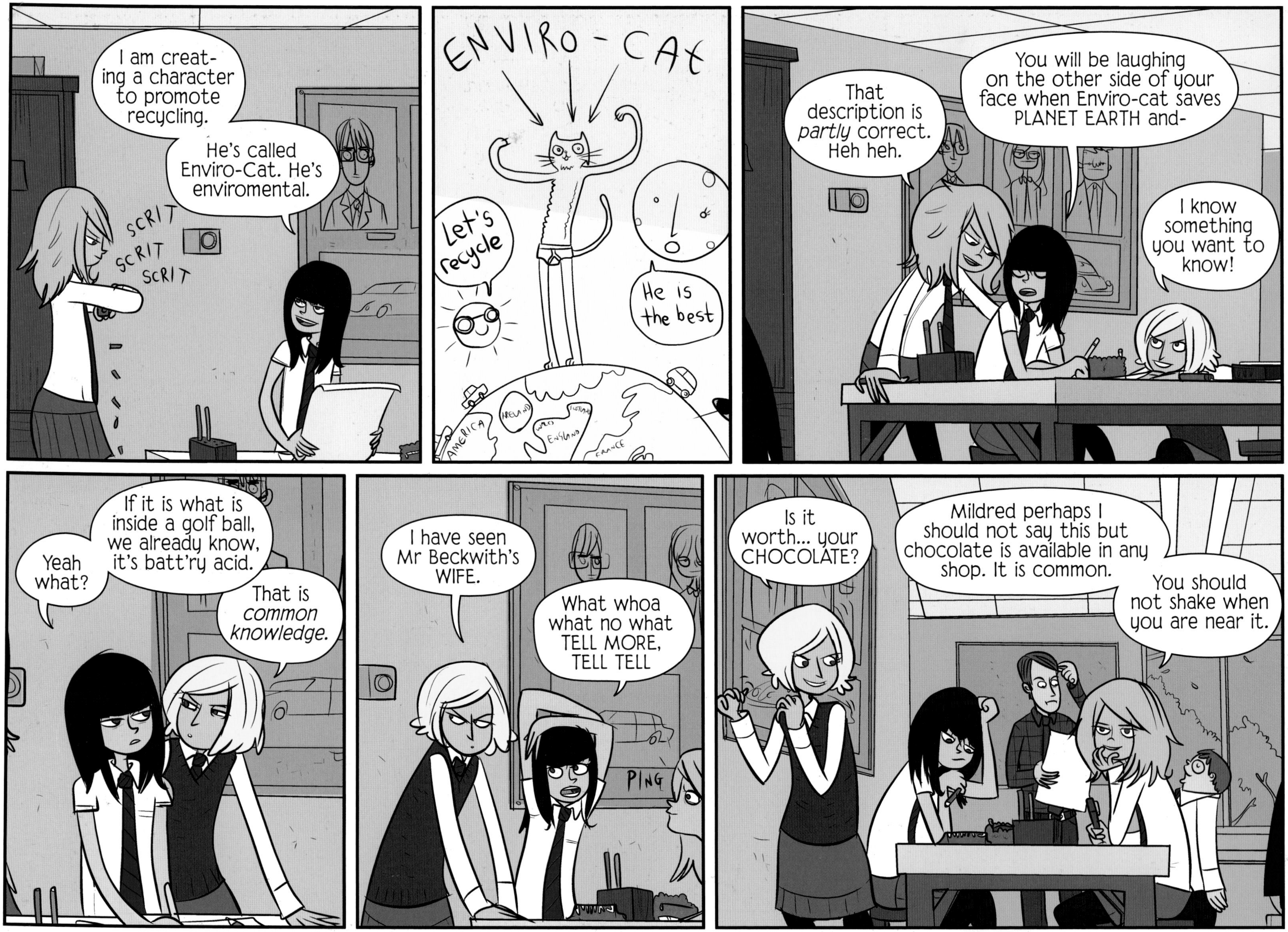
I am creat-ing a character to promote recycling.
He's called Enviro-Cat. He's enviromental.
SCRIT SCRIT SCRIT
ENVIRO-CAT
Let's recycle
He is the best
AMERICA
IRELAND
ENGLAND
FRANCE
That description is *partly* correct. Heh heh.
You will be laughing on the other side of your face when Enviro-cat saves PLANET EARTH and-
I know something you want to know!
Yeah what?
If it is what is inside a golf ball, we already know, it's batt'ry acid.
That is *common knowledge.*
I have seen Mr Beckwith's WIFE.
What whoa what no what TELL MORE, TELL TELL
PING
Is it worth... your CHOCOLATE?
Mildred perhaps I should not say this but chocolate is available in any shop. It is common.
You should not shake when you are near it.

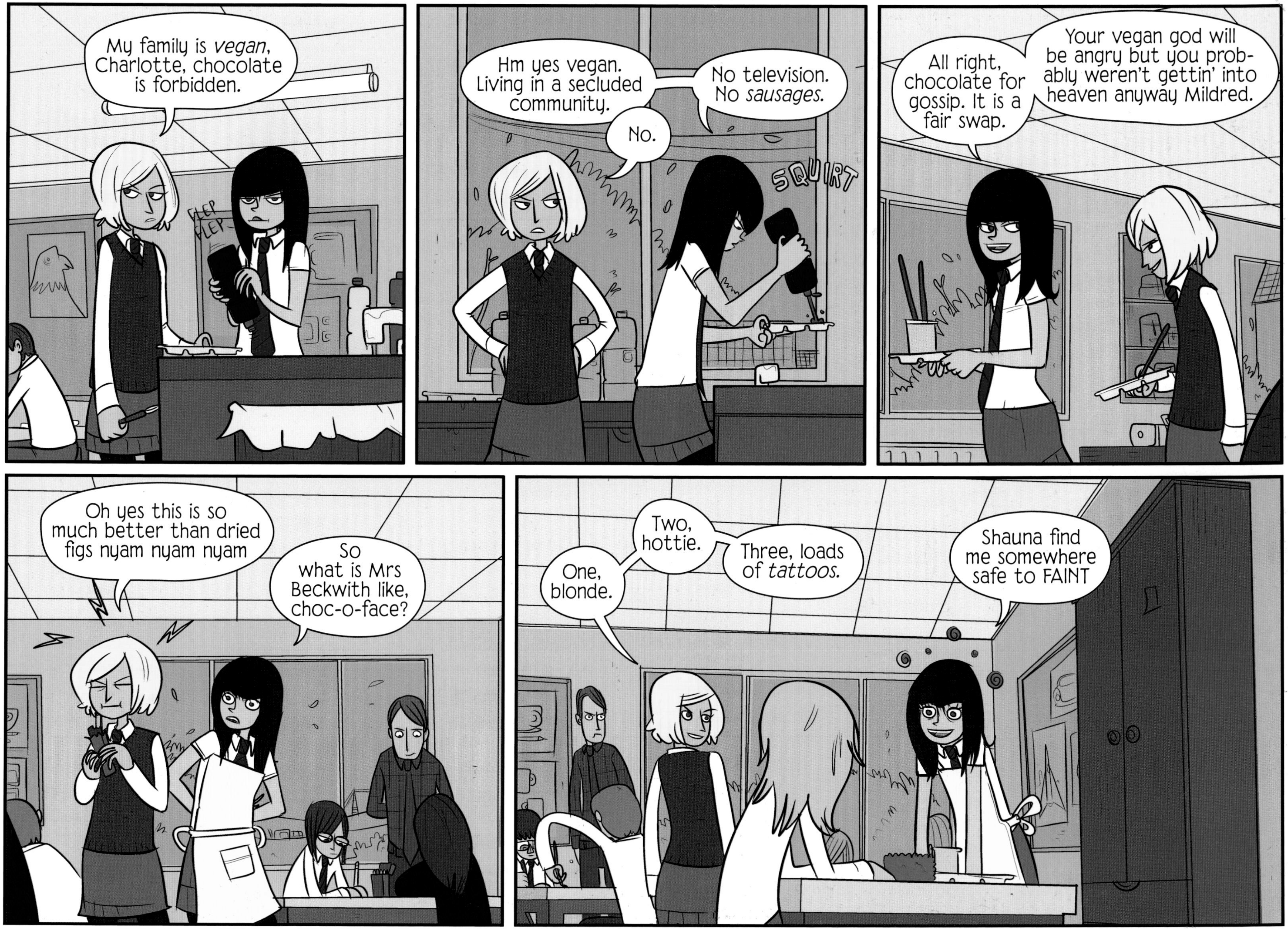
My family is *vegan*, Charlotte, chocolate is forbidden.
FLEP FLEP
Hm yes vegan. Living in a secluded community.
No television. No *sausages.*
No.
SQUIRT
All right, chocolate for gossip. It is a fair swap.
Your vegan god will be angry but you probably weren't gettin' into heaven anyway Mildred.
Oh yes this is so much better than dried figs nyam nyam nyam
So what is Mrs Beckwith like, choc-o-face?
One, blonde.
Two, hottie.
Three, loads of *tattoos.*
Shauna find me somewhere safe to FAINT

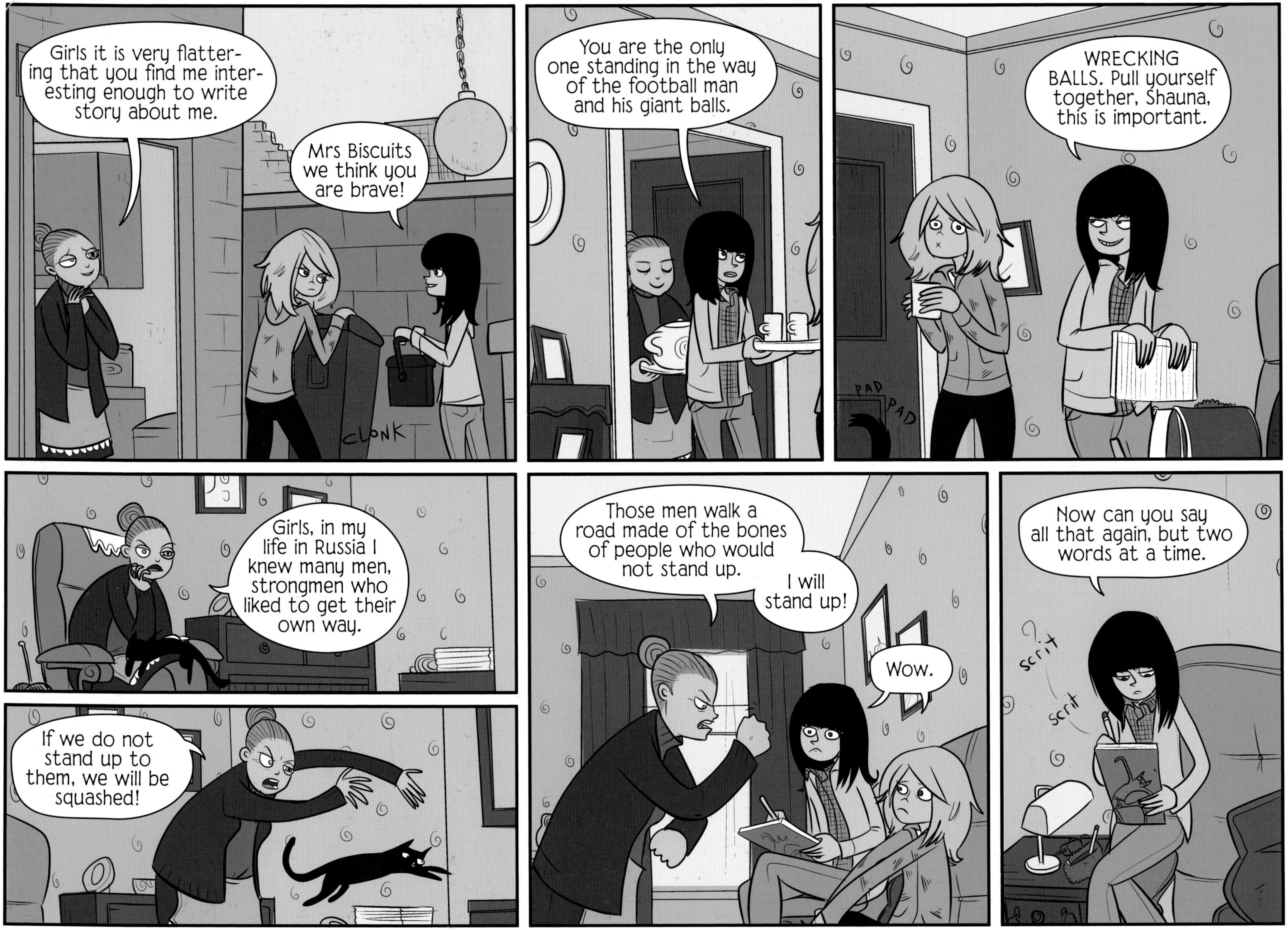
Girls it is very flattering that you find me interesting enough to write story about me.
Mrs Biscuits we think you are brave!
CLONK
You are the only one standing in the way of the football man and his giant balls.
WRECKING BALLS. Pull yourself together, Shauna, this is important.
PAD PAD
Girls, in my life in Russia I knew many men, strongmen who liked to get their own way.
If we do not stand up to them, we will be squashed!
Those men walk a road made of the bones of people who would not stand up.
I will stand up!
Wow.
Now can you say all that again, but two words at a time.
scrit
scrit

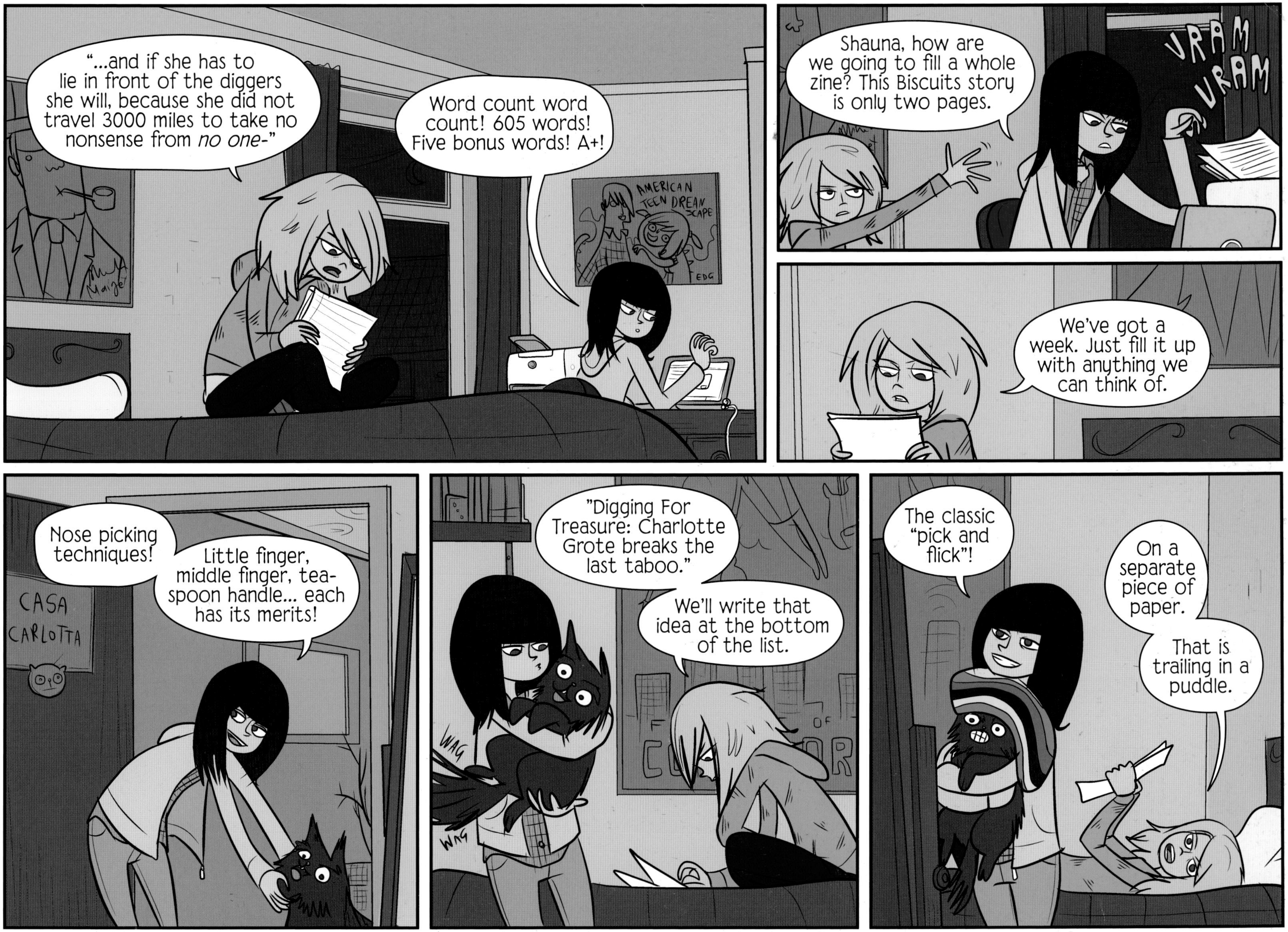
"...and if she has to lie in front of the diggers she will, because she did not travel 3000 miles to take no nonsense from *no one*-"
Word count word count! 605 words! Five bonus words! A+!
AMERICAN TEEN DREAM SCAPE
Shauna, how are we going to fill a whole zine? This Biscuits story is only two pages.
VRAM VRAM
We've got a week. Just fill it up with anything we can think of.
Nose picking techniques!
Little finger, middle finger, tea-spoon handle... each has its merits!
CASA CARLOTTA
"Digging For Treasure: Charlotte Grote breaks the last taboo."
We'll write that idea at the bottom of the list.
WAG
WAG
The classic "pick and flick"!
On a separate piece of paper.
That is trailing in a puddle.

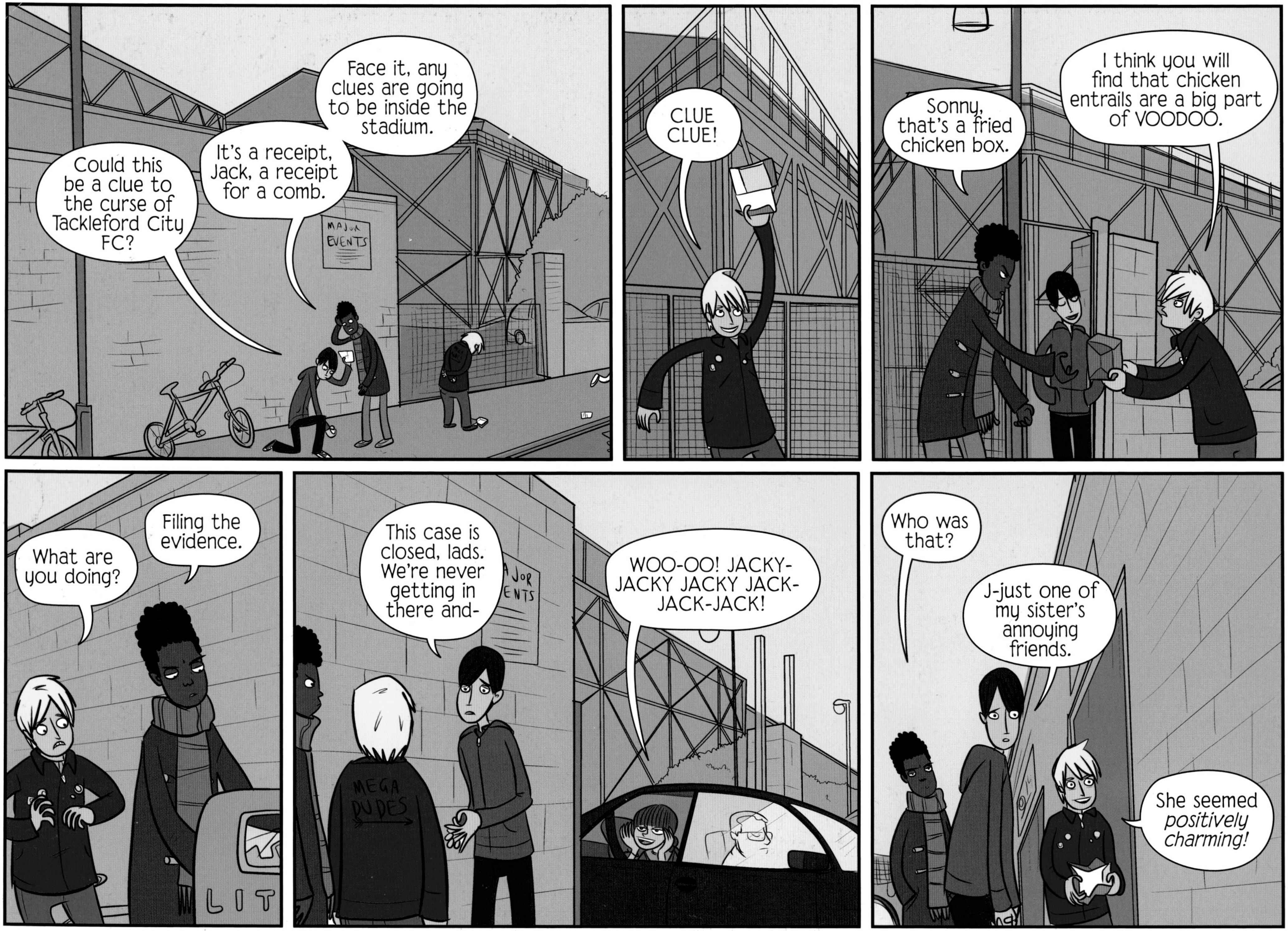
Could this be a clue to the curse of Tackleford City FC?
It's a receipt, Jack, a receipt for a comb.
Face it, any clues are going to be inside the stadium.
MAJOR EVENTS
CLUE CLUE!
Sonny, that's a fried chicken box.
I think you will find that chicken entrails are a big part of VOODOO.
What are you doing?
Filing the evidence.
LIT
This case is closed, lads. We're never getting in there and-
MEGA DUDES
WOO-OO! JACKY-JACKY JACKY JACK-JACK-JACK!
Who was that?
J-just one of my sister's annoying friends.
She seemed *positively charming!*

The Case of The Team Spirit

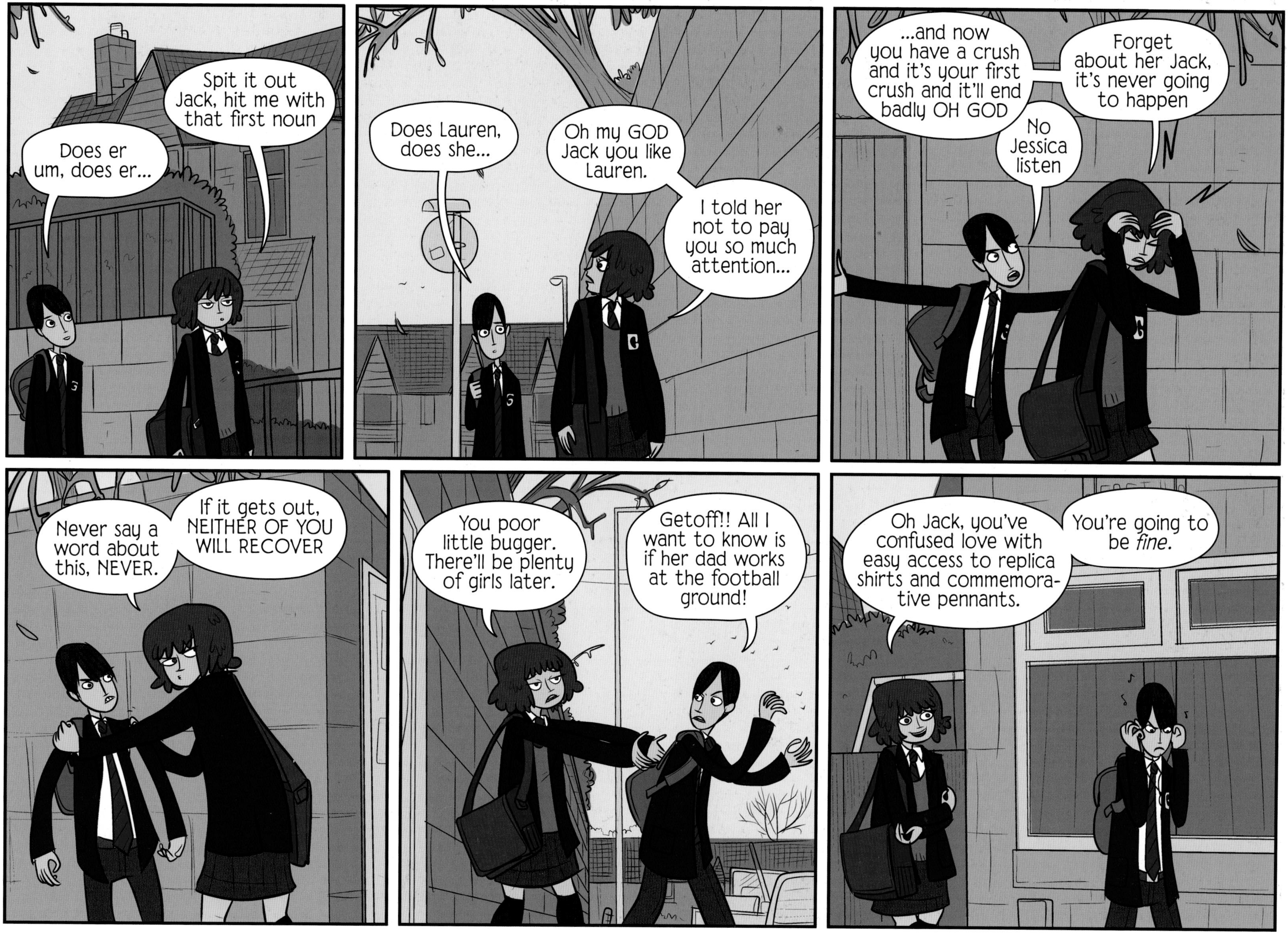
Does er um, does er...
Spit it out Jack, hit me with that first noun
Does Lauren, does she...
Oh my GOD Jack you like Lauren.
I told her not to pay you so much attention...
...and now you have a crush and it's your first crush and it'll end badly OH GOD
Forget about her Jack, it's never going to happen
No Jessica listen
Never say a word about this, NEVER.
If it gets out, NEITHER OF YOU WILL RECOVER
You poor little bugger. There'll be plenty of girls later.
Getoff!! All I want to know is if her dad works at the football ground!
Oh Jack, you've confused love with easy access to replica shirts and commemora-tive pennants.
You're going to be *fine.*

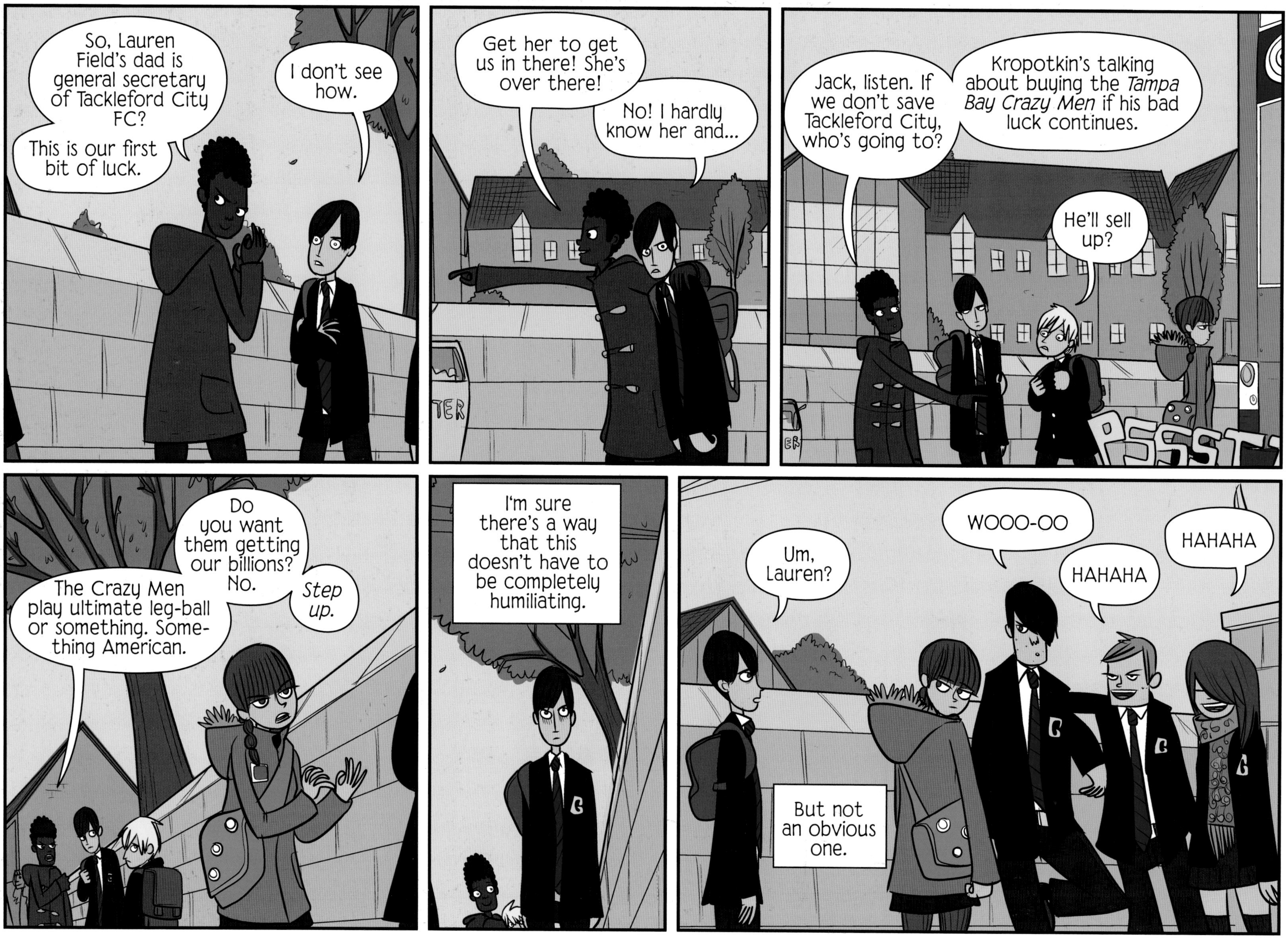
So, Lauren Field's dad is general secretary of Tackleford City FC?
This is our first bit of luck.
I don't see how.
Get her to get us in there! She's over there!
No! I hardly know her and...
Jack, listen. If we don't save Tackleford City, who's going to?
Kropotkin's talking about buying the *Tampa Bay Crazy Men* if his bad luck continues.
He'll sell up?
PSSST
Do you want them getting our billions? No.
The Crazy Men play ultimate leg-ball or something. Something American.
Step up.
I'm sure there's a way that this doesn't have to be completely humiliating.
Um, Lauren?
WOOO-OO
HAHAHA
HAHAHA
But not an obvious one.

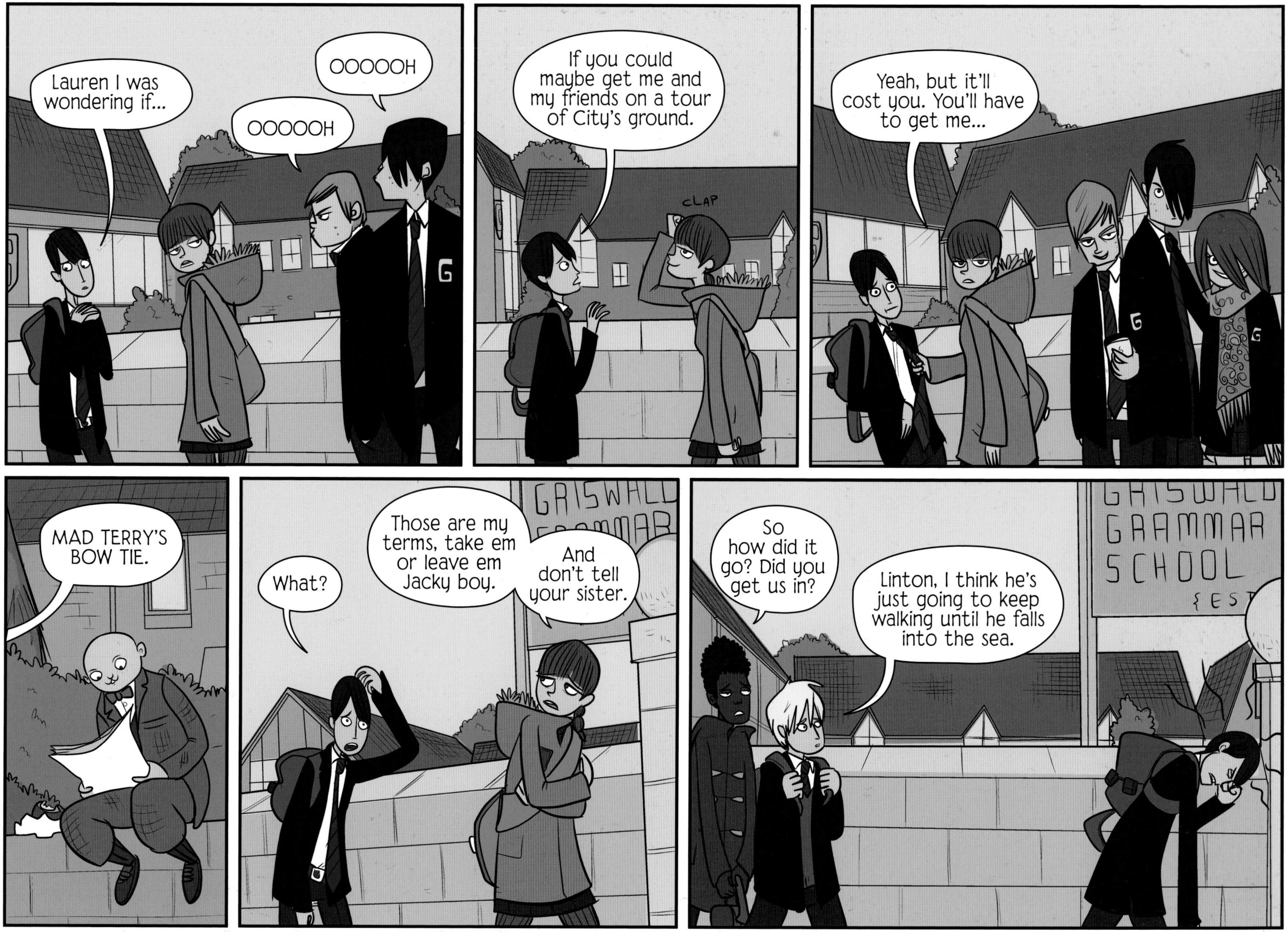
Lauren I was wondering if...
OOOOOH
OOOOOH
If you could maybe get me and my friends on a tour of City's ground.
CLAP
Yeah, but it'll cost you. You'll have to get me...
MAD TERRY'S BOW TIE.
What?
Those are my terms, take em or leave em Jacky boy.
And don't tell your sister.
So how did it go? Did you get us in?
Linton, I think he's just going to keep walking until he falls into the sea.
GRISWALD GRAMMAR SCHOOL

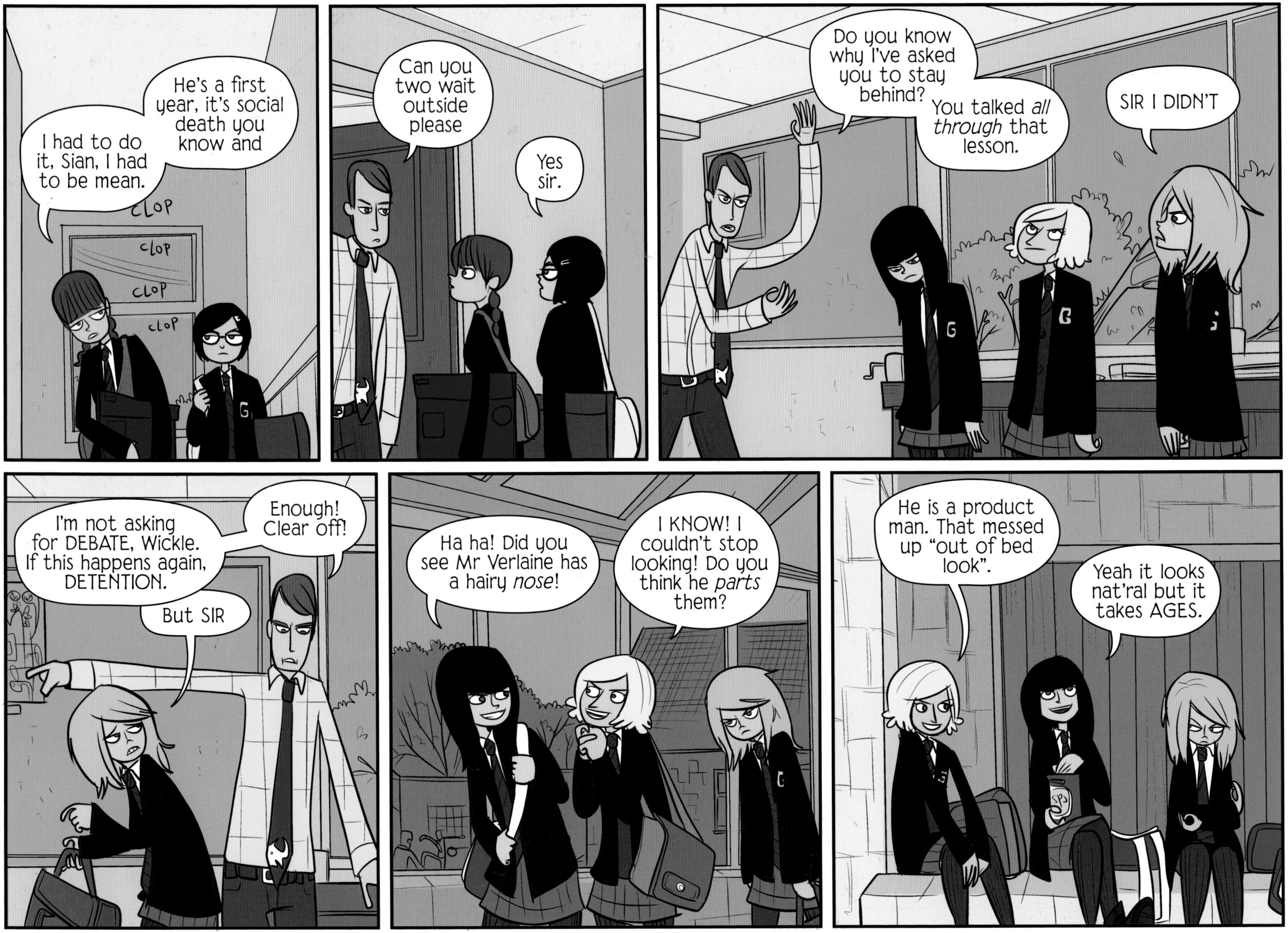
I had to do it, Sian, I had to be mean.
He's a first year, it's social death you know and
CLOP
CLOP
CLOP
CLOP
Can you two wait outside please
Yes sir.
Do you know why I've asked you to stay behind?
You talked *all through* that lesson.
SIR I DIDN'T
I'm not asking for DEBATE, Wickle. If this happens again, DETENTION.
But SIR
Enough! Clear off!
Ha ha! Did you see Mr Verlaine has a hairy *nose*!
I KNOW! I couldn't stop looking! Do you think he *parts* them?
He is a product man. That messed up "out of bed look".
Yeah it looks nat'ral but it takes AGES.

The Case of The Team Spirit

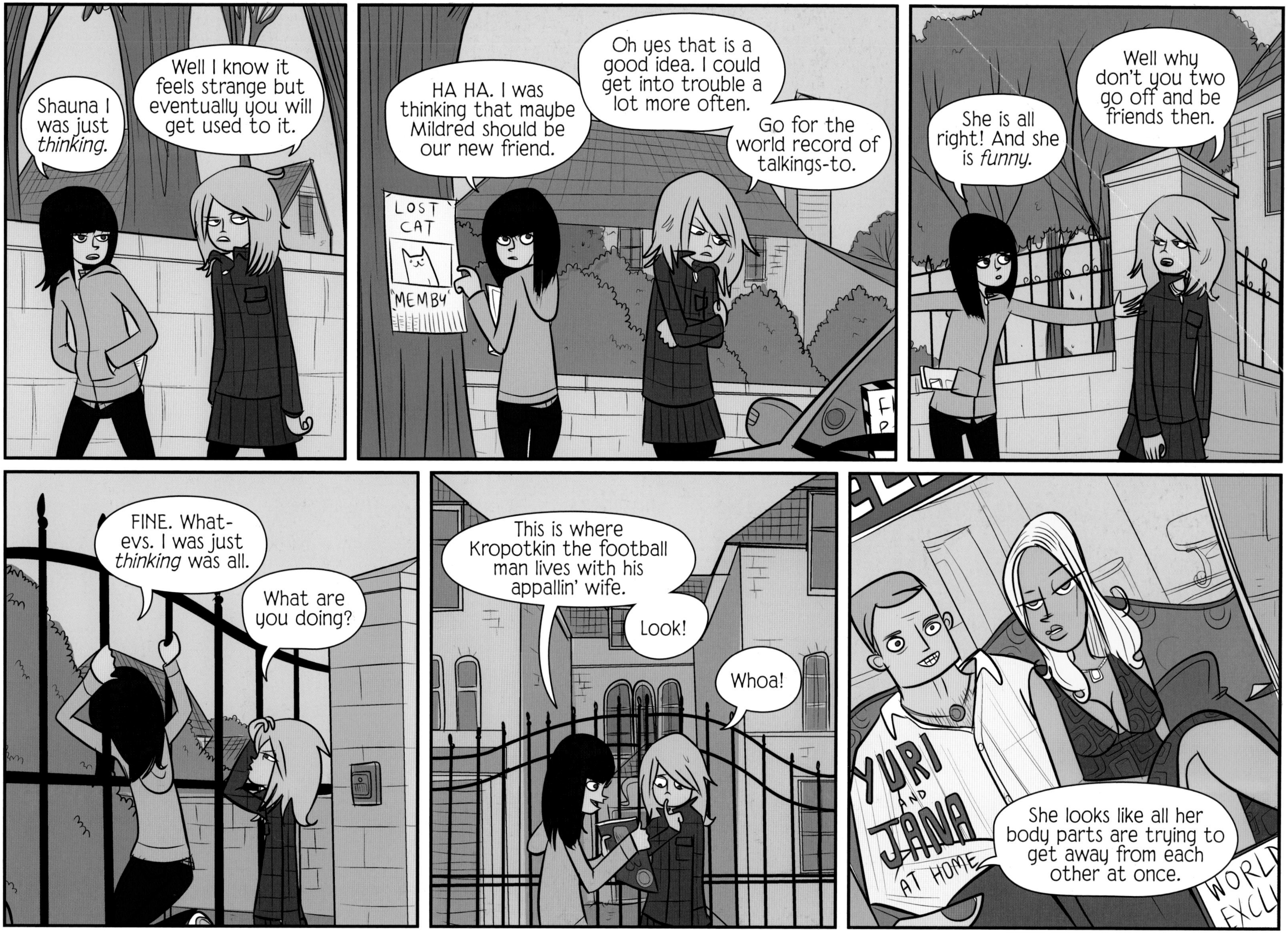
Shauna I was just *thinking.*
Well I know it feels strange but eventually you will get used to it.
HA HA. I was thinking that maybe Mildred should be our new friend.
LOST CAT
"MEMBY"
Oh yes that is a good idea. I could get into trouble a lot more often.
Go for the world record of talkings-to.
She is all right! And she is *funny.*
Well why don't you two go off and be friends then.
FINE. What-evs. I was just *thinking* was all.
What are you doing?
This is where Kropotkin the football man lives with his appallin' wife.
Look!
Whoa!
YURI AND JANA AT HOME
She looks like all her body parts are trying to get away from each other at once.
WORLD

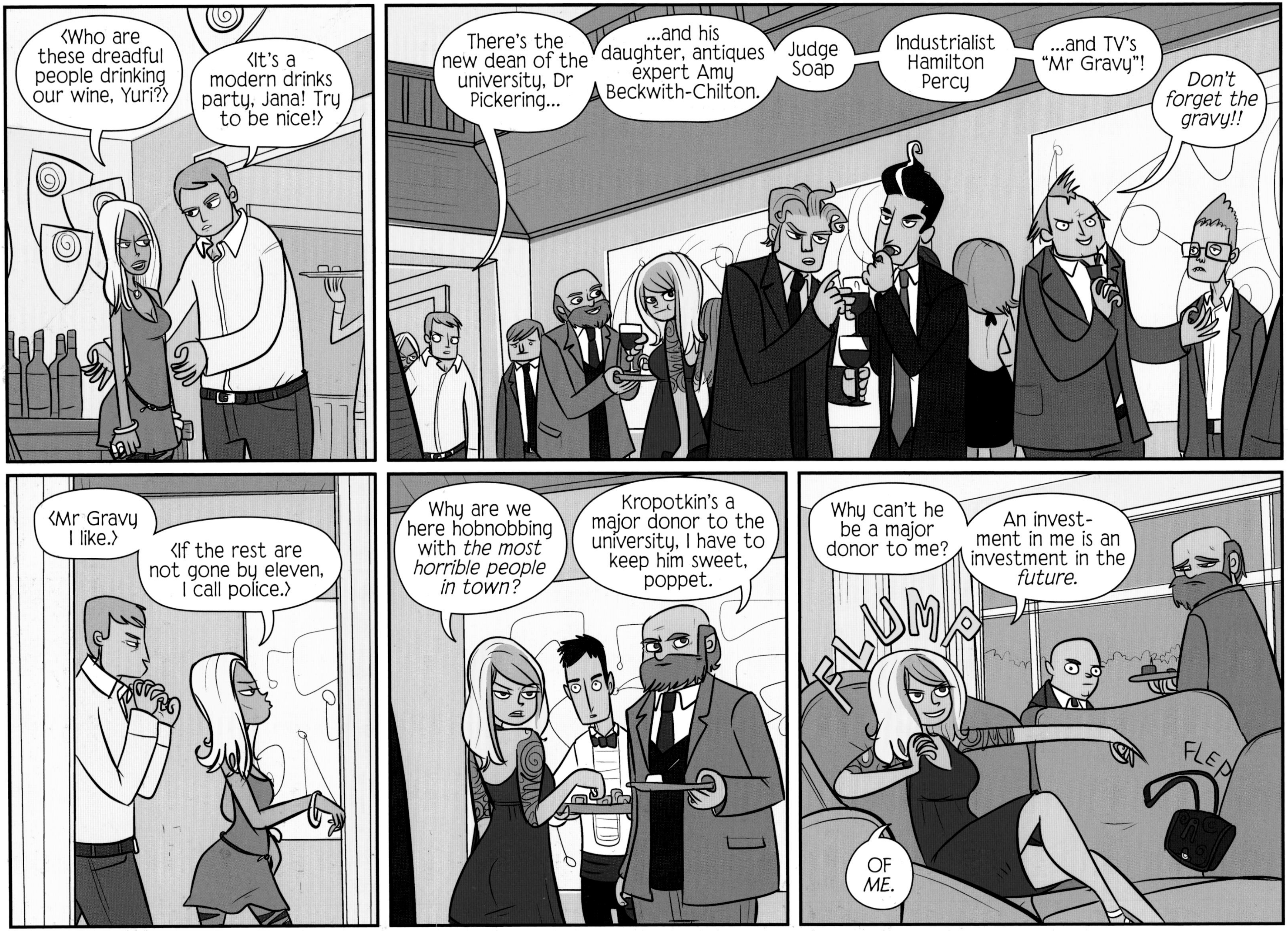
‹Who are these dreadful people drinking our wine, Yuri?›
‹It's a modern drinks party, Jana! Try to be nice!›
There's the new dean of the university, Dr Pickering...
...and his daughter, antiques expert Amy Beckwith-Chilton.
Judge Soap
Industrialist Hamilton Percy
...and TV's "Mr Gravy"!
Don't forget the gravy!!
‹Mr Gravy I like.›
‹If the rest are not gone by eleven, I call police.›
Why are we here hobnobbing with *the most horrible people in town?*
Kropotkin's a major donor to the university, I have to keep him sweet, poppet.
Why can't he be a major donor to me?
An investment in me is an investment in the *future.*
FLUMP
OF *ME.*
FLEP

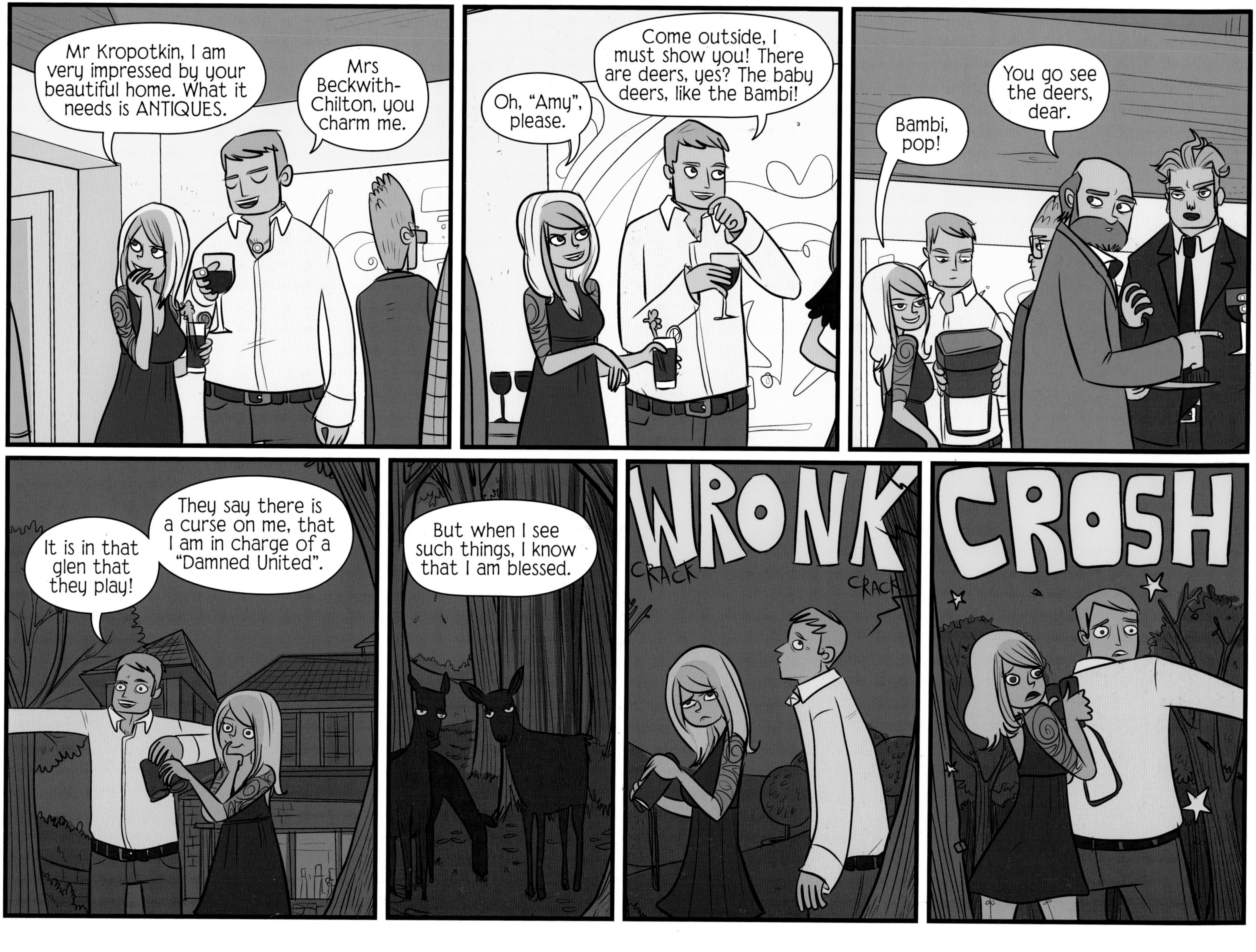
Mr Kropotkin, I am very impressed by your beautiful home. What it needs is ANTIQUES.
Mrs Beckwith-Chilton, you charm me.
Oh, "Amy", please.
Come outside, I must show you! There are deers, yes? The baby deers, like the Bambi!
Bambi, pop!
You go see the deers, dear.
It is in that glen that they play!
They say there is a curse on me, that I am in charge of a "Damned United".
But when I see such things, I know that I am blessed.
WRONK
CRACK
CRACK
CROSH

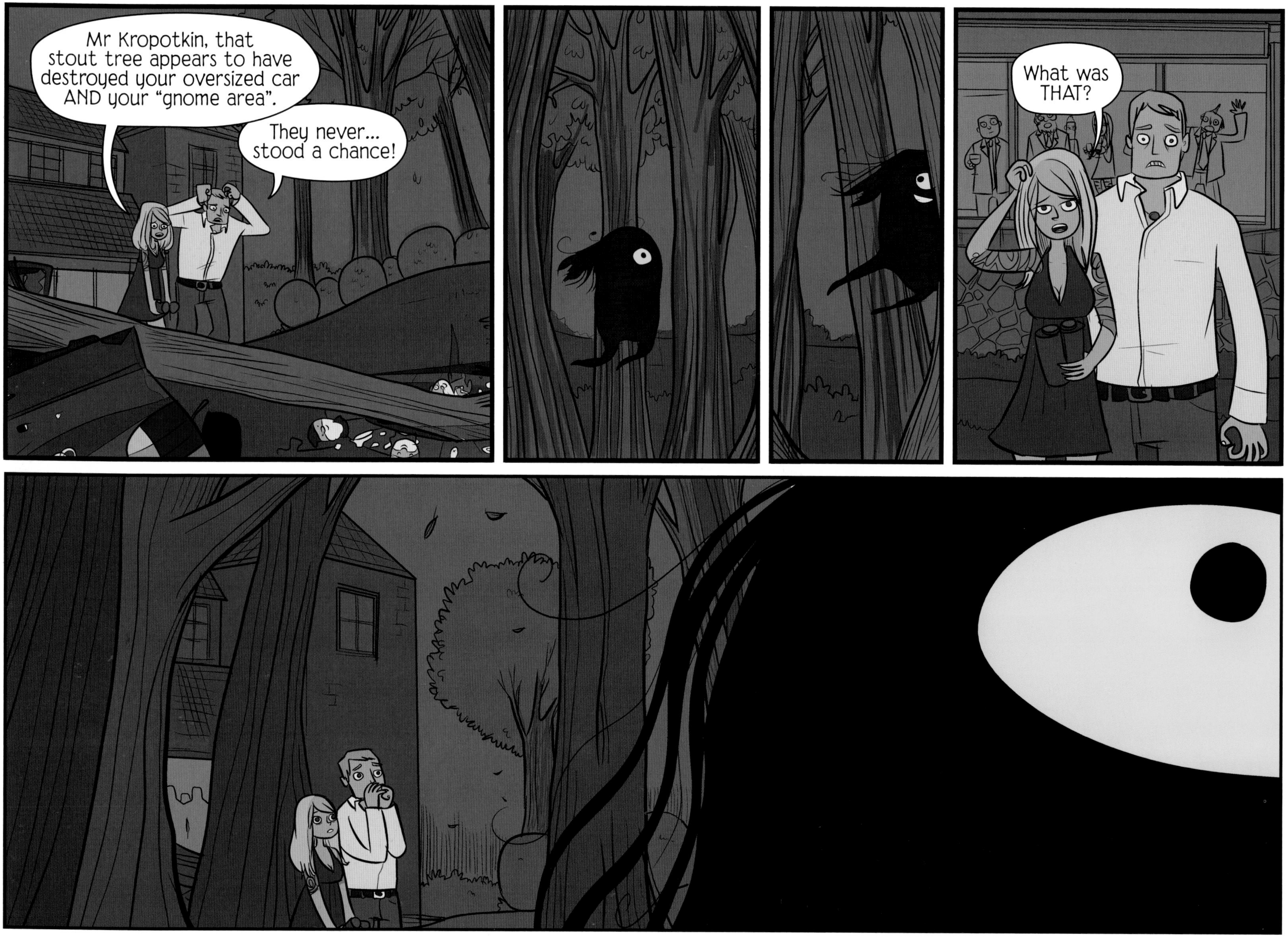
Mr Kropotkin, that stout tree appears to have destroyed your oversized car AND your "gnome area".
They never... stood a chance!
What was THAT?

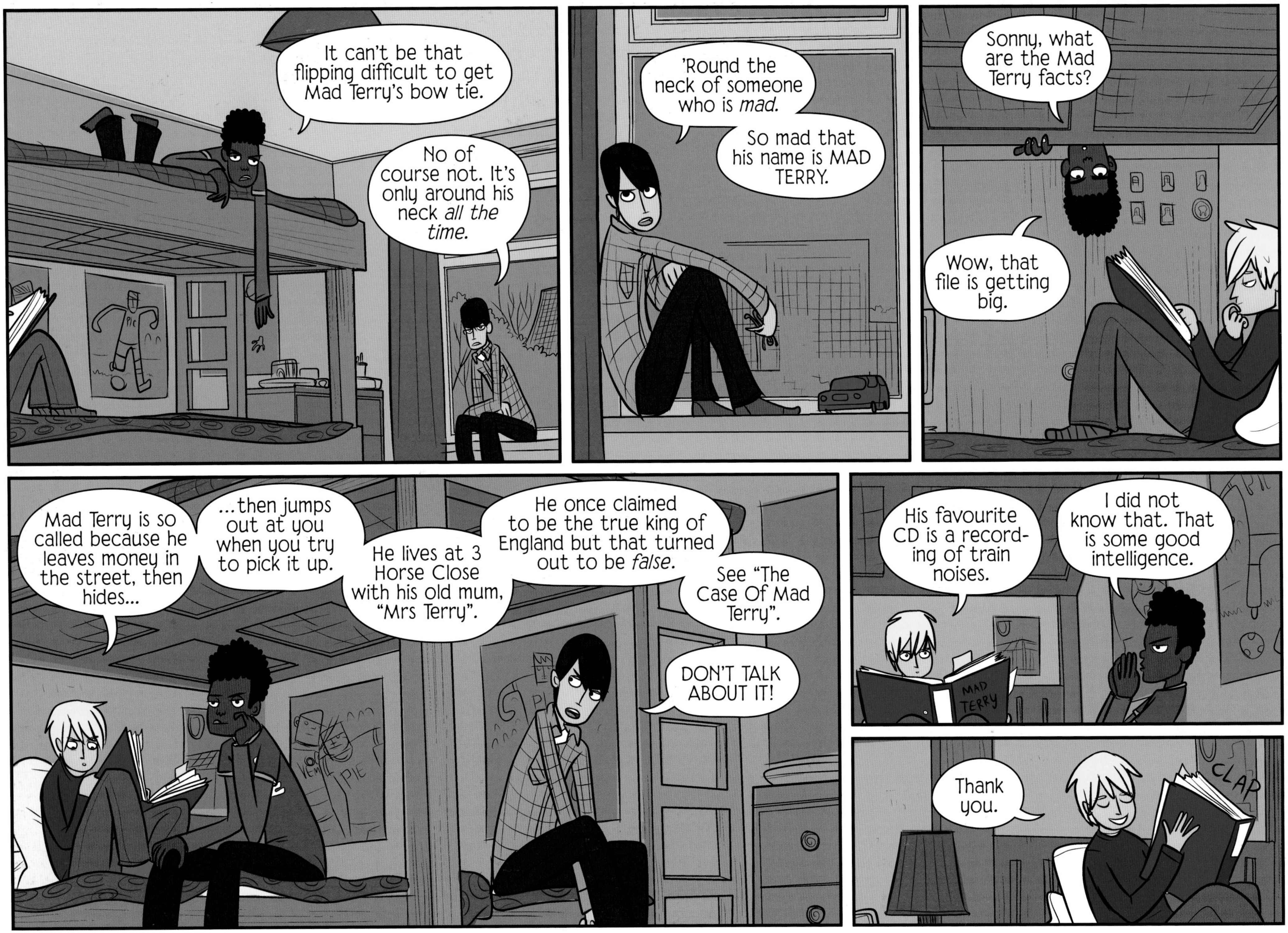
It can't be that flipping difficult to get Mad Terry's bow tie.
No of course not. It's only around his neck *all the time.*
'Round the neck of someone who is *mad.*
So mad that his name is MAD TERRY.
Sonny, what are the Mad Terry facts?
Wow, that file is getting big.
Mad Terry is so called because he leaves money in the street, then hides...
...then jumps out at you when you try to pick it up.
He lives at 3 Horse Close with his old mum, "Mrs Terry".
He once claimed to be the true king of England but that turned out to be *false.*
See "The Case Of Mad Terry".
DON'T TALK ABOUT IT!
His favourite CD is a recording of train noises.
I did not know that. That is some good intelligence.
MAD TERRY
Thank you.
CLAP

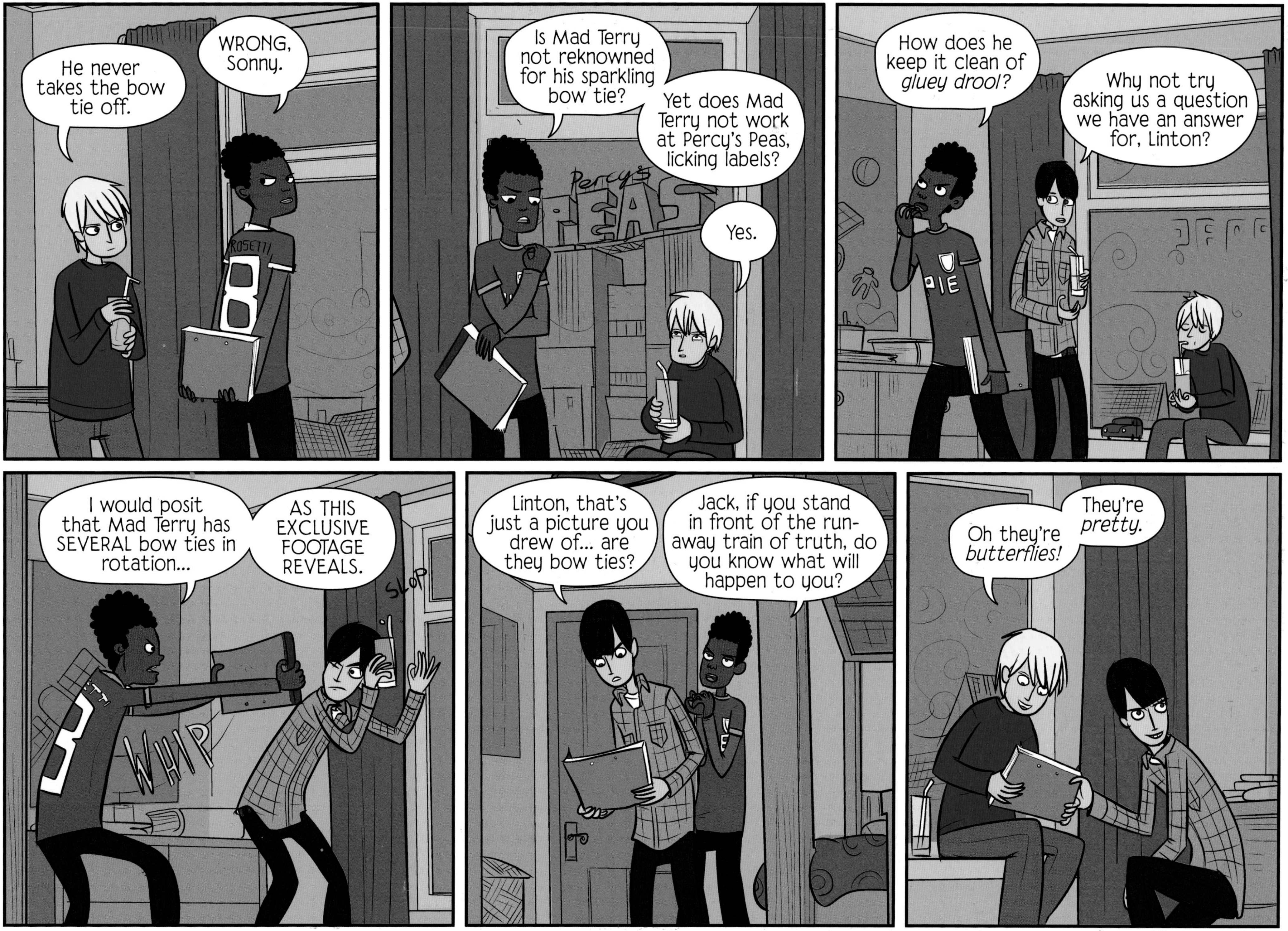
He never takes the bow tie off.
WRONG, Sonny.
ROSETTI
Is Mad Terry not reknowned for his sparkling bow tie?
Yet does Mad Terry not work at Percy's Peas, licking labels?
Percy's PEAS
Yes.
How does he keep it clean of *gluey drool?*
Why not try asking us a question we have an answer for, Linton?
PIE
I would posit that Mad Terry has SEVERAL bow ties in rotation...
AS THIS EXCLUSIVE FOOTAGE REVEALS.
SLOP
WHIP
Linton, that's just a picture you drew of... are they bow ties?
Jack, if you stand in front of the run-away train of truth, do you know what will happen to you?
Oh they're *butterflies!*
They're *pretty.*

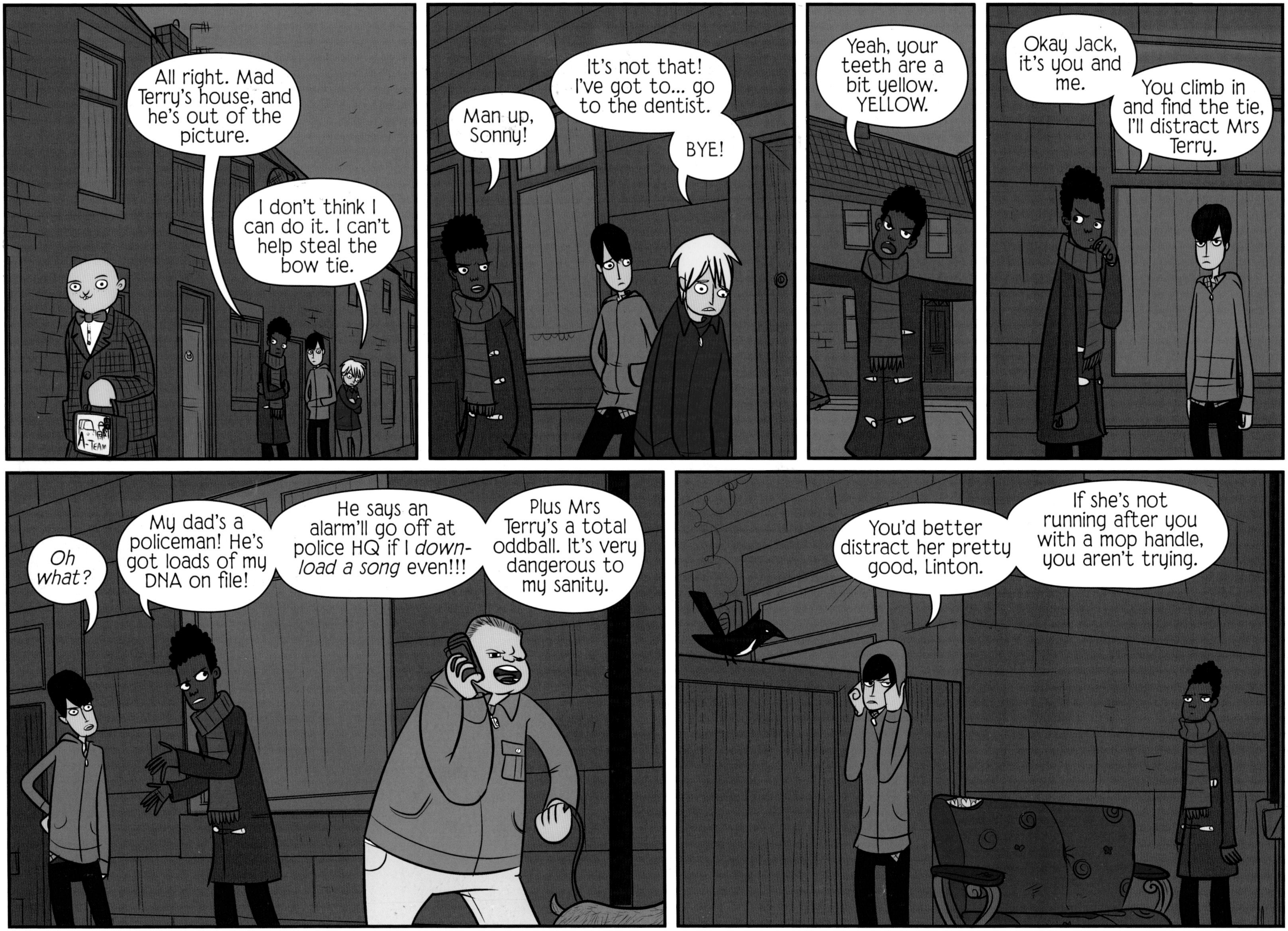
All right. Mad Terry's house, and he's out of the picture.
I don't think I can do it. I can't help steal the bow tie.
A-TEAM
Man up, Sonny!
It's not that! I've got to... go to the dentist.
BYE!
Yeah, your teeth are a bit yellow. YELLOW.
Okay Jack, it's you and me.
You climb in and find the tie, I'll distract Mrs Terry.
Oh what?
My dad's a policeman! He's got loads of my DNA on file!
He says an alarm'll go off at police HQ if I *download a song* even!!!
Plus Mrs Terry's a total oddball. It's very dangerous to my sanity.
You'd better distract her pretty good, Linton.
If she's not running after you with a mop handle, you aren't trying.

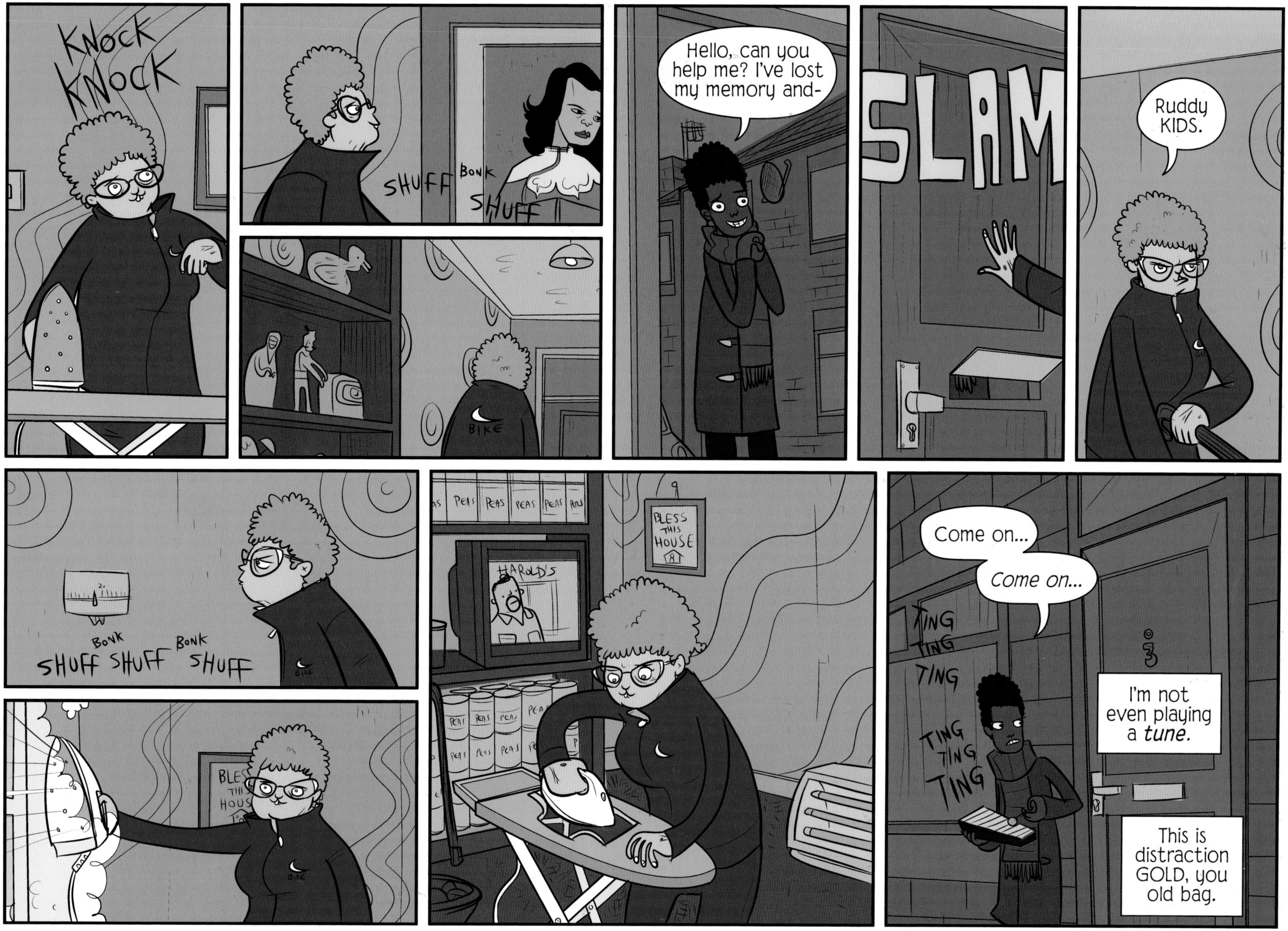
KNOCK KNOCK
SHUFF BONK SHUFF
Hello, can you help me? I've lost my memory and-
SLAM
Ruddy KIDS.
BIKE
BONK BONK
SHUFF SHUFF SHUFF
PEAS
HAROLD'S
BLESS THIS HOUSE
Come on...
Come on...
TING TING TING
TING TING TING
I'm not even playing a *tune.*
This is distraction GOLD, you old bag.

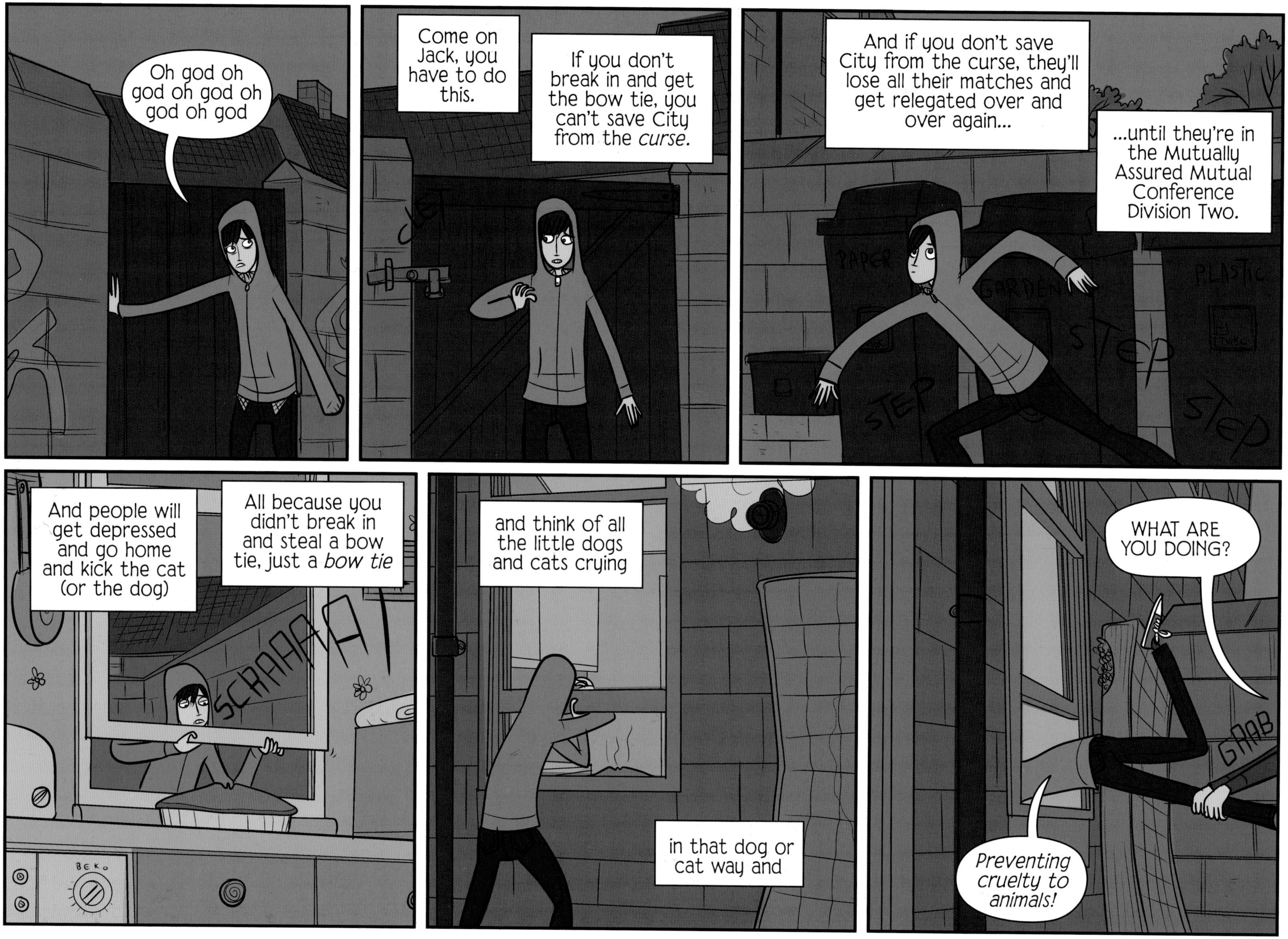
Oh god oh god oh god oh god oh god oh god
Come on Jack, you have to do this.
If you don't break in and get the bow tie, you can't save City from the *curse.*
JET
And if you don't save City from the curse, they'll lose all their matches and get relegated over and over again...
...until they're in the Mutually Assured Mutual Conference Division Two.
PAPER
GARDEN
PLASTIC
STEP
STEP
STEP
And people will get depressed and go home and kick the cat (or the dog)
All because you didn't break in and steal a bow tie, just a *bow tie*
SCRAAAA
BEKO
and think of all the little dogs and cats crying
in that dog or cat way and
WHAT ARE YOU DOING?
Preventing cruelty to animals!
GRAB

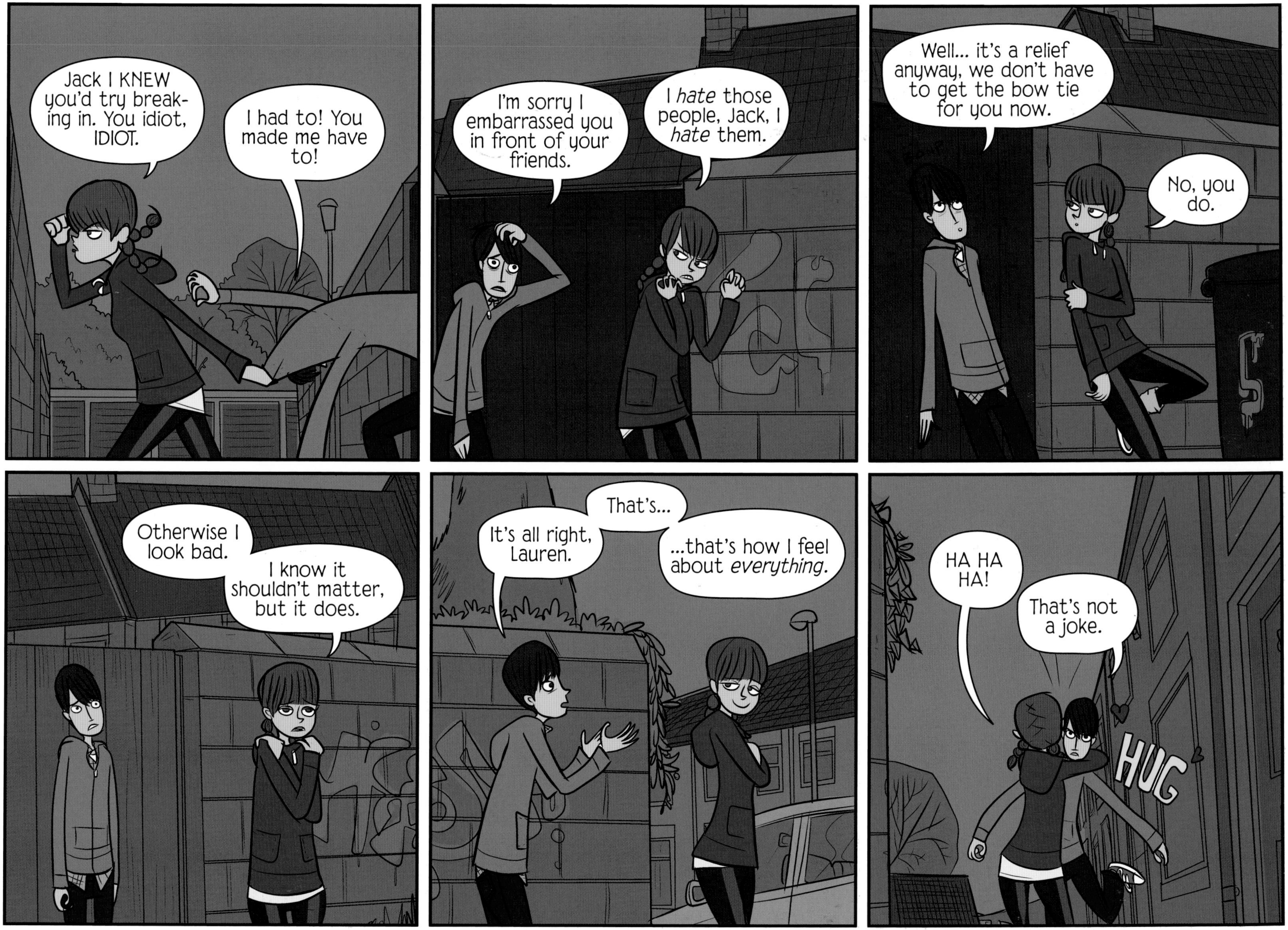
Jack I KNEW you'd try breaking in. You idiot, IDIOT.
I had to! You made me have to!
I'm sorry I embarrassed you in front of your friends.
I *hate* those people, Jack, I *hate* them.
Well... it's a relief anyway, we don't have to get the bow tie for you now.
No, you do.
Otherwise I look bad.
I know it shouldn't matter, but it does.
It's all right, Lauren.
That's...
...that's how I feel about *everything*.
HA HA HA!
That's not a joke.
HUG

Bad Machinery, Volume One

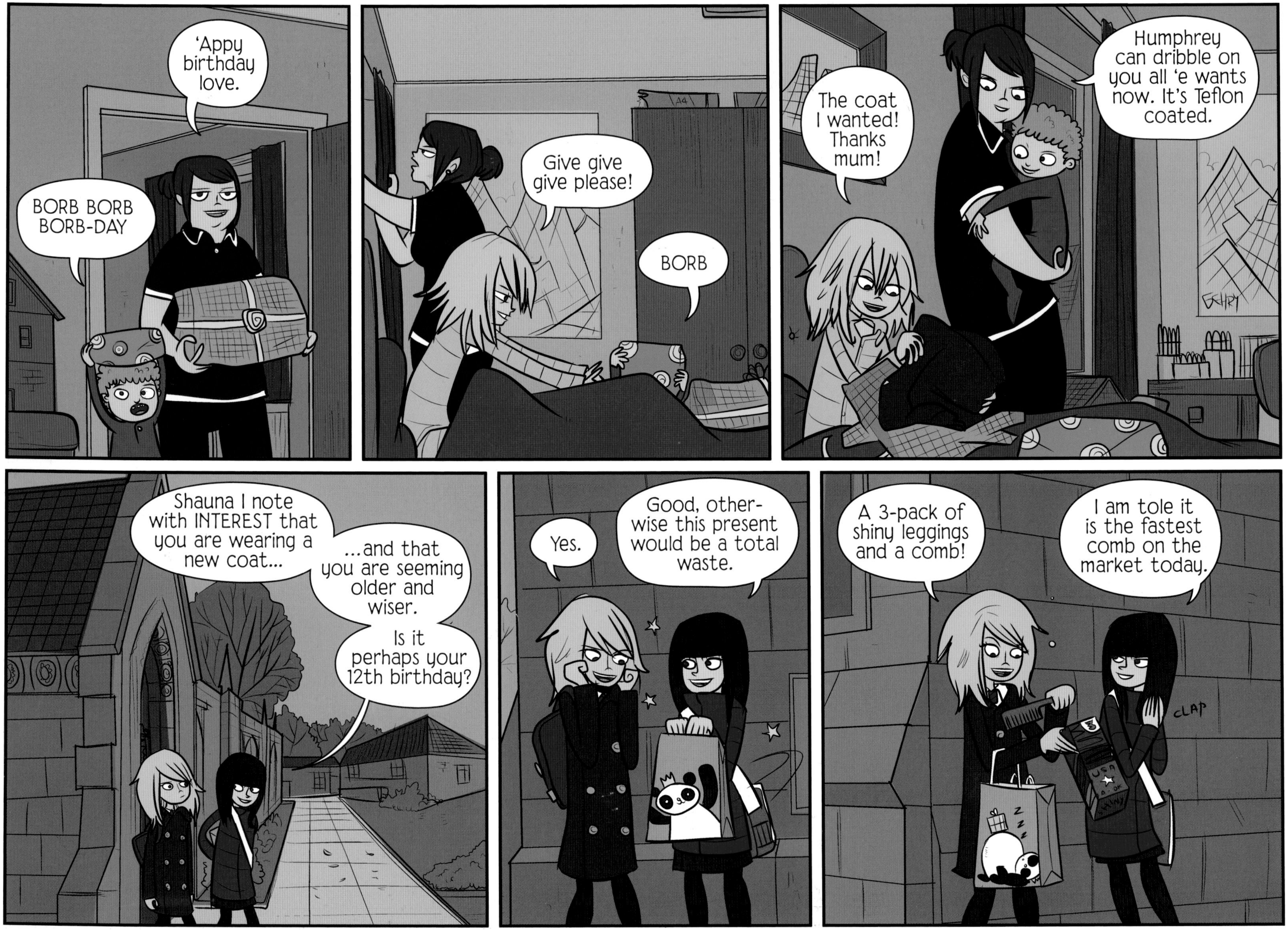
'Appy birthday love.
BORB BORB BORB-DAY
Give give give please!
BORB
The coat I wanted! Thanks mum!
Humphrey can dribble on you all 'e wants now. It's Teflon coated.
Shauna I note with INTEREST that you are wearing a new coat...
...and that you are seeming older and wiser.
Is it perhaps your 12th birthday?
Yes.
Good, other-wise this present would be a total waste.
A 3-pack of shiny leggings and a comb!
I am tole it is the fastest comb on the market today.
CLAP

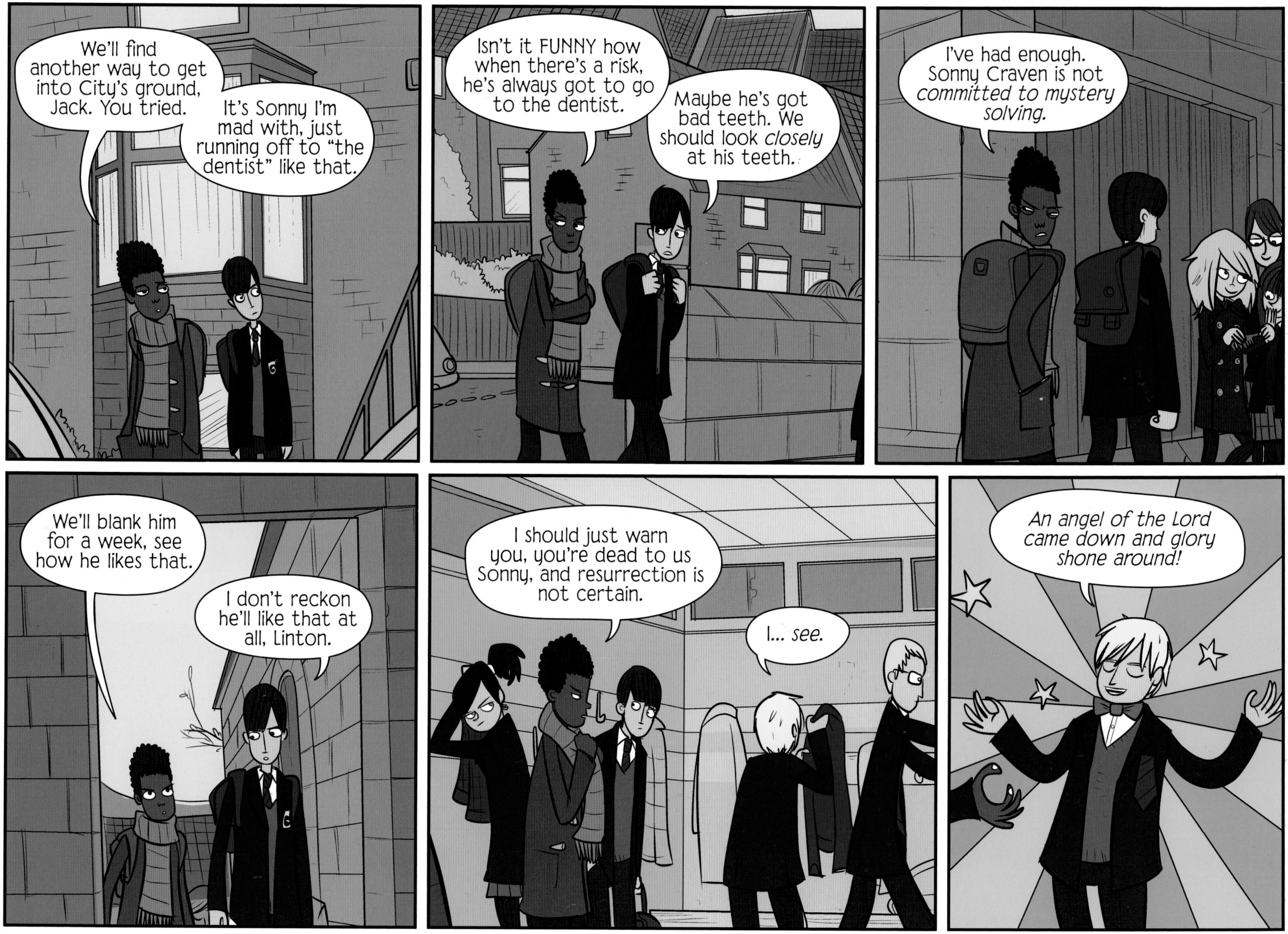
We'll find another way to get into City's ground, Jack. You tried.
It's Sonny I'm mad with, just running off to "the dentist" like that.
Isn't it FUNNY how when there's a risk, he's always got to go to the dentist.
Maybe he's got bad teeth. We should look *closely* at his teeth.
I've had enough. Sonny Craven is not *committed to mystery solving.*
We'll blank him for a week, see how he likes that.
I don't reckon he'll like that at all, Linton.
I should just warn you, you're dead to us Sonny, and resurrection is not certain.
I... *see.*
An angel of the Lord came down and glory shone around!

Bad Machinery, Volume One

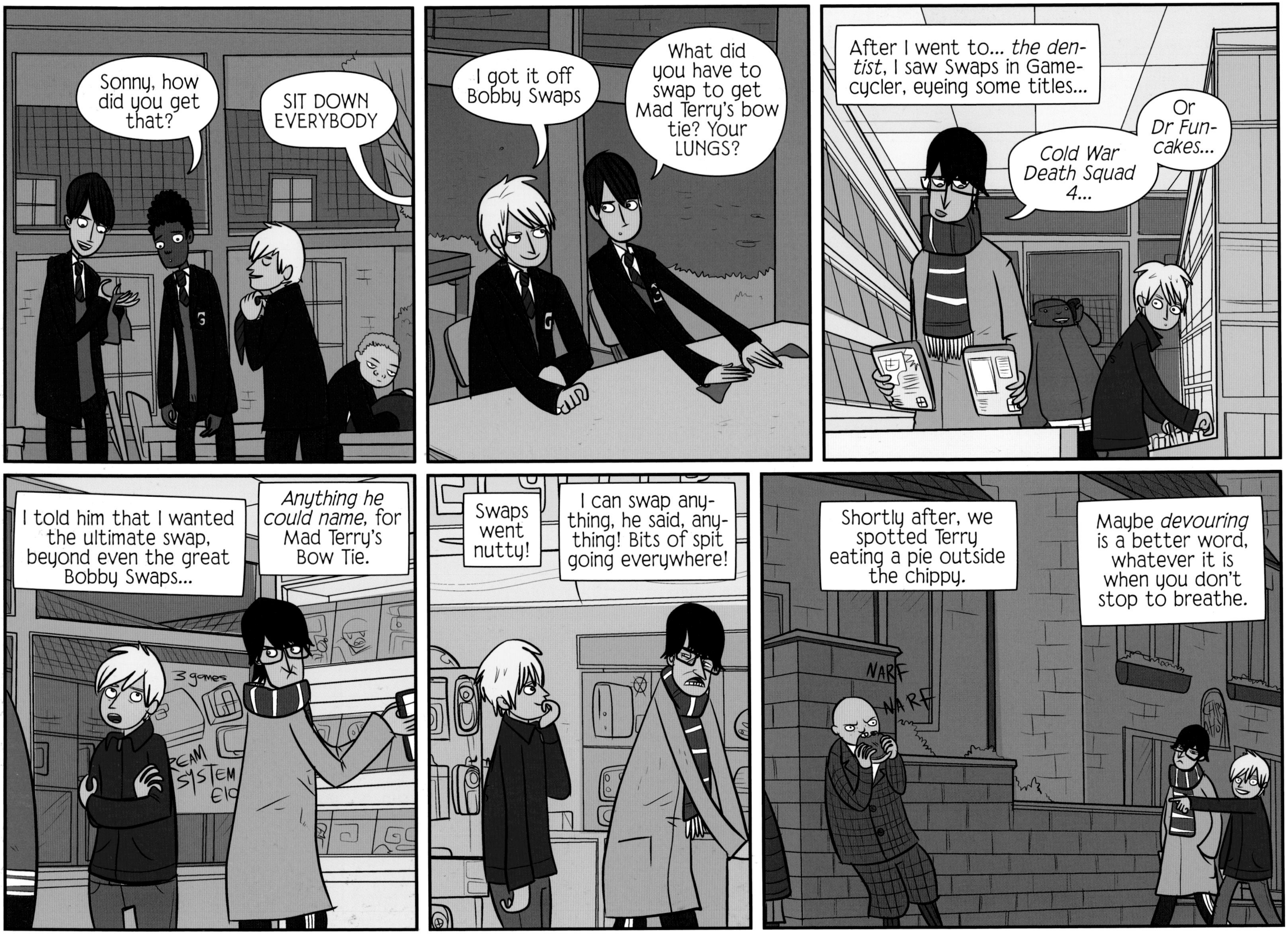
Sonny, how did you get that?
SIT DOWN EVERYBODY
I got it off Bobby Swaps
What did you have to swap to get Mad Terry's bow tie? Your LUNGS?
After I went to... *the dentist*, I saw Swaps in Gamecycler, eyeing some titles...
Cold War Death Squad 4...
Or *Dr Funcakes...*
I told him that I wanted the ultimate swap, beyond even the great Bobby Swaps...
Anything he could name, for Mad Terry's Bow Tie.
3 games
Swaps went nutty!
I can swap anything, he said, anything! Bits of spit going everywhere!
Shortly after, we spotted Terry eating a pie outside the chippy.
Maybe *devouring* is a better word, whatever it is when you don't stop to breathe.
NARF
NARF

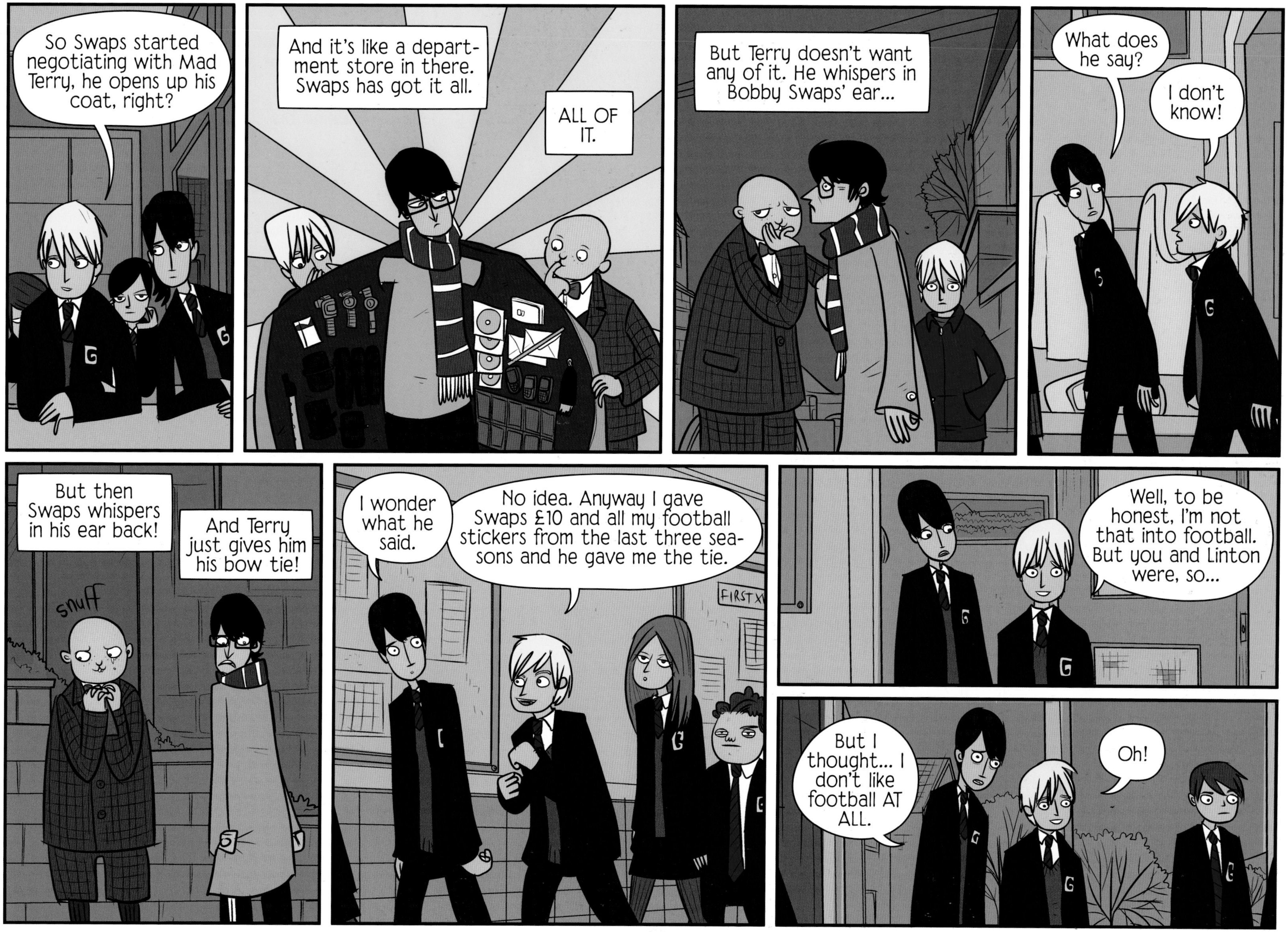
So Swaps started negotiating with Mad Terry, he opens up his coat, right?
And it's like a department store in there. Swaps has got it all.
ALL OF IT.
But Terry doesn't want any of it. He whispers in Bobby Swaps' ear...
What does he say?
I don't know!
But then Swaps whispers in his ear back!
And Terry just gives him his bow tie!
snuff
I wonder what he said.
No idea. Anyway I gave Swaps £10 and all my football stickers from the last three seasons and he gave me the tie.
Well, to be honest, I'm not that into football. But you and Linton were, so...
But I thought... I don't like football AT ALL.
Oh!

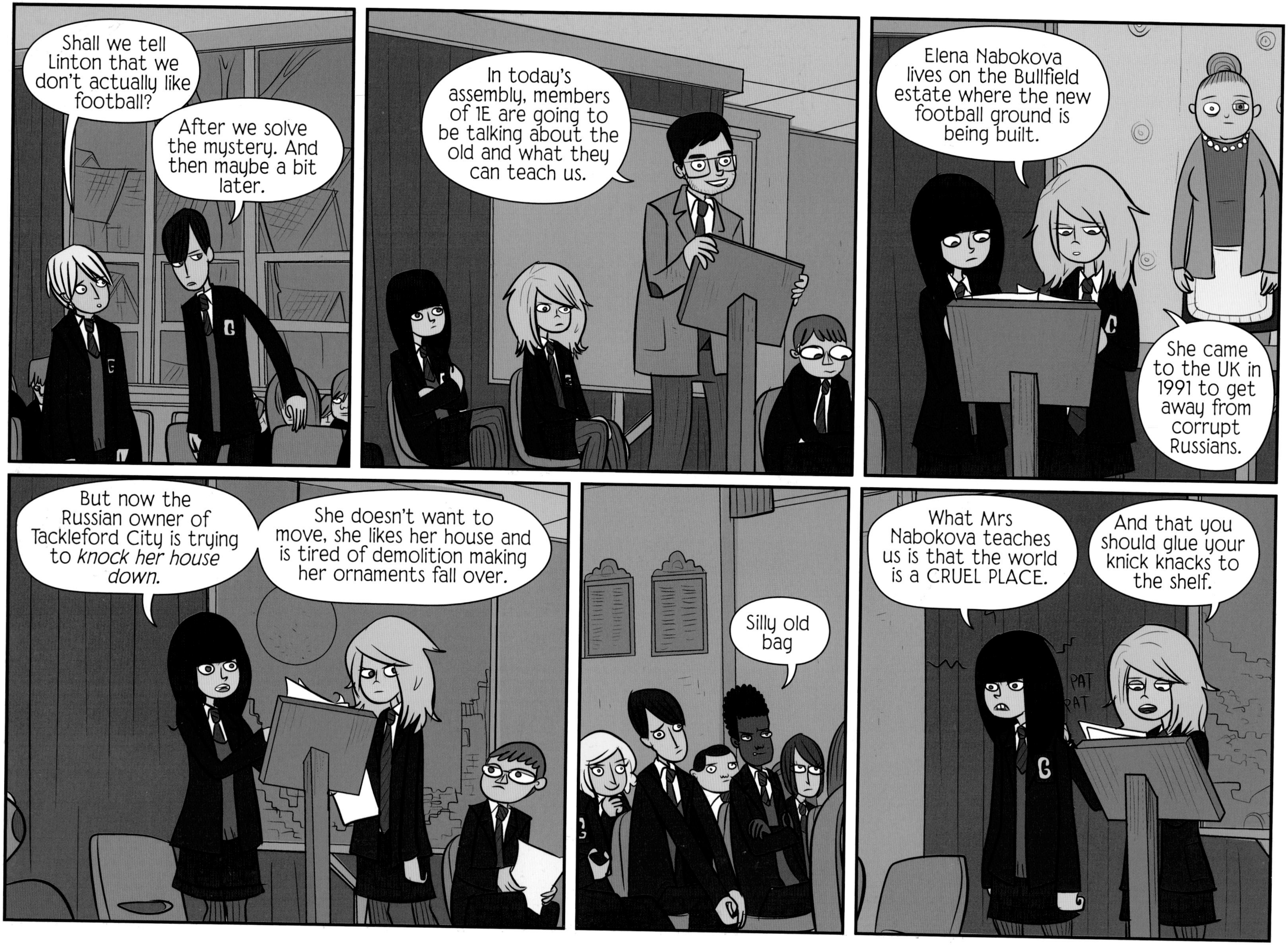
Shall we tell Linton that we don't actually like football?
After we solve the mystery. And then maybe a bit later.
In today's assembly, members of 1E are going to be talking about the old and what they can teach us.
Elena Nabokova lives on the Bullfield estate where the new football ground is being built.
She came to the UK in 1991 to get away from corrupt Russians.
But now the Russian owner of Tackleford City is trying to *knock her house down.*
She doesn't want to move, she likes her house and is tired of demolition making her ornaments fall over.
Silly old bag
What Mrs Nabokova teaches us is that the world is a CRUEL PLACE.
And that you should glue your knick knacks to the shelf.
PAT PAT

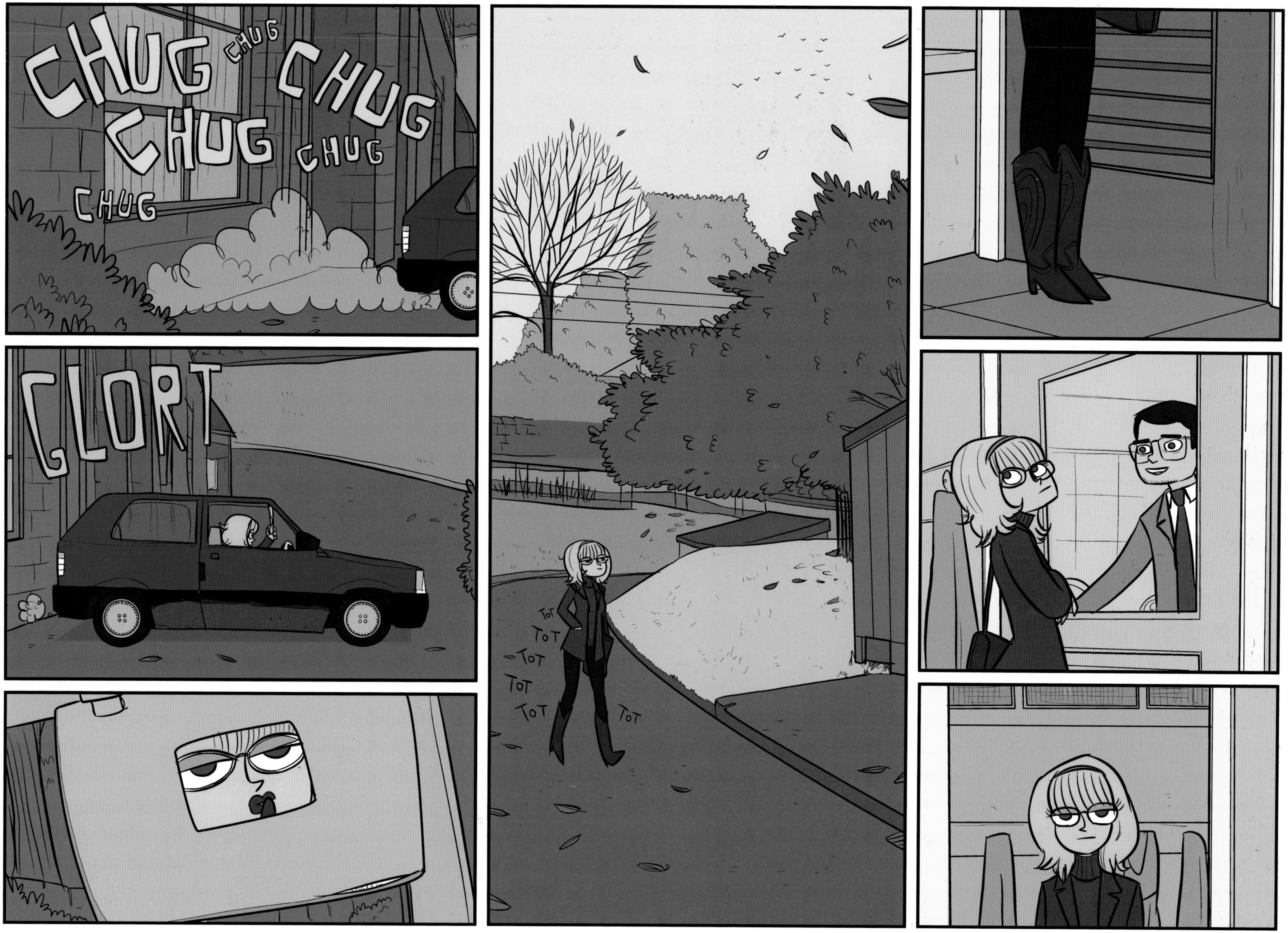
CHUG
CHUG
CHUG
CHUG
CHUG
CHUG
CHUG
GLORT
TOT
TOT
TOT
TOT
TOT
TOT

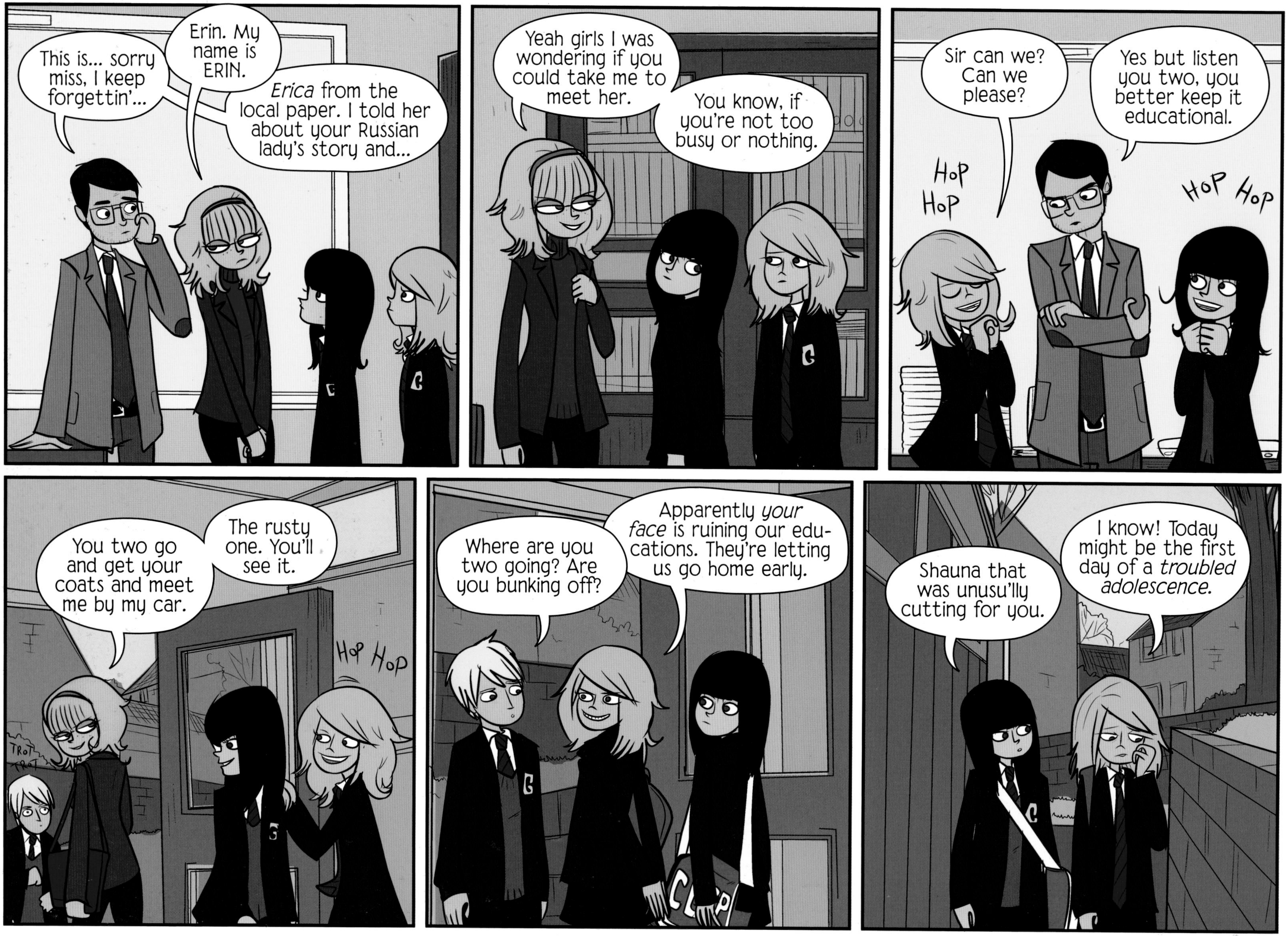
This is... sorry miss, I keep forgettin'...
Erin. My name is ERIN.
Erica from the local paper. I told her about your Russian lady's story and...
Yeah girls I was wondering if you could take me to meet her.
You know, if you're not too busy or nothing.
Sir can we? Can we please?
Yes but listen you two, you better keep it educational.
HOP HOP
HOP HOP
You two go and get your coats and meet me by my car.
The rusty one. You'll see it.
HOP HOP
TROT TROT
Where are you two going? Are you bunking off?
Apparently *your face* is ruining our educations. They're letting us go home early.
Shauna that was unusu'lly cutting for you.
I know! Today might be the first day of a *troubled adolescence*.

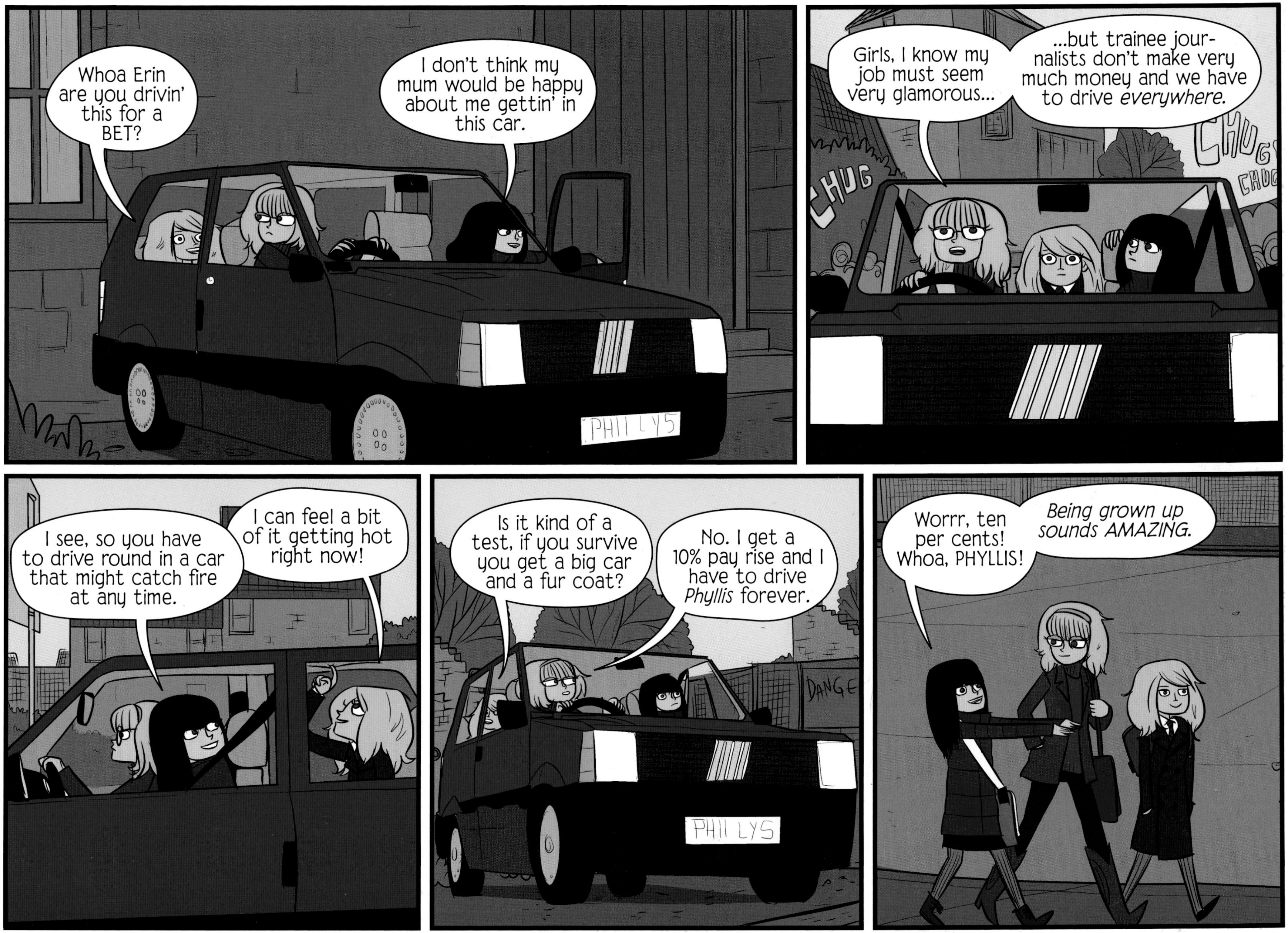
Whoa Erin are you drivin' this for a BET?
I don't think my mum would be happy about me gettin' in this car.
PHIL LYS
Girls, I know my job must seem very glamorous...
...but trainee journalists don't make very much money and we have to drive *everywhere.*
CHUG
CHUG
I see, so you have to drive round in a car that might catch fire at any time.
I can feel a bit of it getting hot right now!
Is it kind of a test, if you survive you get a big car and a fur coat?
No. I get a 10% pay rise and I have to drive *Phyllis* forever.
PHIL LYS
Worrr, ten per cents! Whoa, PHYLLIS!
Being grown up sounds AMAZING.

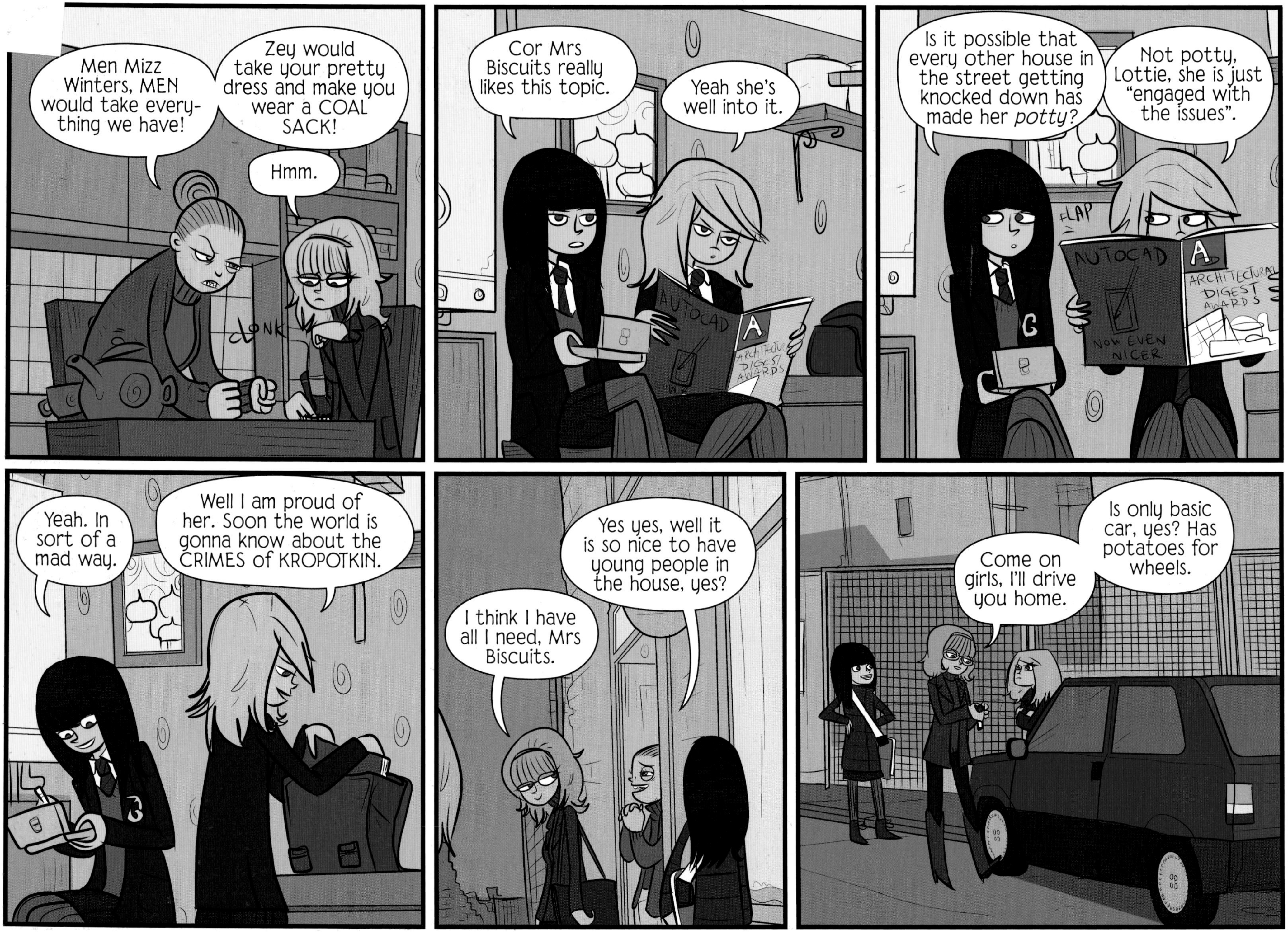
Men Mizz Winters, MEN would take everything we have!
Zey would take your pretty dress and make you wear a COAL SACK!
Hmm.
CLONK
Cor Mrs Biscuits really likes this topic.
Yeah she's well into it.
AUTOCAD
Is it possible that every other house in the street getting knocked down has made her *potty*?
Not potty, Lottie, she is just "engaged with the issues".
FLAP
AUTOCAD
ARCHITECTURAL DIGEST AWARDS
NOW EVEN NICER
Yeah. In sort of a mad way.
Well I am proud of her. Soon the world is gonna know about the CRIMES of KROPOTKIN.
Yes yes, well it is so nice to have young people in the house, yes?
I think I have all I need, Mrs Biscuits.
Come on girls, I'll drive you home.
Is only basic car, yes? Has potatoes for wheels.

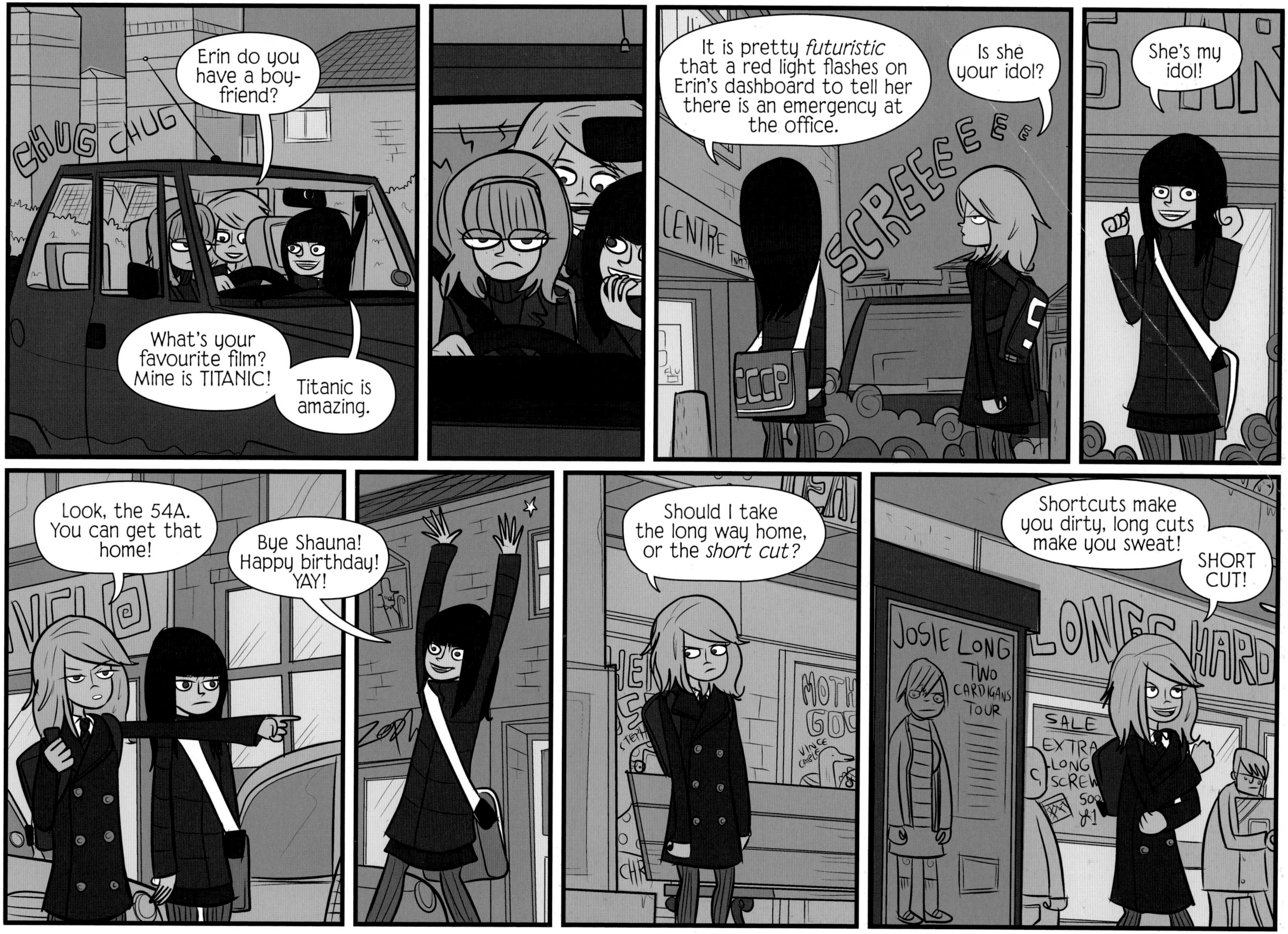
CHUG CHUG
Erin do you have a boy-friend?
What's your favourite film? Mine is TITANIC!
Titanic is amazing.
It is pretty *futuristic* that a red light flashes on Erin's dashboard to tell her there is an emergency at the office.
Is she your idol?
SCREEEEEEE
CENTRE
CCCP
She's my idol!
Look, the 54A. You can get that home!
Bye Shauna! Happy birthday! YAY!
Should I take the long way home, or the *short cut?*
JOSIE LONG
TWO CARDIGANS TOUR
Shortcuts make you dirty, long cuts make you sweat!
SHORT CUT!
SALE
EXTRA LONG SCREWS

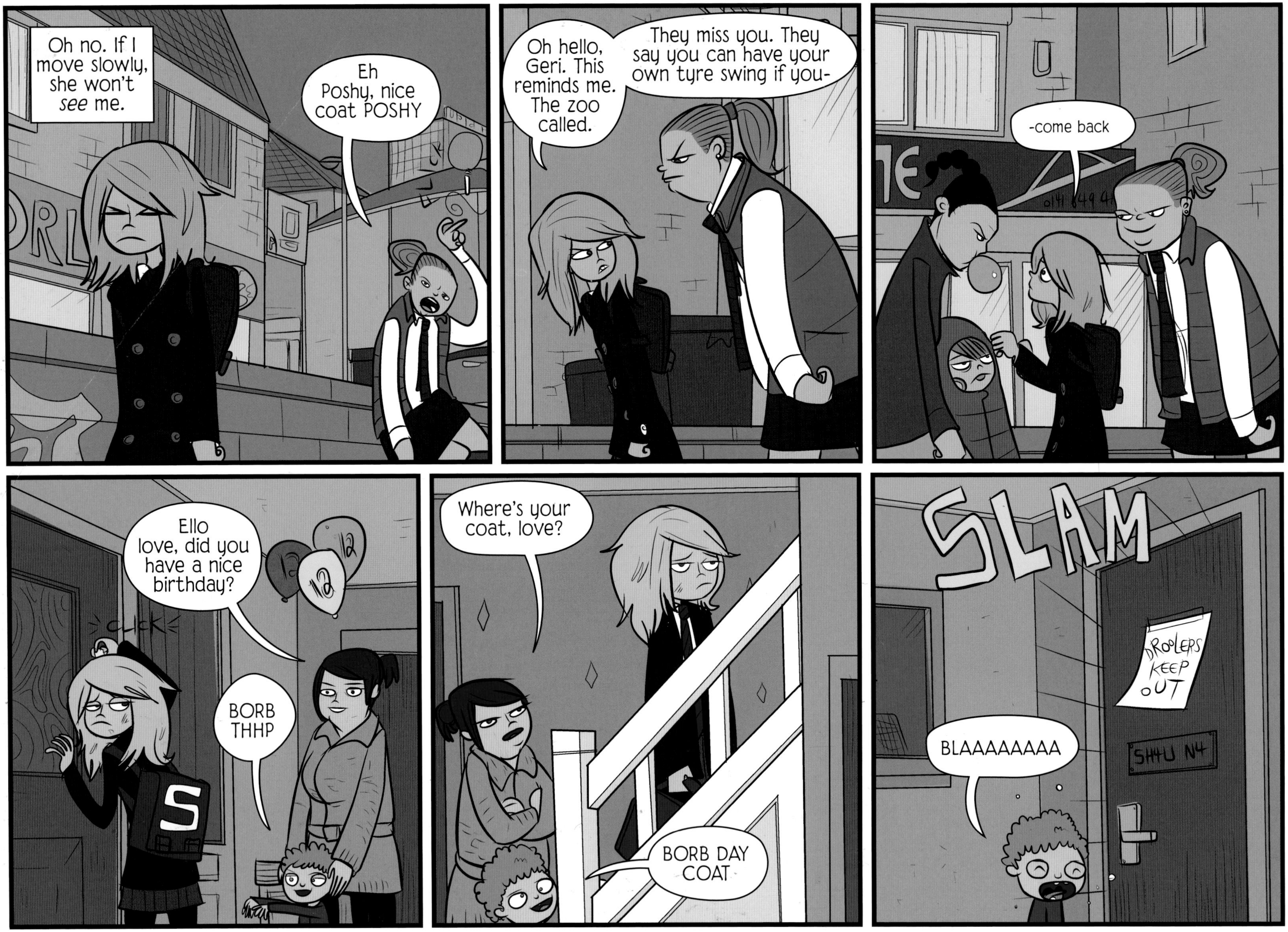
Oh no. If I move slowly, she won't *see* me.
Eh Poshy, nice coat POSHY
Oh hello, Geri. This reminds me. The zoo called.
They miss you. They say you can have your own tyre swing if you-
-come back
Ello love, did you have a nice birthday?
CLICK
BORB THHP
Where's your coat, love?
BORB DAY COAT
SLAM
DROOLERS KEEP OUT
BLAAAAAAAA

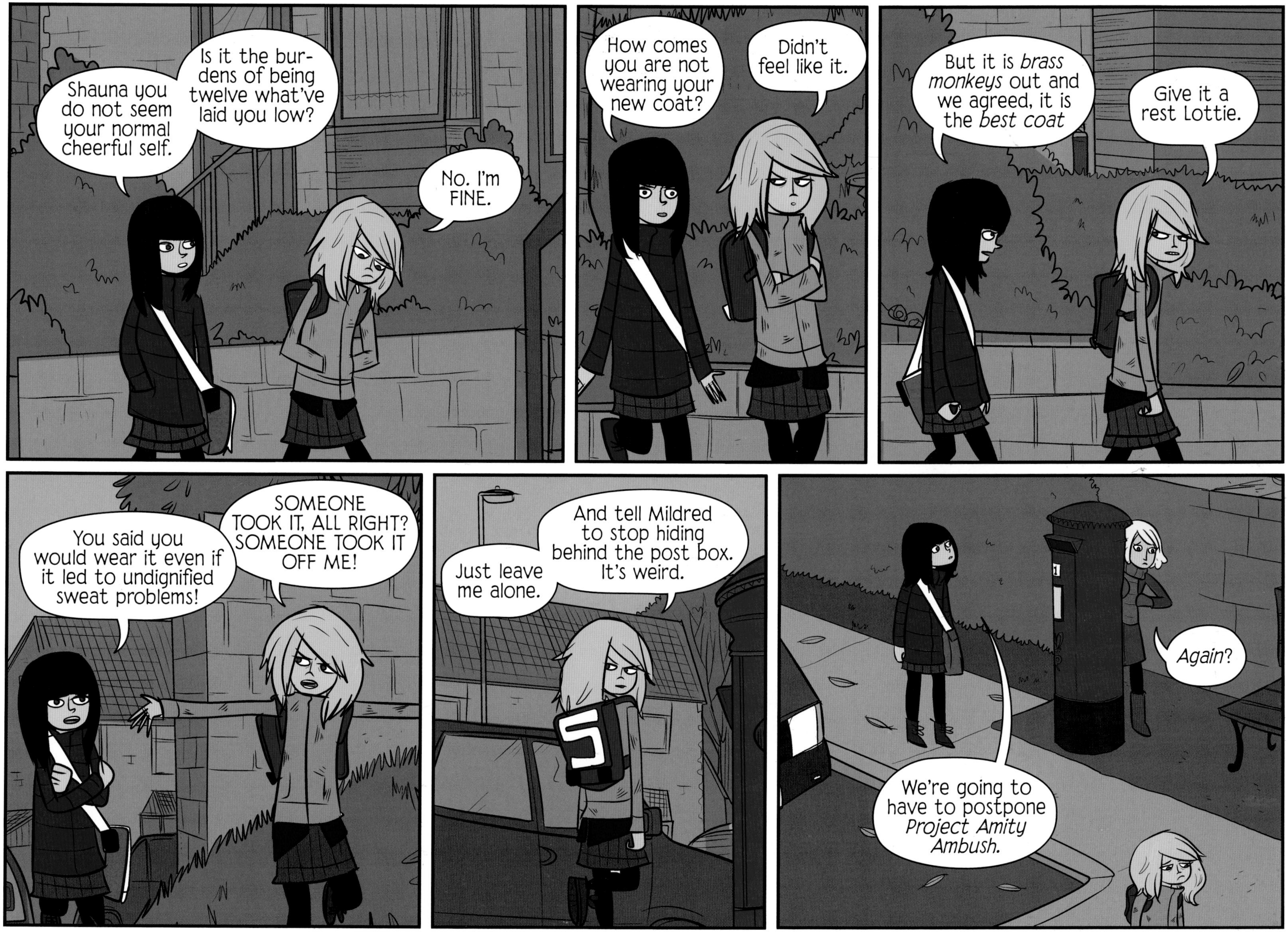
Shauna you do not seem your normal cheerful self.
Is it the burdens of being twelve what've laid you low?
No. I'm FINE.
How comes you are not wearing your new coat?
Didn't feel like it.
But it is *brass monkeys* out and we agreed, it is the *best coat*
Give it a rest Lottie.
You said you would wear it even if it led to undignified sweat problems!
SOMEONE TOOK IT, ALL RIGHT? SOMEONE TOOK IT OFF ME!
Just leave me alone.
And tell Mildred to stop hiding behind the post box. It's weird.
Again?
We're going to have to postpone *Project Amity Ambush.*

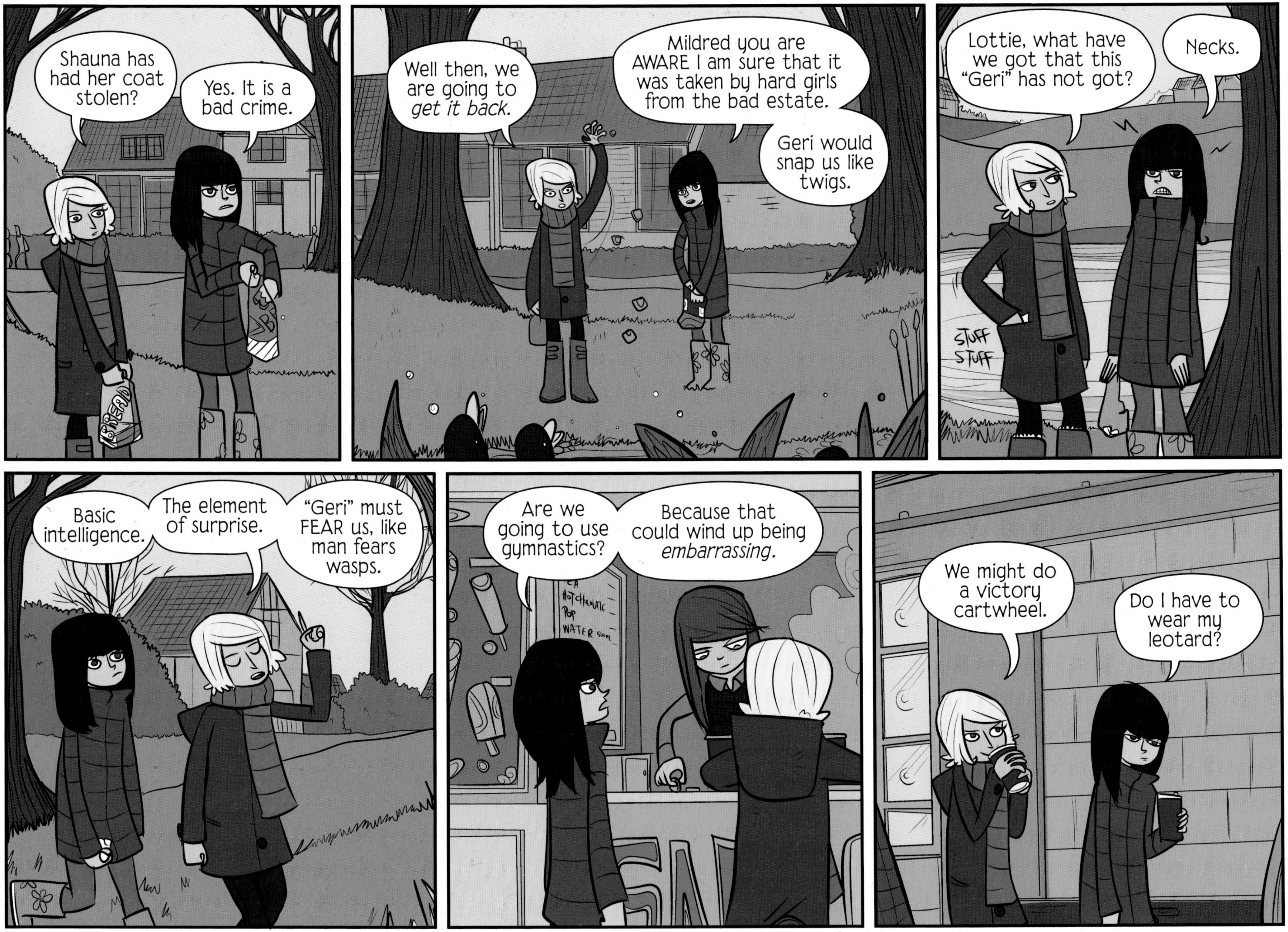

Shauna has had her coat stolen?
Yes. It is a bad crime.
Well then, we are going to *get it back.*
Mildred you are AWARE I am sure that it was taken by hard girls from the bad estate.
Geri would snap us like twigs.
Lottie, what have we got that this "Geri" has not got?
Necks.
STUFF
STUFF
Basic intelligence.
The element of surprise.
"Geri" must FEAR us, like man fears wasps.
Are we going to use gymnastics?
Because that could wind up being *embarrassing*.
We might do a victory cartwheel.
Do I have to wear my leotard?

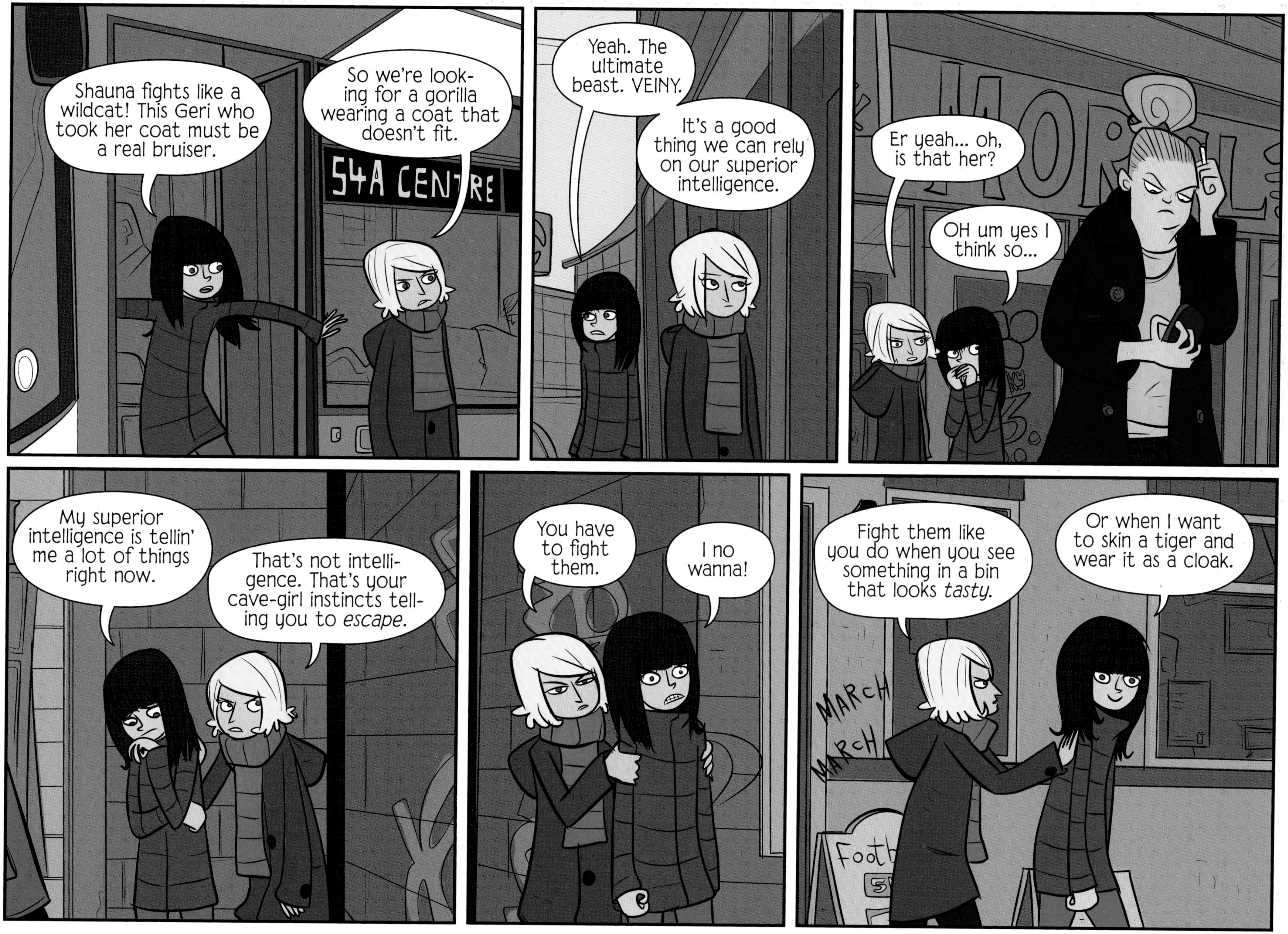
Shauna fights like a wildcat! This Geri who took her coat must be a real bruiser.
So we're looking for a gorilla wearing a coat that doesn't fit.
54A CENTRE
Yeah. The ultimate beast. VEINY.
It's a good thing we can rely on our superior intelligence.
Er yeah... oh, is that her?
OH um yes I think so...
My superior intelligence is tellin' me a lot of things right now.
That's not intelligence. That's your cave-girl instincts telling you to *escape.*
You have to fight them.
I no wanna!
Fight them like you do when you see something in a bin that looks *tasty.*
Or when I want to skin a tiger and wear it as a cloak.
MARCH
MARCH

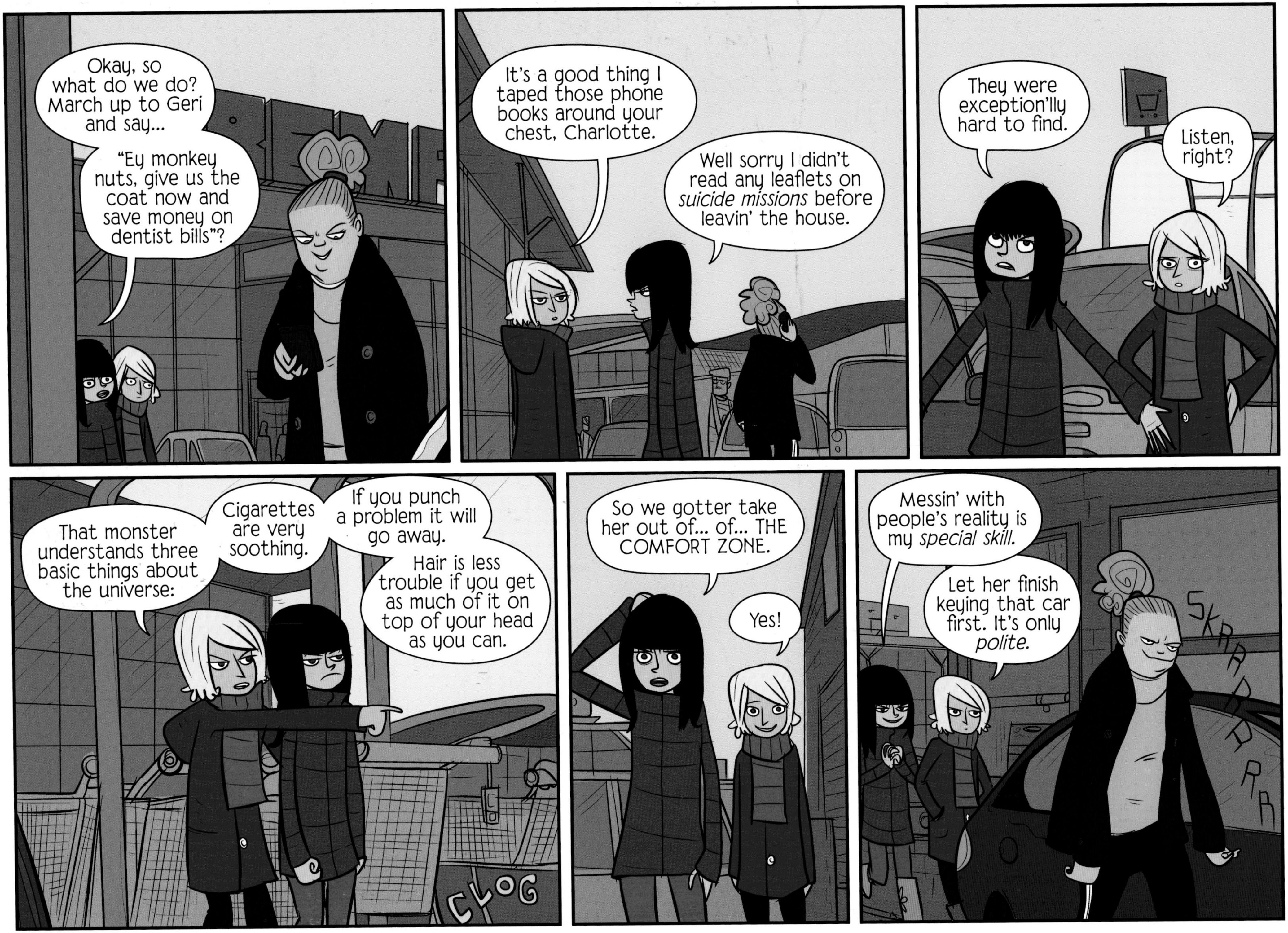
Okay, so what do we do? March up to Geri and say...
"Ey monkey nuts, give us the coat now and save money on dentist bills"?
It's a good thing I taped those phone books around your chest, Charlotte.
Well sorry I didn't read any leaflets on *suicide missions* before leavin' the house.
They were exception'lly hard to find.
Listen, right?
That monster understands three basic things about the universe:
Cigarettes are very soothing.
If you punch a problem it will go away.
Hair is less trouble if you get as much of it on top of your head as you can.
CLOG
So we gotter take her out of... of... THE COMFORT ZONE.
Yes!
Messin' with people's reality is my *special skill.*
Let her finish keying that car first. It's only *polite.*
SKRRRRRR

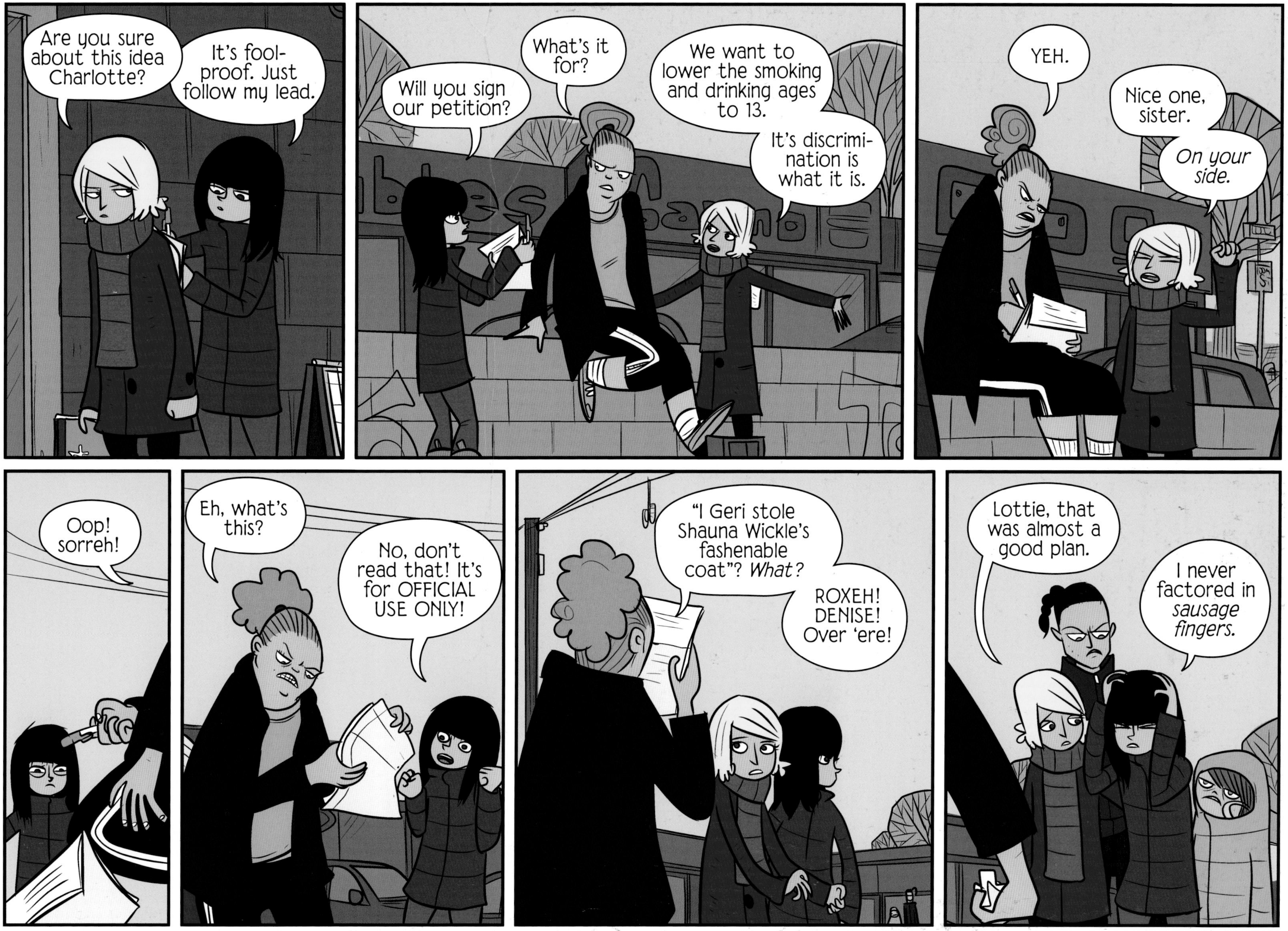
Are you sure about this idea Charlotte?
It's fool-proof. Just follow my lead.
Will you sign our petition?
What's it for?
We want to lower the smoking and drinking ages to 13.
It's discrimi-nation is what it is.
YEH.
Nice one, sister.
On your side.
Oop! sorreh!
Eh, what's this?
No, don't read that! It's for OFFICIAL USE ONLY!
"I Geri stole Shauna Wickle's fashenable coat"? *What?*
ROXEH! DENISE! Over 'ere!
Lottie, that was almost a good plan.
I never factored in *sausage fingers.*

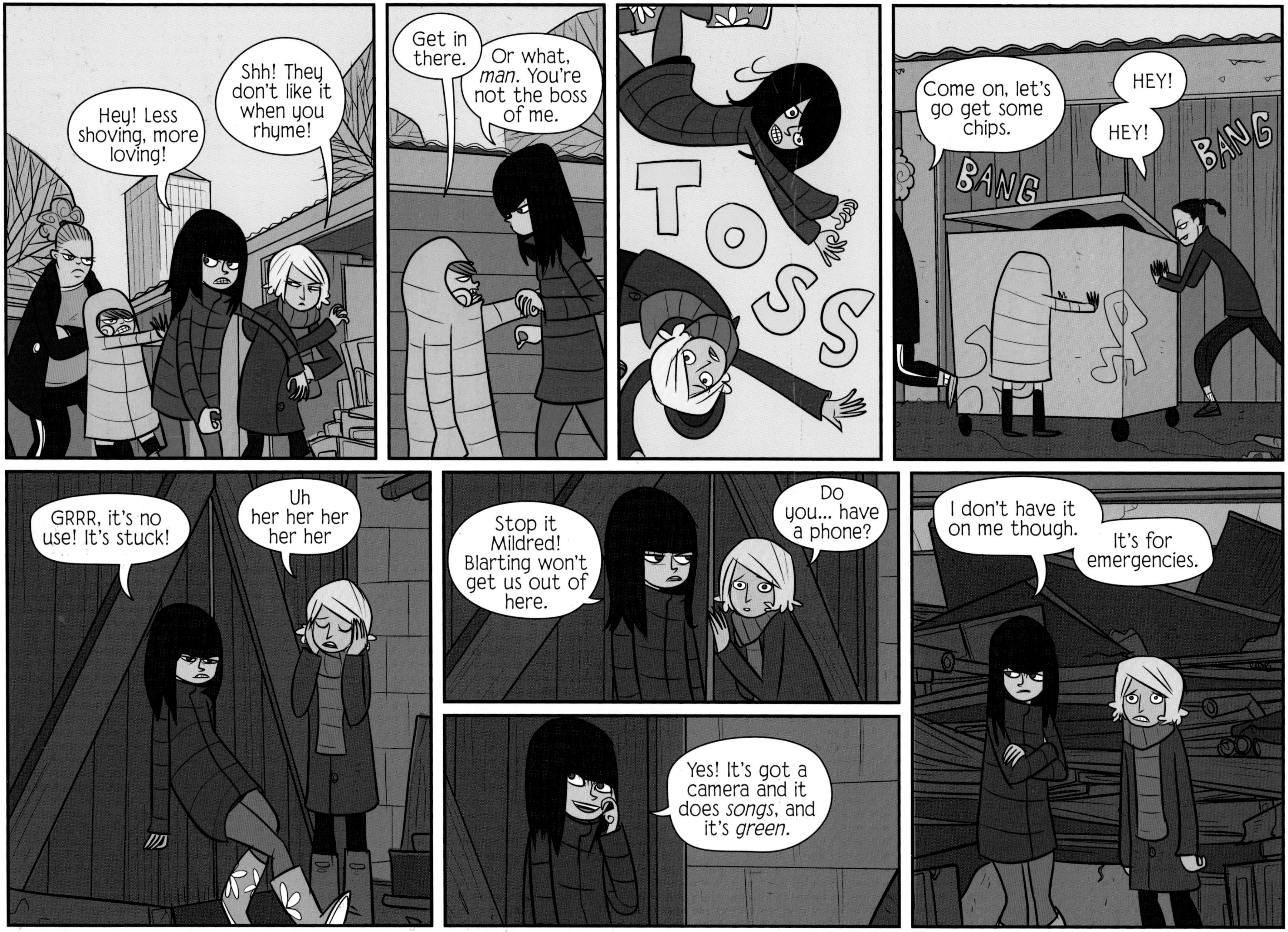
Hey! Less shoving, more loving!
Shh! They don't like it when you rhyme!
Get in there.
Or what, *man*. You're not the boss of me.
TOSS
Come on, let's go get some chips.
HEY!
HEY!
BANG
BANG
GRRR, it's no use! It's stuck!
Uh her her her her her
Stop it Mildred! Blarting won't get us out of here.
Do you... have a phone?
Yes! It's got a camera and it does *songs*, and it's *green*.
I don't have it on me though.
It's for emergencies.

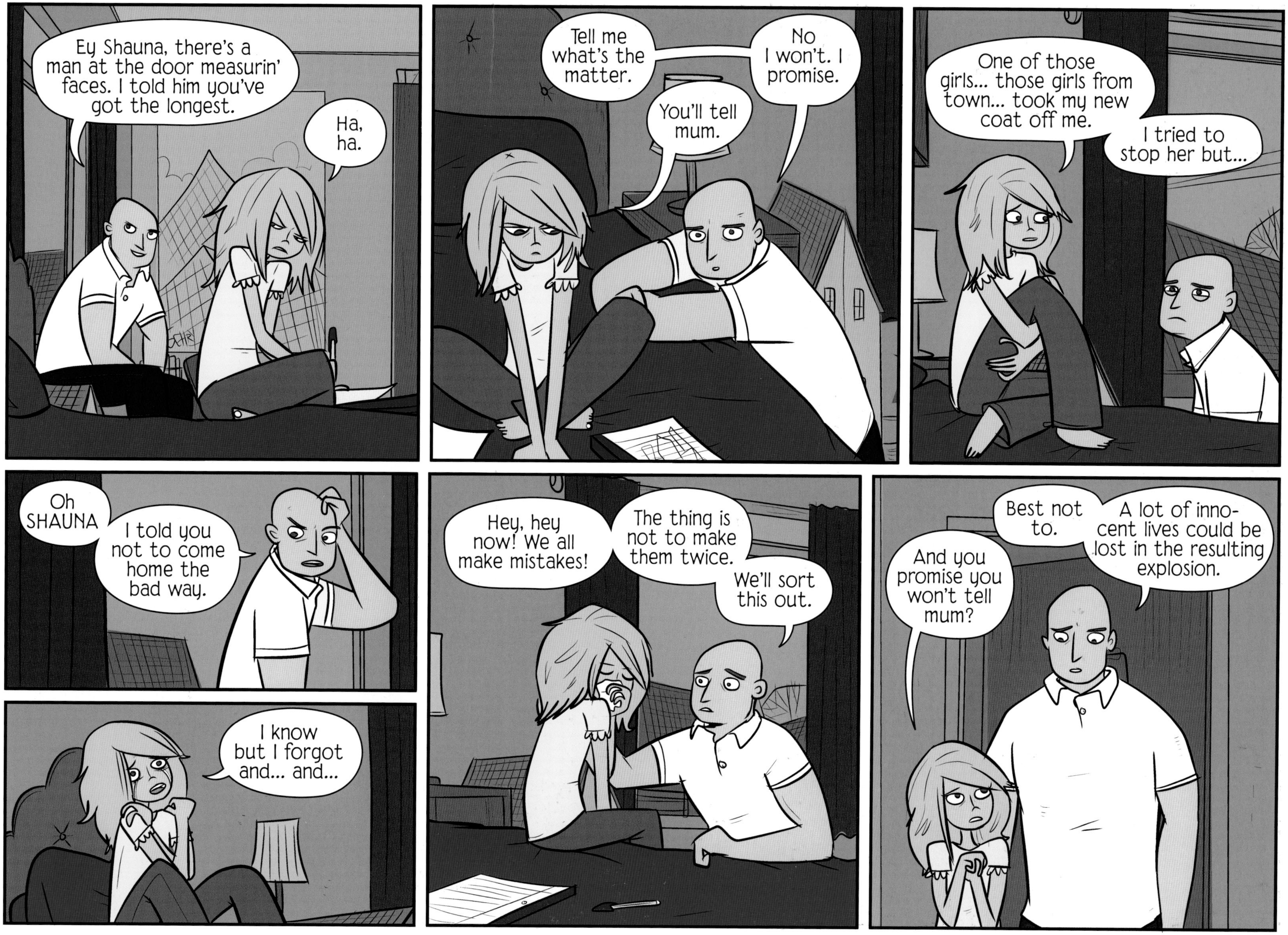
Ey Shauna, there's a man at the door measurin' faces. I told him you've got the longest.
Ha, ha.
Tell me what's the matter.
You'll tell mum.
No I won't. I promise.
One of those girls... those girls from town... took my new coat off me.
I tried to stop her but...
Oh SHAUNA
I told you not to come home the bad way.
I know but I forgot and... and...
Hey, hey now! We all make mistakes!
The thing is not to make them twice.
We'll sort this out.
And you promise you won't tell mum?
Best not to.
A lot of innocent lives could be lost in the resulting explosion.

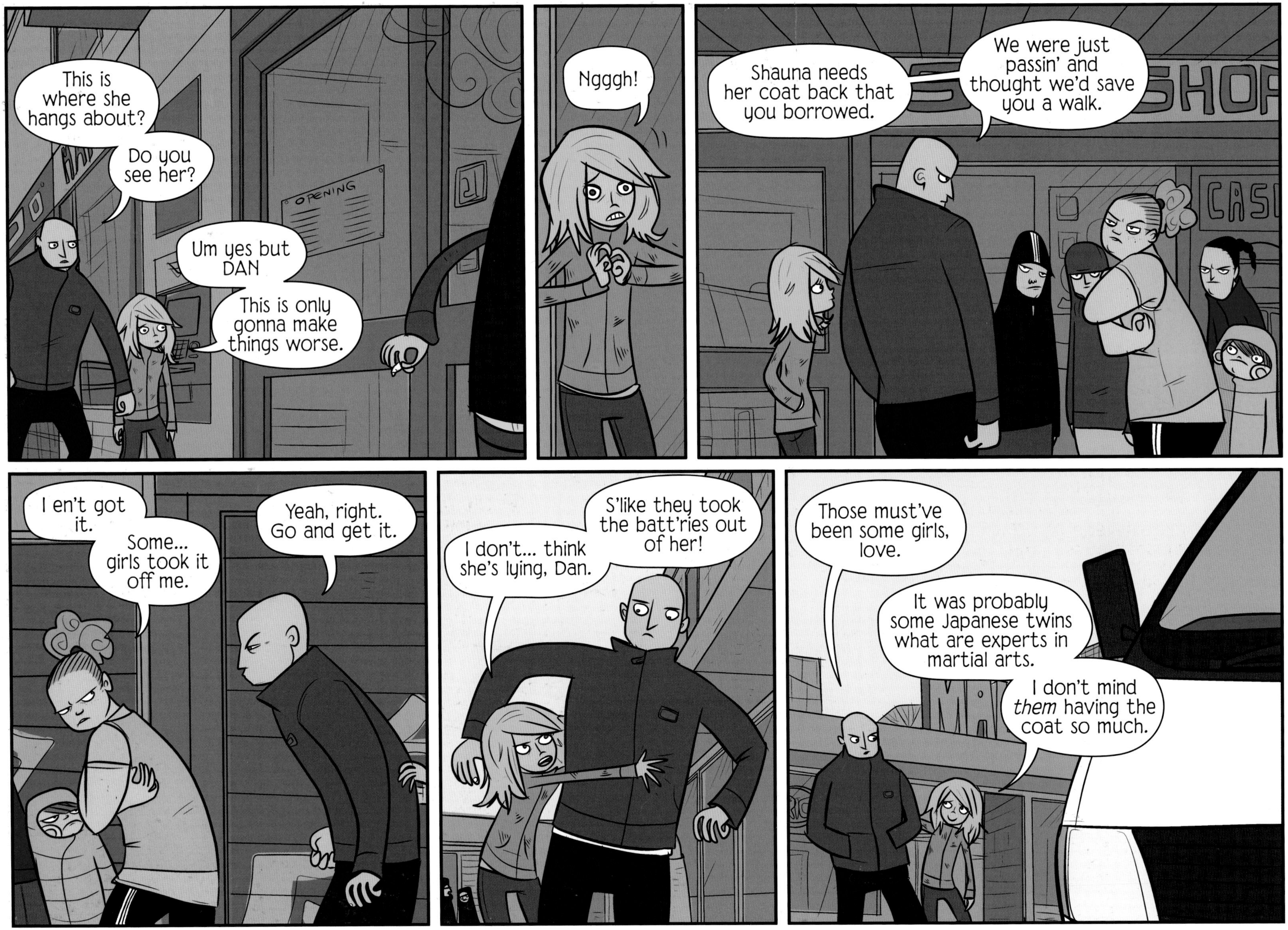
This is where she hangs about?
Do you see her?
Um yes but DAN
This is only gonna make things worse.
OPENING
Ngggh!
Shauna needs her coat back that you borrowed.
We were just passin' and thought we'd save you a walk.
I en't got it.
Some... girls took it off me.
Yeah, right. Go and get it.
I don't... think she's lying, Dan.
S'like they took the batt'ries out of her!
Those must've been some girls, love.
It was probably some Japanese twins what are experts in martial arts.
I don't mind *them* having the coat so much.

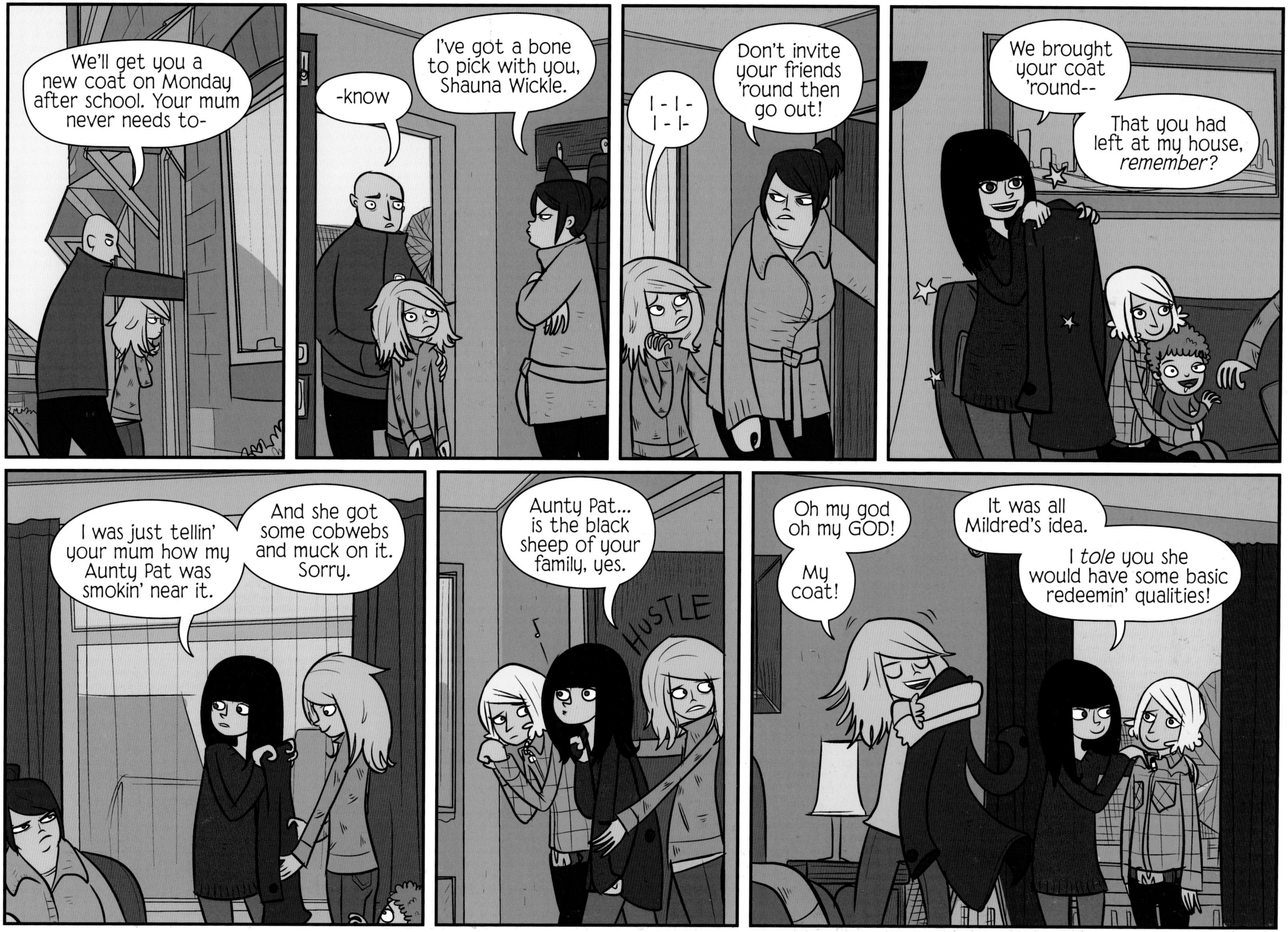
We'll get you a new coat on Monday after school. Your mum never needs to-
-know
I've got a bone to pick with you, Shauna Wickle.
I - I - I - I-
Don't invite your friends 'round then go out!
We brought your coat 'round--
That you had left at my house, *remember?*
I was just tellin' your mum how my Aunty Pat was smokin' near it.
And she got some cobwebs and muck on it. Sorry.
Aunty Pat... is the black sheep of your family, yes.
HUSTLE
Oh my god oh my GOD!
My coat!
It was all Mildred's idea.
I *tole* you she would have some basic redeemin' qualities!

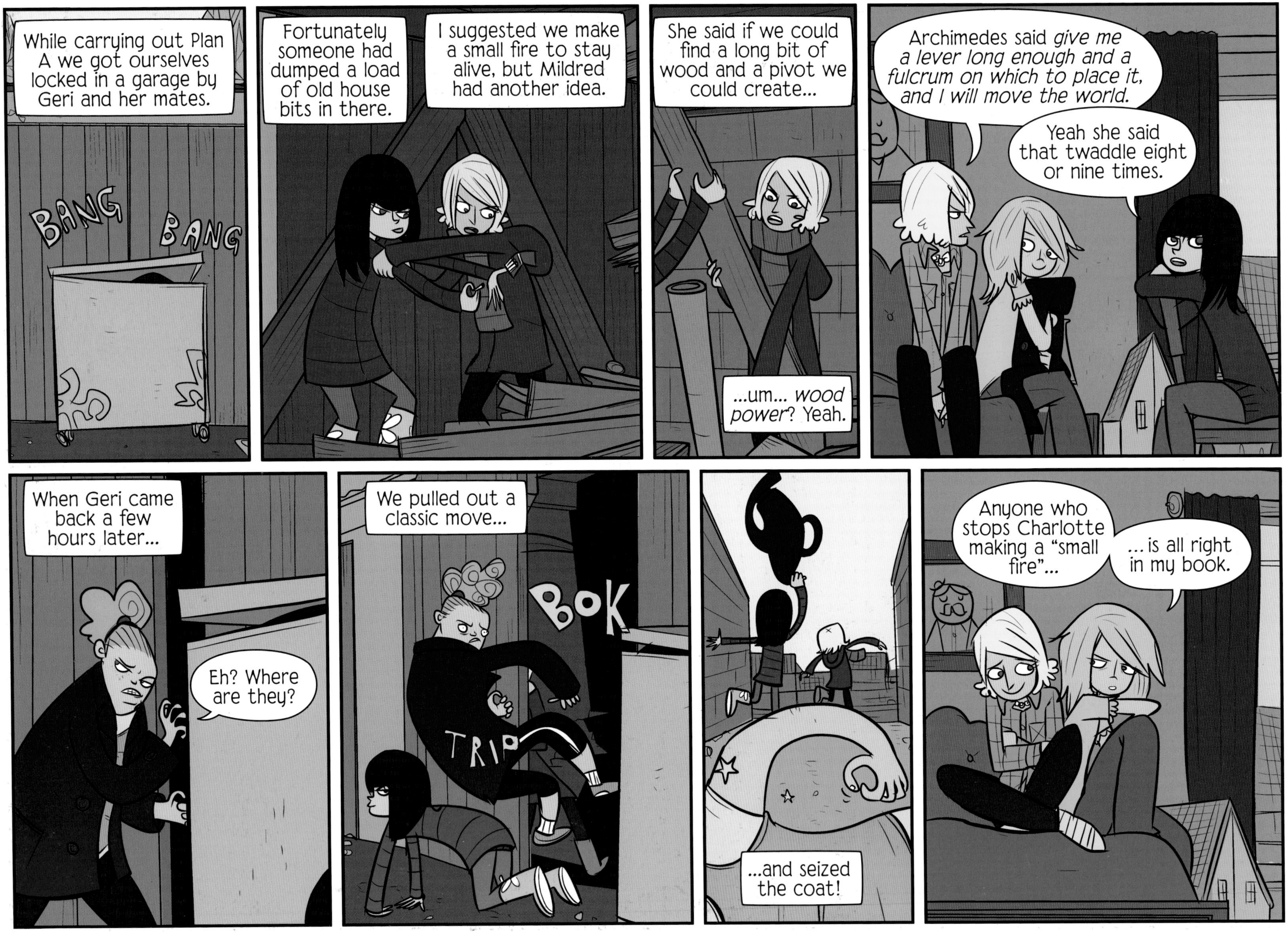
While carrying out Plan A we got ourselves locked in a garage by Geri and her mates.
BANG
BANG
Fortunately someone had dumped a load of old house bits in there.
I suggested we make a small fire to stay alive, but Mildred had another idea.
She said if we could find a long bit of wood and a pivot we could create...
...um... *wood power*? Yeah.
Archimedes said *give me a lever long enough and a fulcrum on which to place it, and I will move the world.*
Yeah she said that twaddle eight or nine times.
When Geri came back a few hours later...
Eh? Where are they?
We pulled out a classic move...
BOK
TRIP
...and seized the coat!
Anyone who stops Charlotte making a "small fire"...
...is all right in my book.

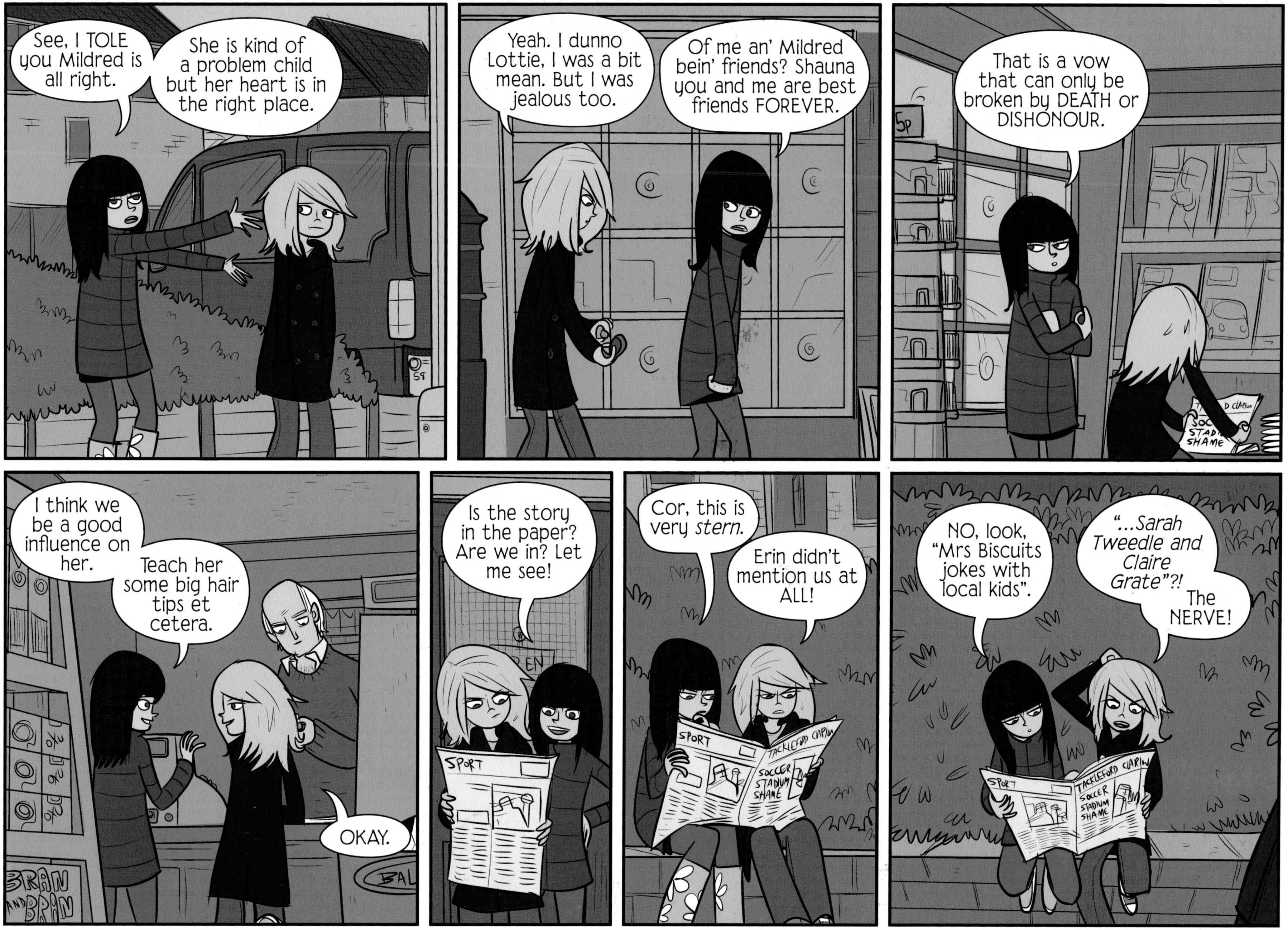

See, I TOLE you Mildred is all right.
She is kind of a problem child but her heart is in the right place.
Yeah. I dunno Lottie, I was a bit mean. But I was jealous too.
Of me an' Mildred bein' friends? Shauna you and me are best friends FOREVER.
That is a vow that can only be broken by DEATH or DISHONOUR.
SOCCER STADIUM SHAME
I think we be a good influence on her.
Teach her some big hair tips et cetera.
OKAY.
Is the story in the paper? Are we in? Let me see!
SPORT
Cor, this is very *stern.*
Erin didn't mention us at ALL!
SPORT
TACKLEFORD CLARION
SOCCER STADIUM SHAME
NO, look, "Mrs Biscuits jokes with local kids".
"*...Sarah Tweedle and Claire Grate*"?! The NERVE!
SPORT
TACKLEFORD CLARION
SOCCER STADIUM SHAME

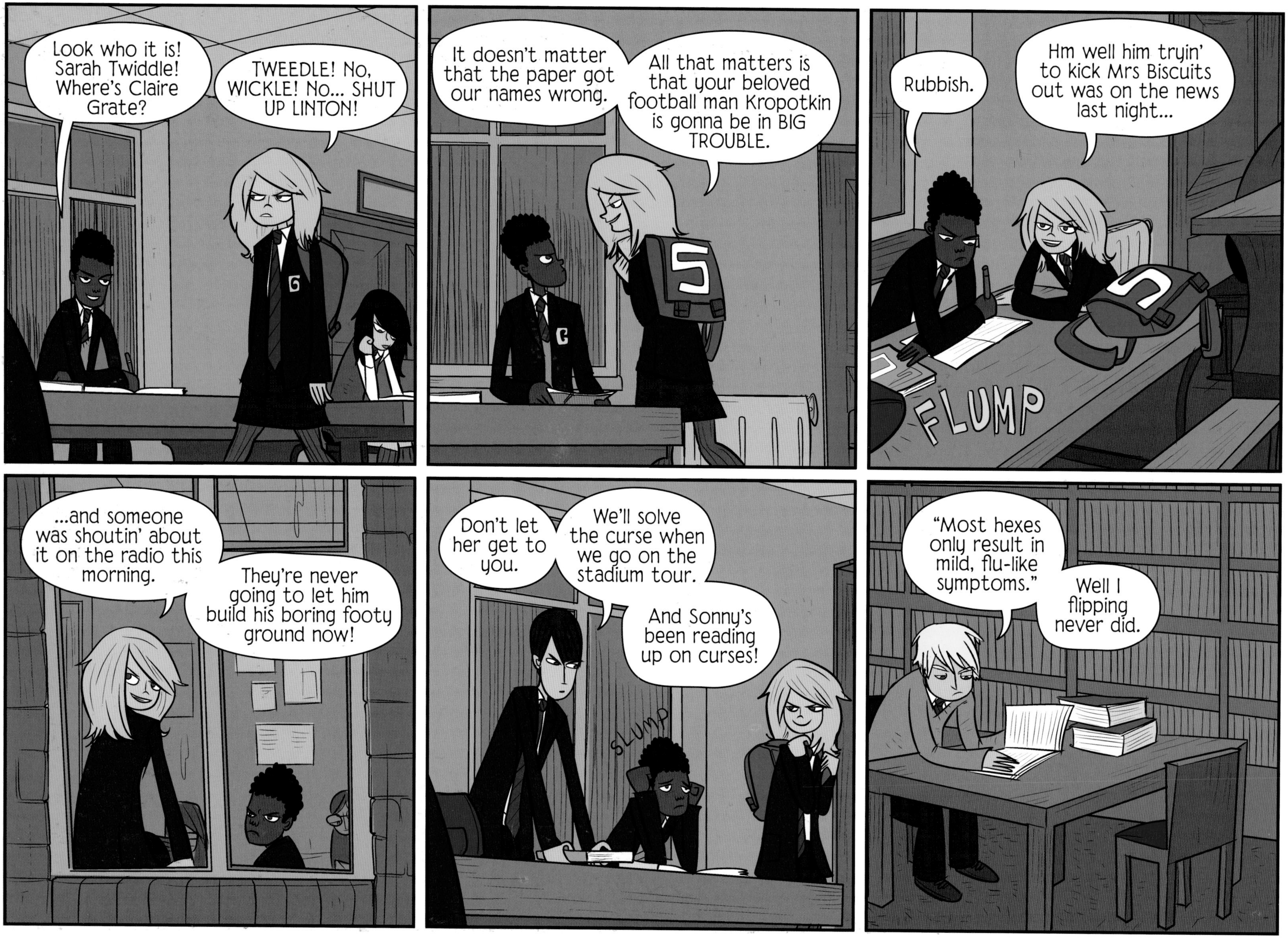
Look who it is! Sarah Twiddle! Where's Claire Grate?
TWEEDLE! No, WICKLE! No... SHUT UP LINTON!
It doesn't matter that the paper got our names wrong.
All that matters is that your beloved football man Kropotkin is gonna be in BIG TROUBLE.
Rubbish.
Hm well him tryin' to kick Mrs Biscuits out was on the news last night...
FLUMP
...and someone was shoutin' about it on the radio this morning.
They're never going to let him build his boring footy ground now!
Don't let her get to you.
We'll solve the curse when we go on the stadium tour.
And Sonny's been reading up on curses!
SLUMP
"Most hexes only result in mild, flu-like symptoms."
Well I flipping never did.

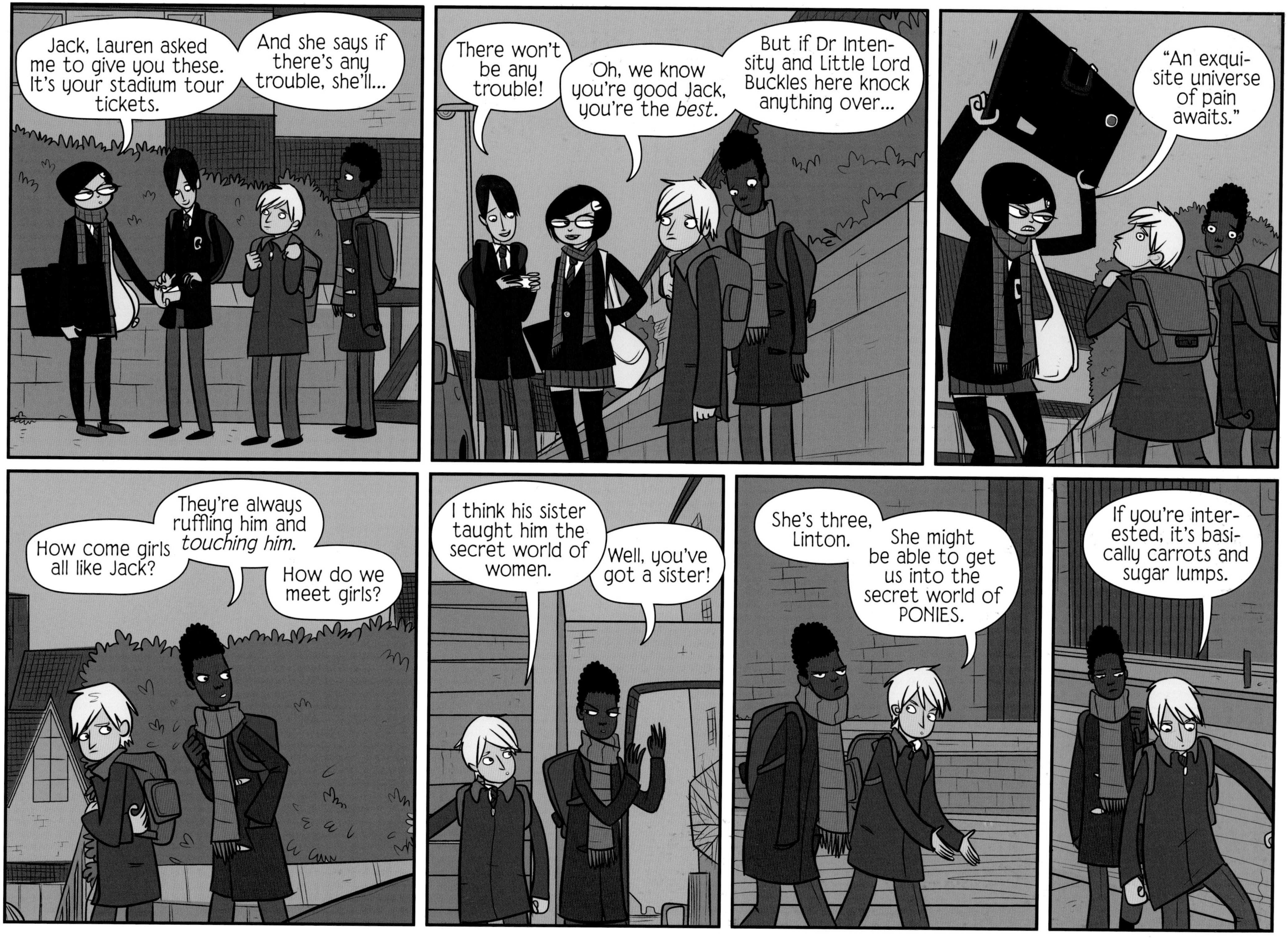
Jack, Lauren asked me to give you these. It's your stadium tour tickets.
And she says if there's any trouble, she'll...
There won't be any trouble!
Oh, we know you're good Jack, you're the *best.*
But if Dr Intensity and Little Lord Buckles here knock anything over...
"An exquisite universe of pain awaits."
How come girls all like Jack?
They're always ruffling him and *touching him.*
How do we meet girls?
I think his sister taught him the secret world of women.
Well, you've got a sister!
She's three, Linton.
She might be able to get us into the secret world of PONIES.
If you're interested, it's basically carrots and sugar lumps.

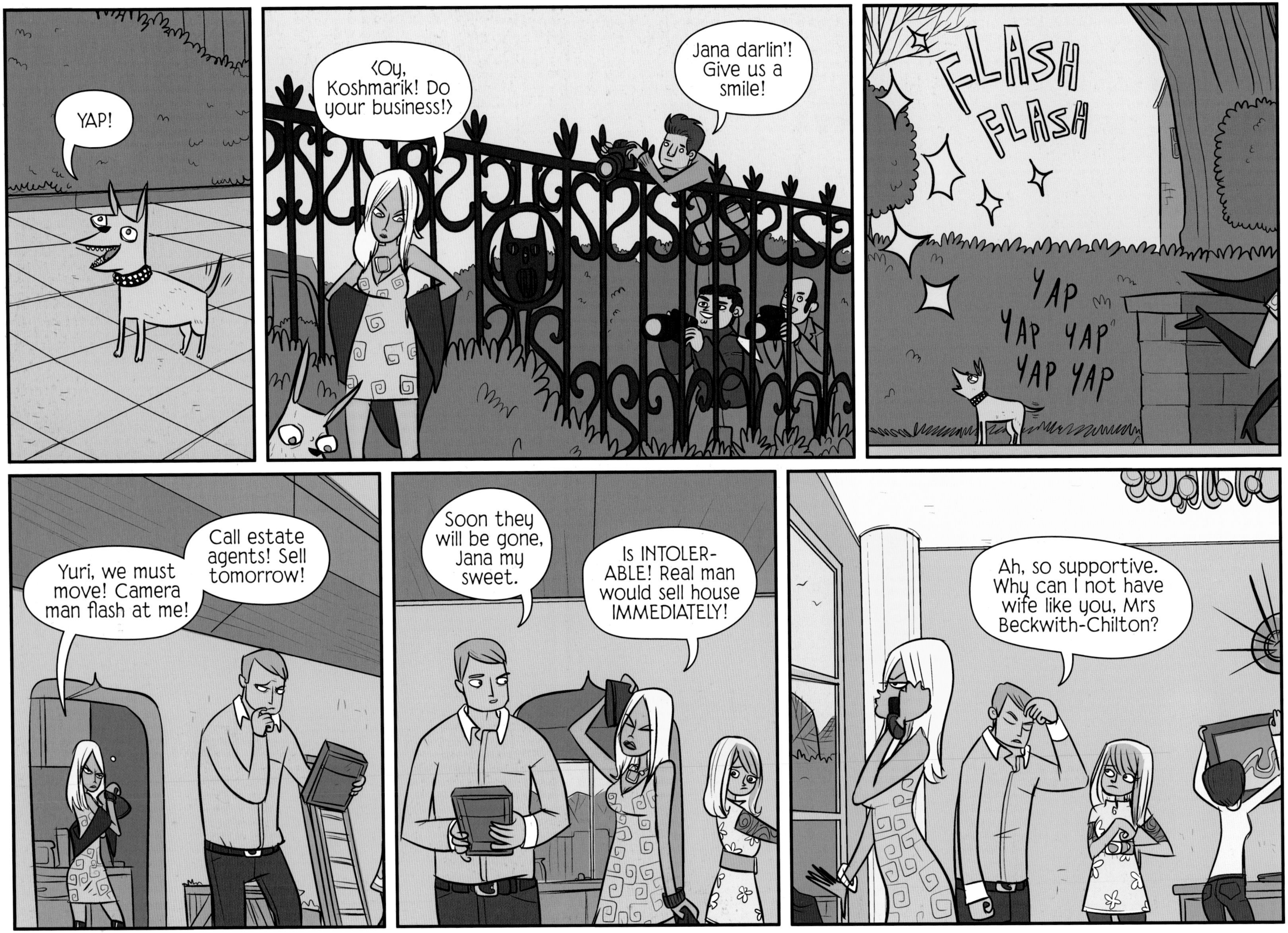
YAP!
‹Oy, Koshmarik! Do your business!›
Jana darlin'! Give us a smile!
FLASH
FLASH
YAP
YAP YAP
YAP YAP
Yuri, we must move! Camera man flash at me!
Call estate agents! Sell tomorrow!
Soon they will be gone, Jana my sweet.
Is INTOLERABLE! Real man would sell house IMMEDIATELY!
Ah, so supportive. Why can I not have wife like you, Mrs Beckwith-Chilton?

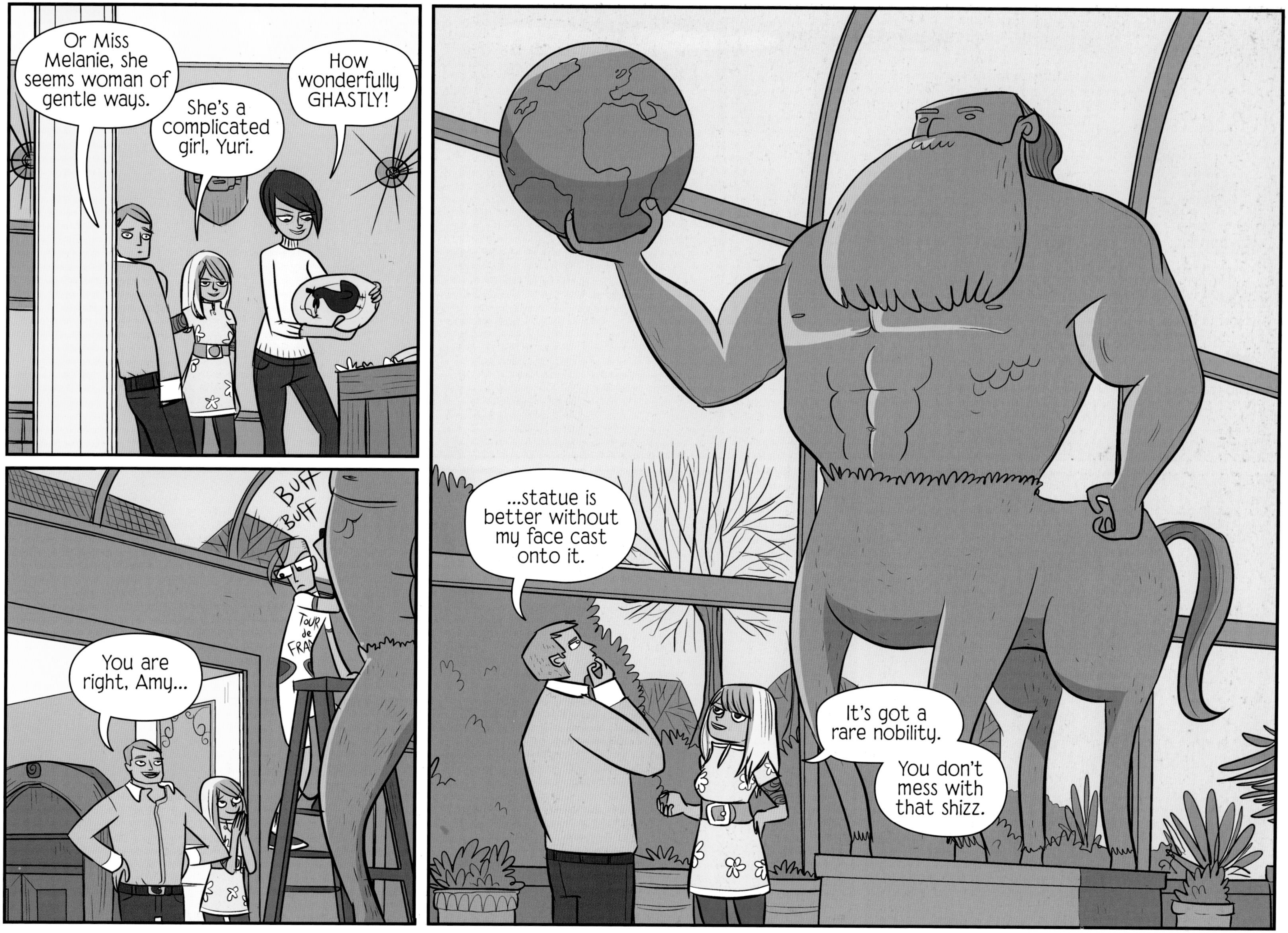
Or Miss Melanie, she seems woman of gentle ways.
She's a complicated girl, Yuri.
How wonderfully GHASTLY!
BUFF BUFF
TOUR de FRA
You are right, Amy...
...statue is better without my face cast onto it.
It's got a rare nobility.
You don't mess with that shizz.

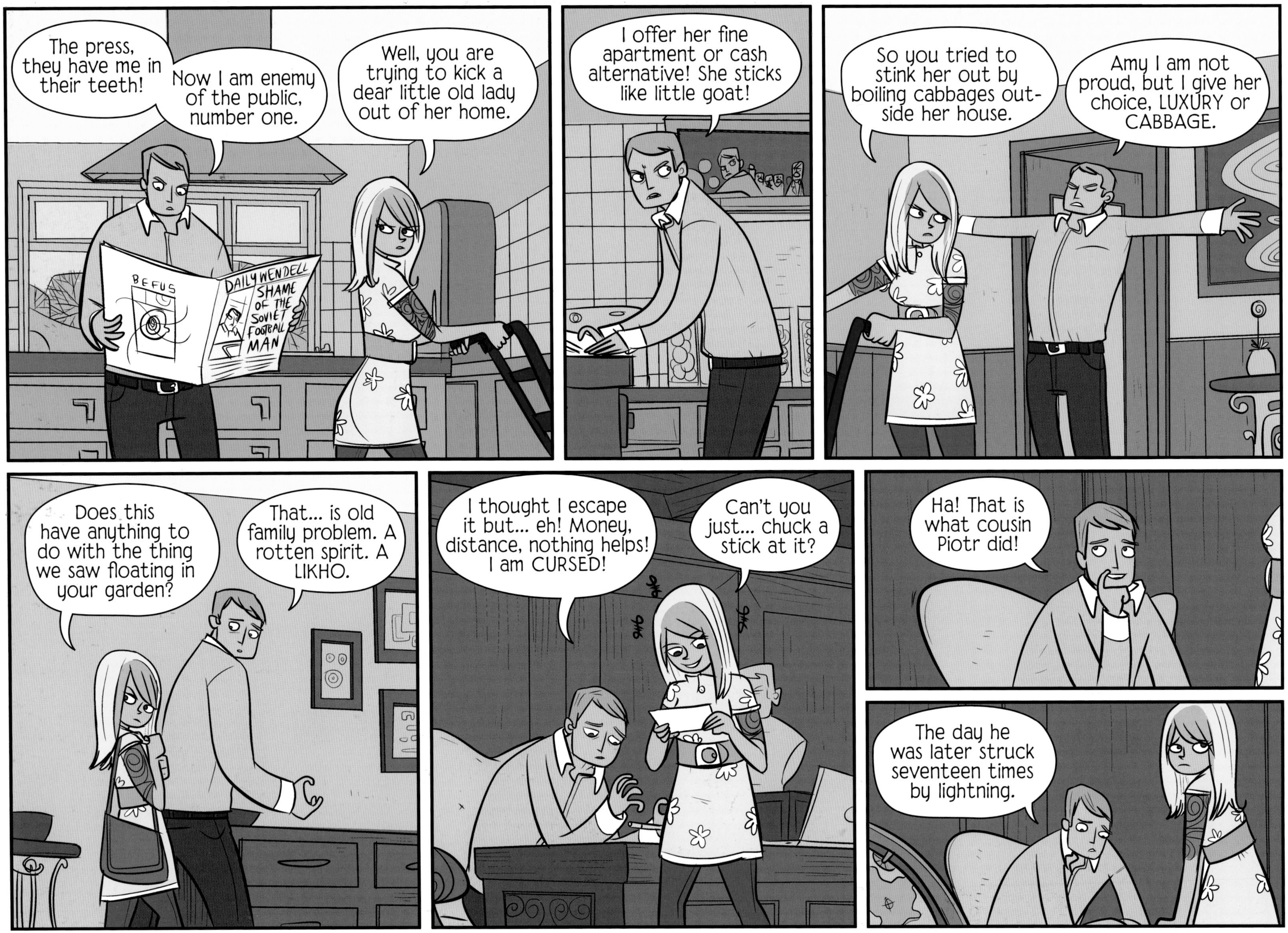
The press, they have me in their teeth!
Now I am enemy of the public, number one.
BEFUS
DAILY WENDELL
SHAME OF THE SOVIET FOOTBALL MAN
Well, you are trying to kick a dear little old lady out of her home.
I offer her fine apartment or cash alternative! She sticks like little goat!
So you tried to stink her out by boiling cabbages outside her house.
Amy I am not proud, but I give her choice, LUXURY or CABBAGE.
Does this have anything to do with the thing we saw floating in your garden?
That... is old family problem. A rotten spirit. A LIKHO.
I thought I escape it but... eh! Money, distance, nothing helps! I am CURSED!
Can't you just... chuck a stick at it?
Ha! That is what cousin Piotr did!
The day he was later struck seventeen times by lightning.

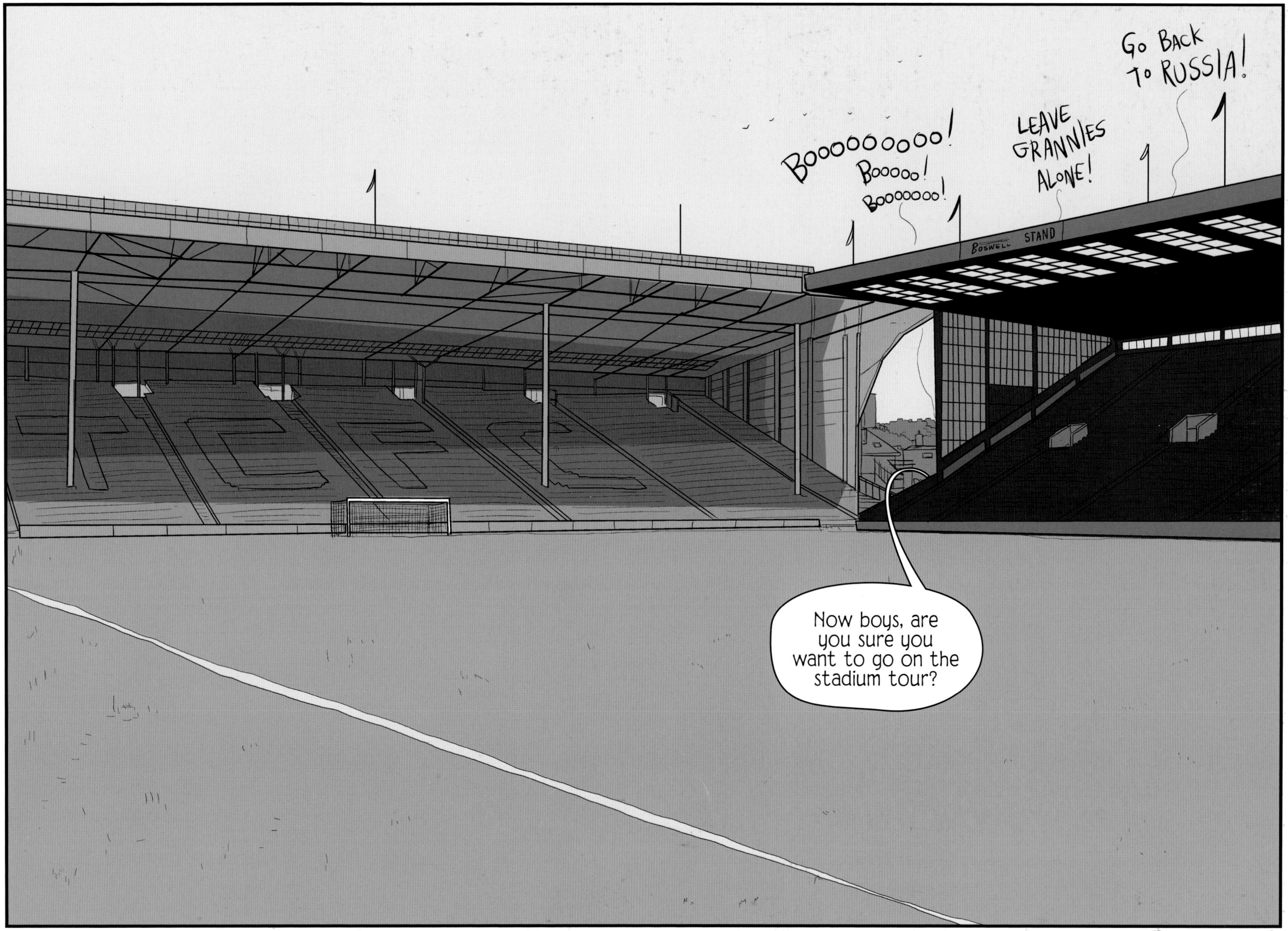
BOSWELL STAND
Boooooooooo!
Booooo!
Booooooo!
LEAVE GRANNIES ALONE!
Go BACK TO RUSSIA!
Now boys, are you sure you want to go on the stadium tour?

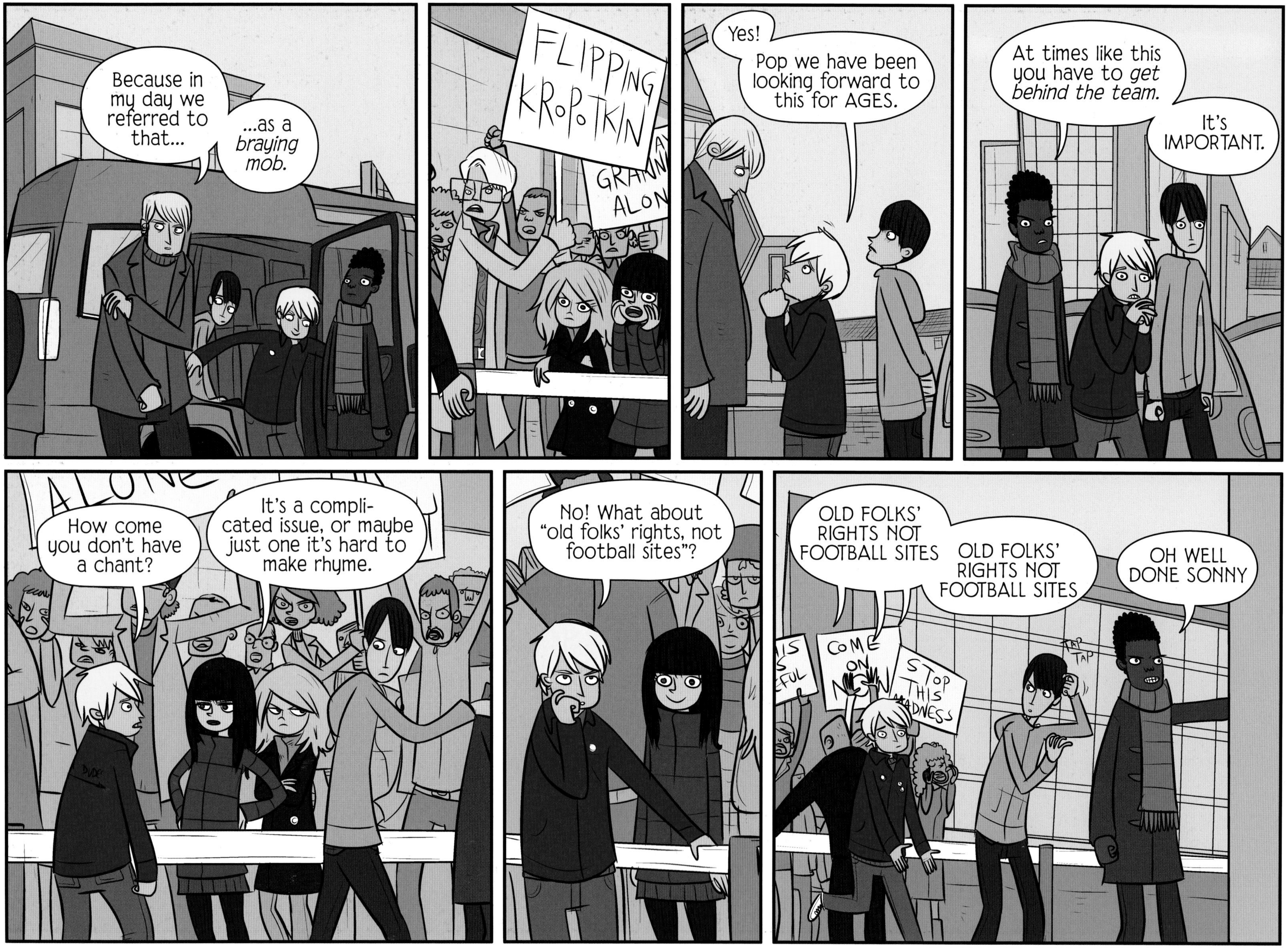
Because in my day we referred to that...
...as a *braying mob.*
FLIPPING KROPOTKIN
Yes!
Pop we have been looking forward to this for AGES.
At times like this you have to *get behind the team.*
It's IMPORTANT.
How come you don't have a chant?
It's a compli-cated issue, or maybe just one it's hard to make rhyme.
No! What about "old folks' rights, not football sites"?
OLD FOLKS' RIGHTS NOT FOOTBALL SITES
OLD FOLKS' RIGHTS NOT FOOTBALL SITES
OH WELL DONE SONNY
COME ON
STOP THIS MADNESS
TAP TAP

The Case of The Team Spirit

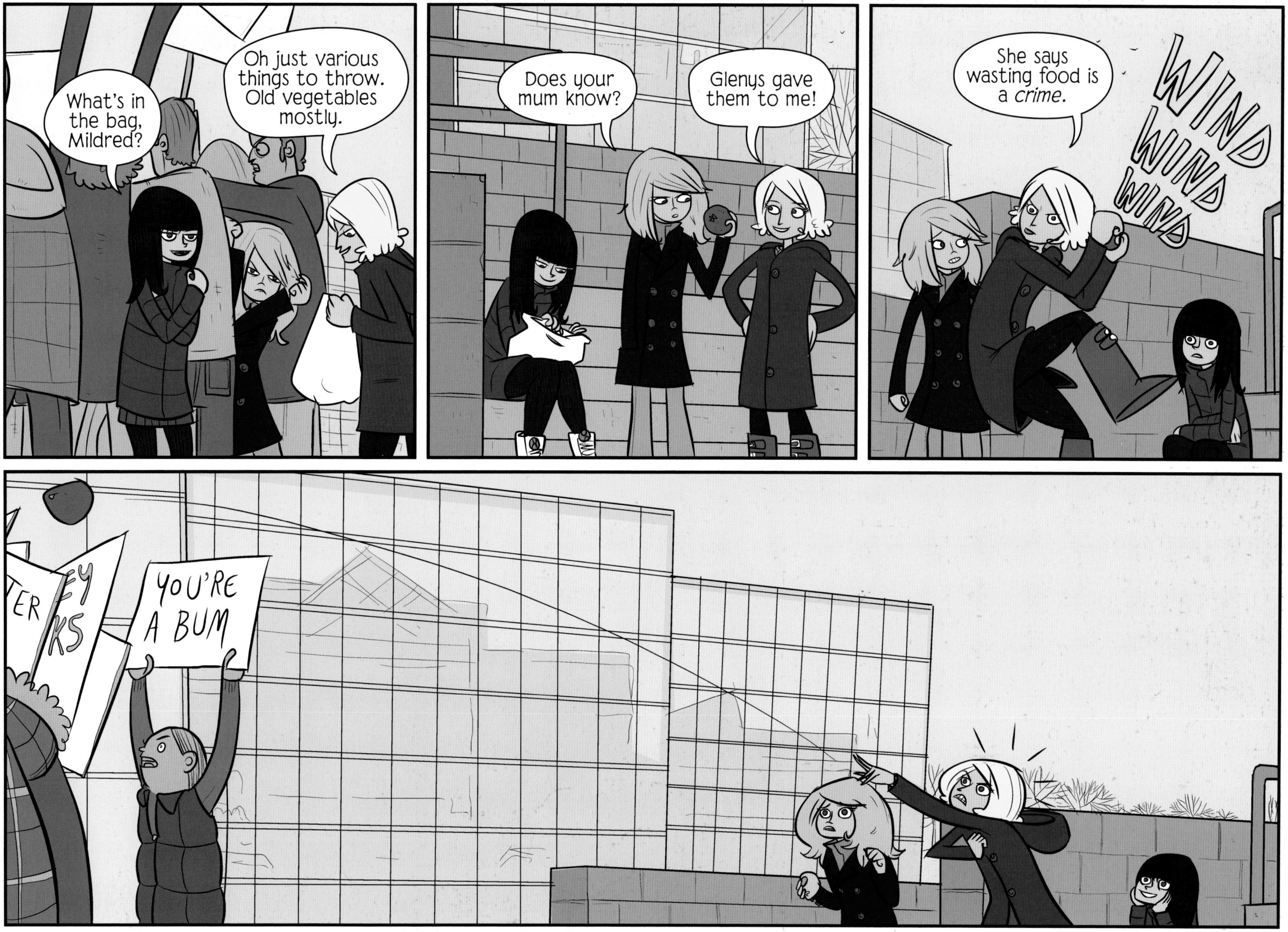
What's in the bag, Mildred?
Oh just various things to throw. Old vegetables mostly.
Does your mum know?
Glenys gave them to me!
She says wasting food is a *crime*.
WIND
WIND
WIND
YOU'RE A BUM

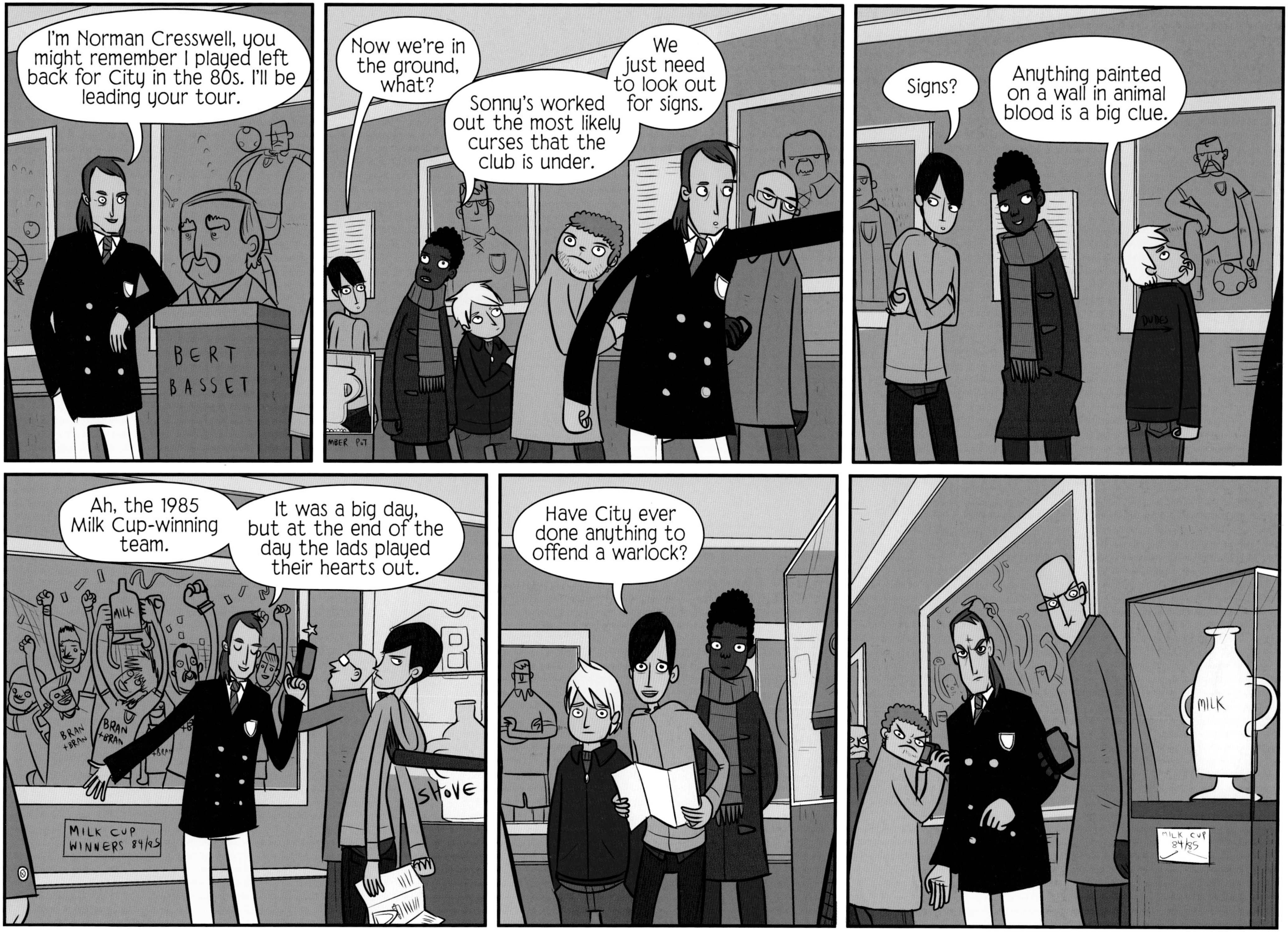
I'm Norman Cresswell, you might remember I played left back for City in the 80s. I'll be leading your tour.
BERT BASSET
Now we're in the ground, what?
Sonny's worked out the most likely curses that the club is under.
We just need to look out for signs.
Signs?
Anything painted on a wall in animal blood is a big clue.
Ah, the 1985 Milk Cup-winning team.
It was a big day, but at the end of the day the lads played their hearts out.
MILK
MILK CUP WINNERS 84/85
Have City ever done anything to offend a warlock?
MILK
MILK CUP 84/85

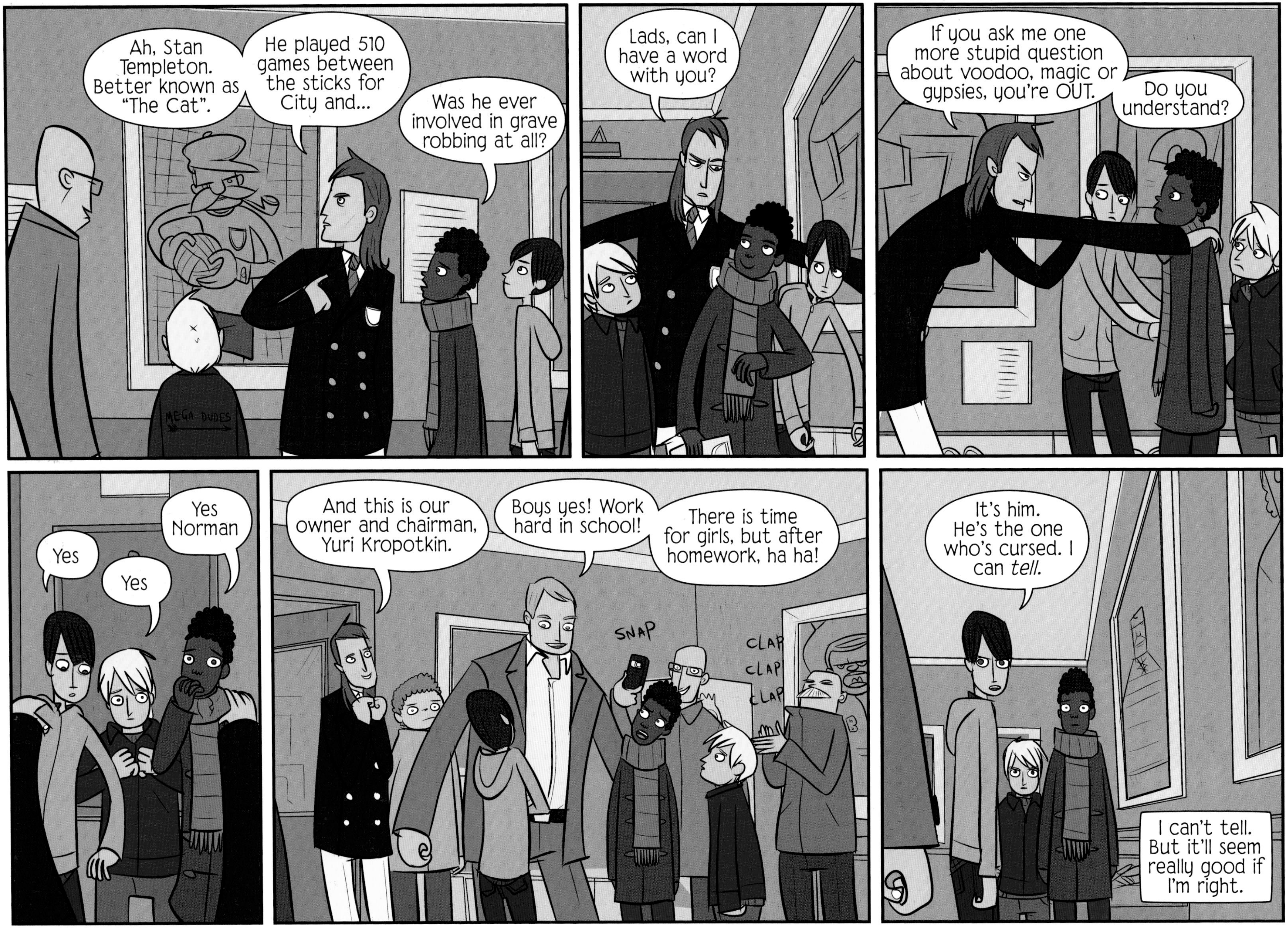
Ah, Stan Templeton. Better known as "The Cat".
He played 510 games between the sticks for City and...
Was he ever involved in grave robbing at all?
MEGA DUDES
Lads, can I have a word with you?
If you ask me one more stupid question about voodoo, magic or gypsies, you're OUT.
Do you understand?
Yes
Yes
Yes Norman
And this is our owner and chairman, Yuri Kropotkin.
Boys yes! Work hard in school!
There is time for girls, but after homework, ha ha!
SNAP
CLAP
CLAP
CLAP
It's him. He's the one who's cursed. I can *tell.*
I can't tell. But it'll seem really good if I'm right.

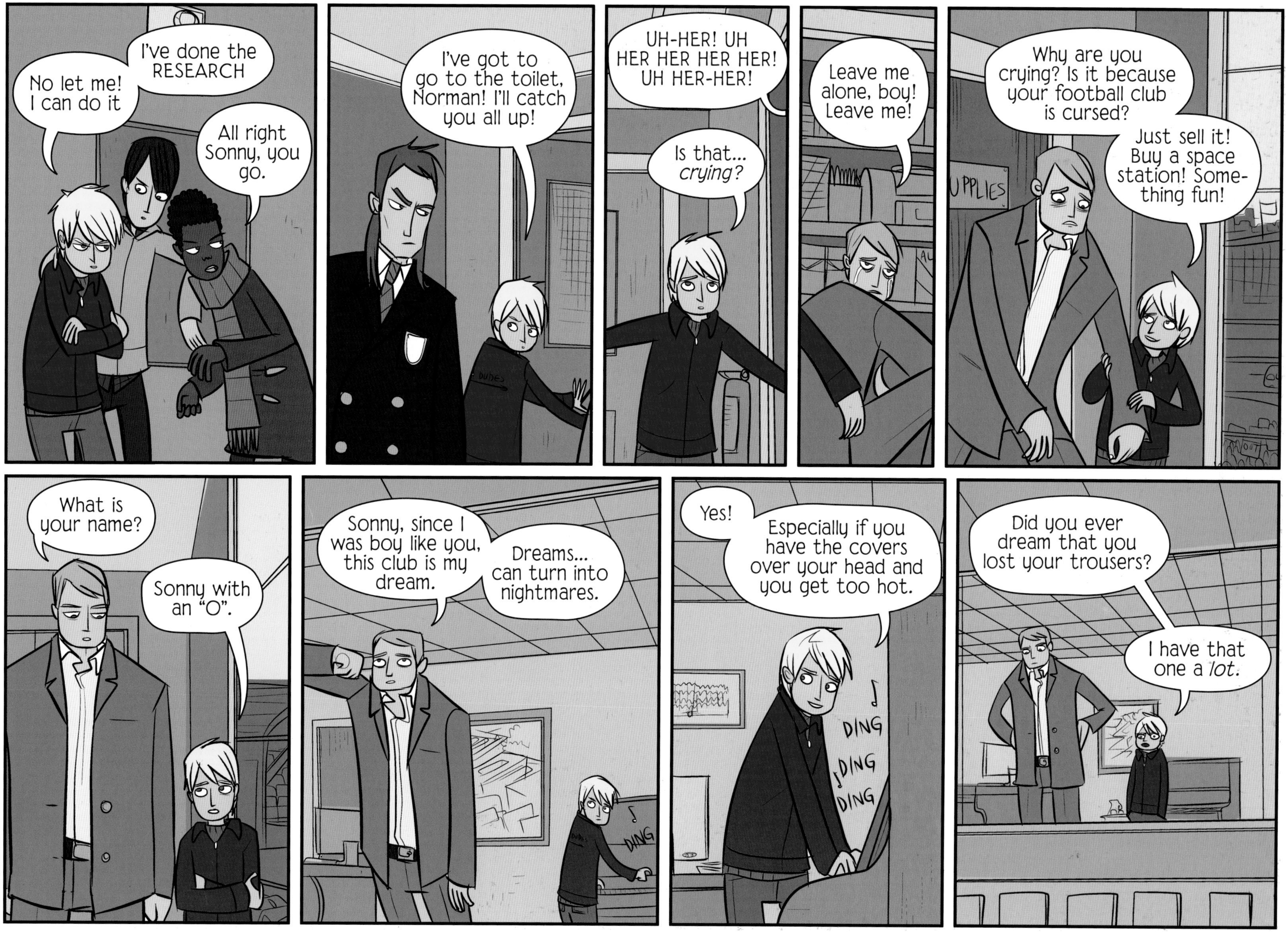
No let me! I can do it
I've done the RESEARCH
All right Sonny, you go.
I've got to go to the toilet, Norman! I'll catch you all up!
UH-HER! UH HER HER HER HER! UH HER-HER!
Is that... *crying?*
Leave me alone, boy! Leave me!
Why are you crying? Is it because your football club is cursed?
Just sell it! Buy a space station! Something fun!
UPPLIES
What is your name?
Sonny with an "O".
Sonny, since I was boy like you, this club is my dream.
Dreams... can turn into nightmares.
DING
Yes!
Especially if you have the covers over your head and you get too hot.
DING
DING
DING
Did you ever dream that you lost your trousers?
I have that one a *lot.*

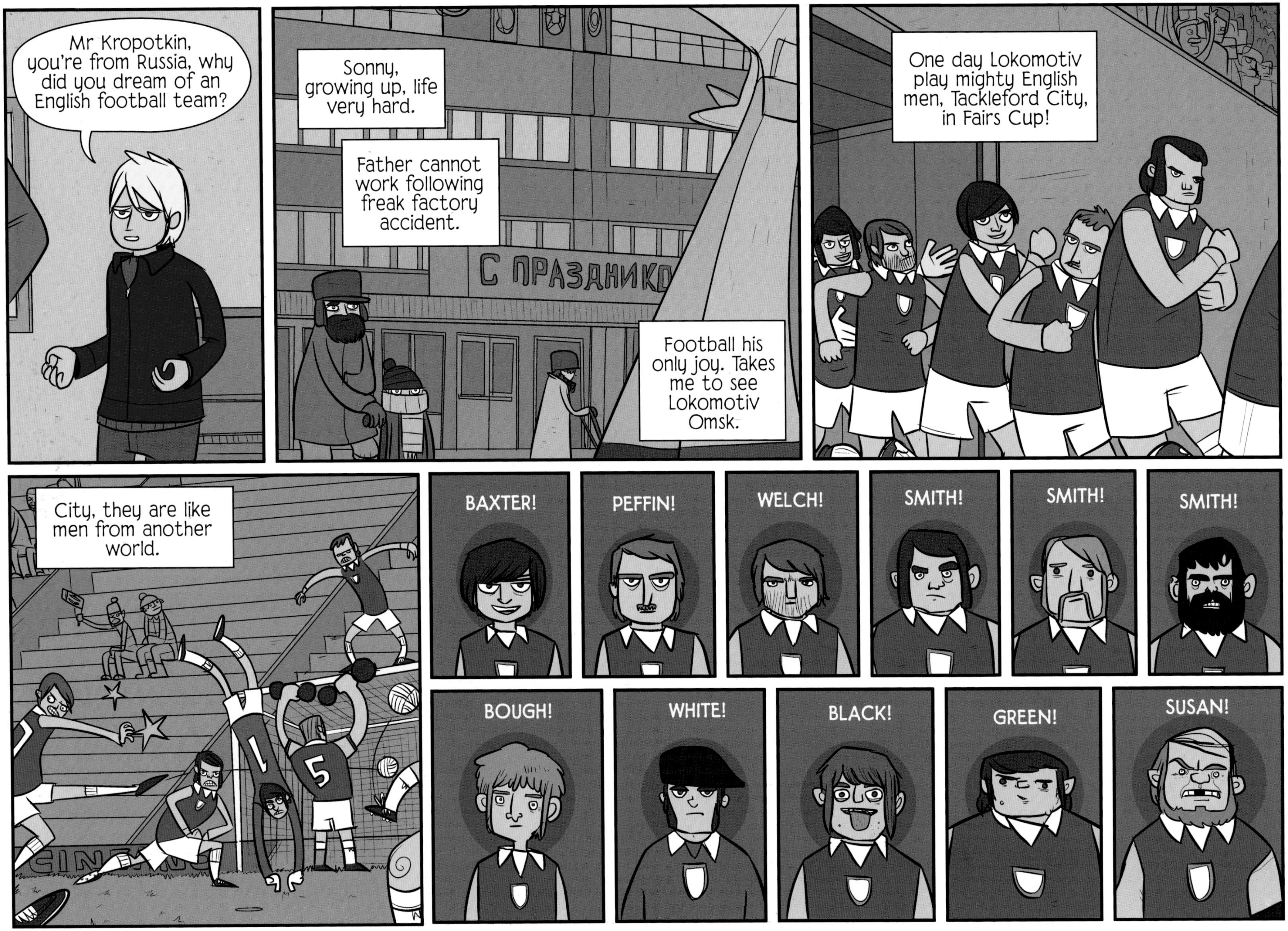
Mr Kropotkin, you're from Russia, why did you dream of an English football team?
Sonny, growing up, life very hard.
Father cannot work following freak factory accident.
С ПРАЗДНИКО
Football his only joy. Takes me to see Lokomotiv Omsk.
One day Lokomotiv play mighty English men, Tackleford City, in Fairs Cup!
City, they are like men from another world.
BAXTER!
PEFFIN!
WELCH!
SMITH!
SMITH!
SMITH!
BOUGH!
WHITE!
BLACK!
GREEN!
SUSAN!

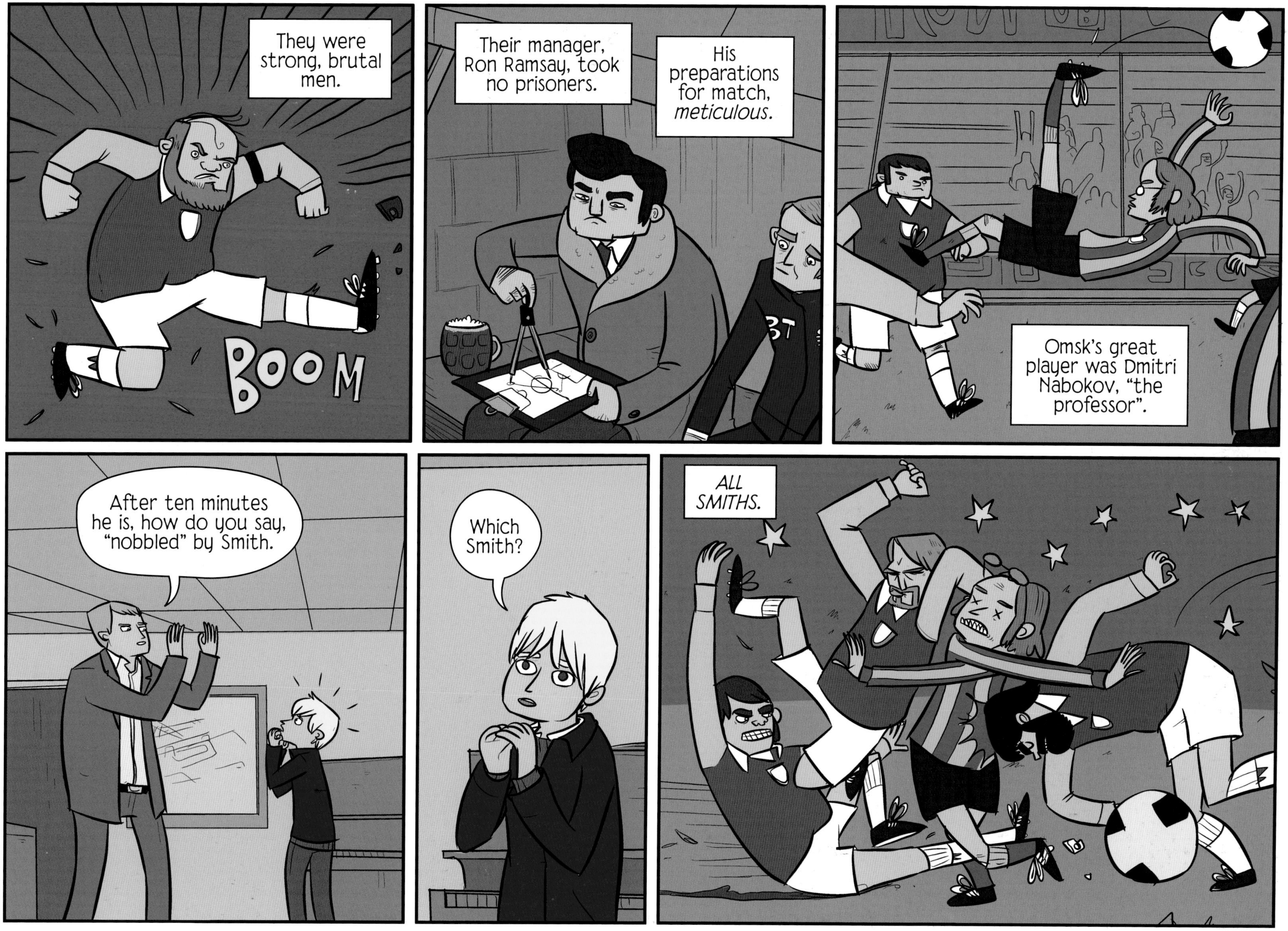
They were strong, brutal men.
BOOM
Their manager, Ron Ramsay, took no prisoners.
His preparations for match, *meticulous.*
Omsk's great player was Dmitri Nabokov, "the professor".
After ten minutes he is, how do you say, "nobbled" by Smith.
Which Smith?
ALL SMITHS.

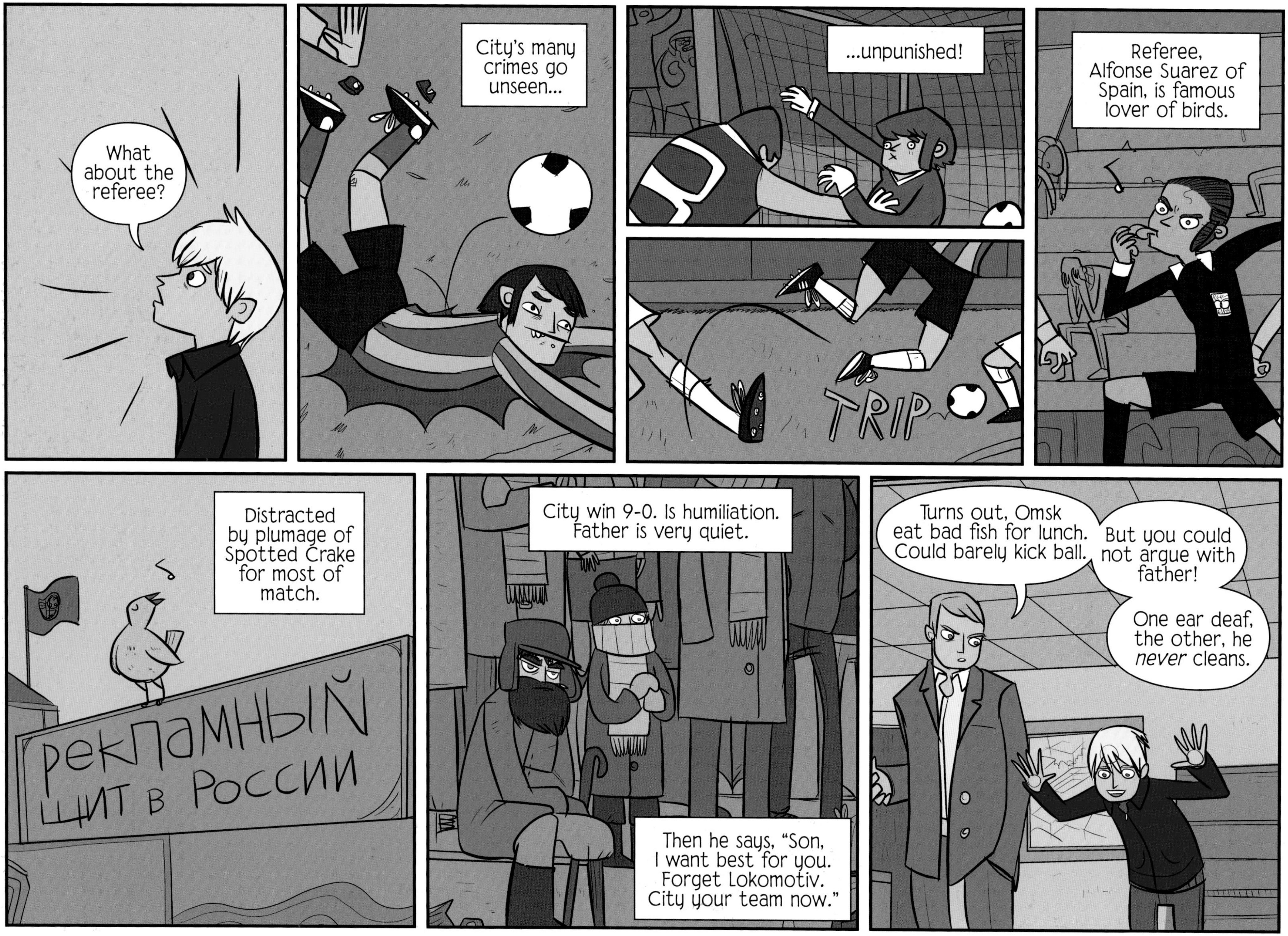
What about the referee?
City's many crimes go unseen...
...unpunished!
TRIP
Referee, Alfonse Suarez of Spain, is famous lover of birds.
Distracted by plumage of Spotted Crake for most of match.
РЕКЛАМНЫЙ ЩИТ В РОССИИ
City win 9-0. Is humiliation. Father is very quiet.
Then he says, "Son, I want best for you. Forget Lokomotiv. City your team now."
Turns out, Omsk eat bad fish for lunch. Could barely kick ball.
But you could not argue with father!
One ear deaf, the other, he *never* cleans.

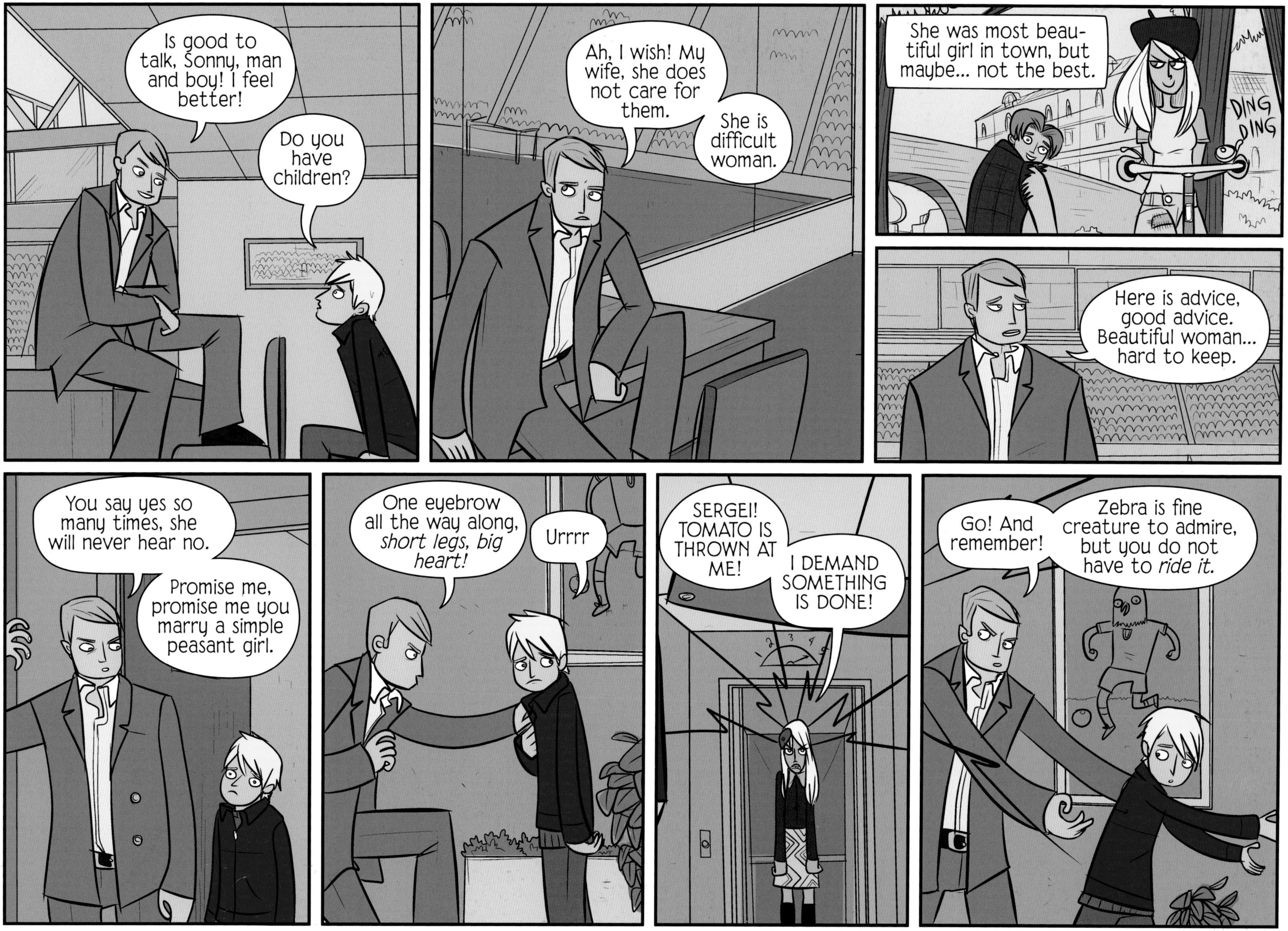
Is good to talk, Sonny, man and boy! I feel better!
Do you have children?
Ah, I wish! My wife, she does not care for them.
She is difficult woman.
She was most beau-tiful girl in town, but maybe... not the best.
DING DING
Here is advice, good advice. Beautiful woman... hard to keep.
You say yes so many times, she will never hear no.
Promise me, promise me you marry a simple peasant girl.
One eyebrow all the way along, *short legs, big heart!*
Urrrr
SERGEI! TOMATO IS THROWN AT ME!
I DEMAND SOMETHING IS DONE!
Go! And remember!
Zebra is fine creature to admire, but you do not have to *ride it.*

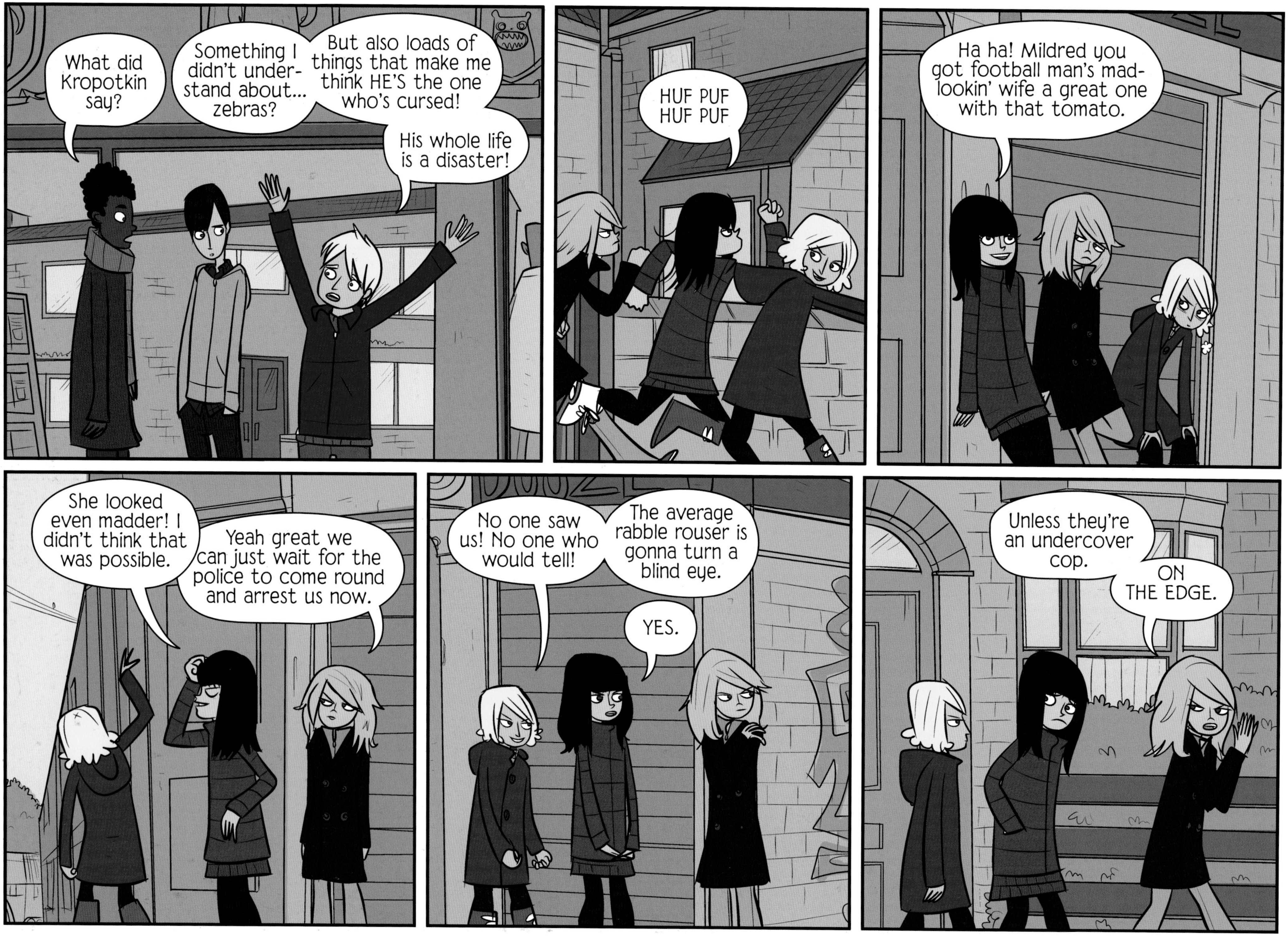
What did Kropotkin say?
Something I didn't understand about... zebras?
But also loads of things that make me think HE'S the one who's cursed!
His whole life is a disaster!
HUF PUF HUF PUF
Ha ha! Mildred you got football man's mad-lookin' wife a great one with that tomato.
She looked even madder! I didn't think that was possible.
Yeah great we can just wait for the police to come round and arrest us now.
No one saw us! No one who would tell!
The average rabble rouser is gonna turn a blind eye.
YES.
Unless they're an undercover cop.
ON THE EDGE.

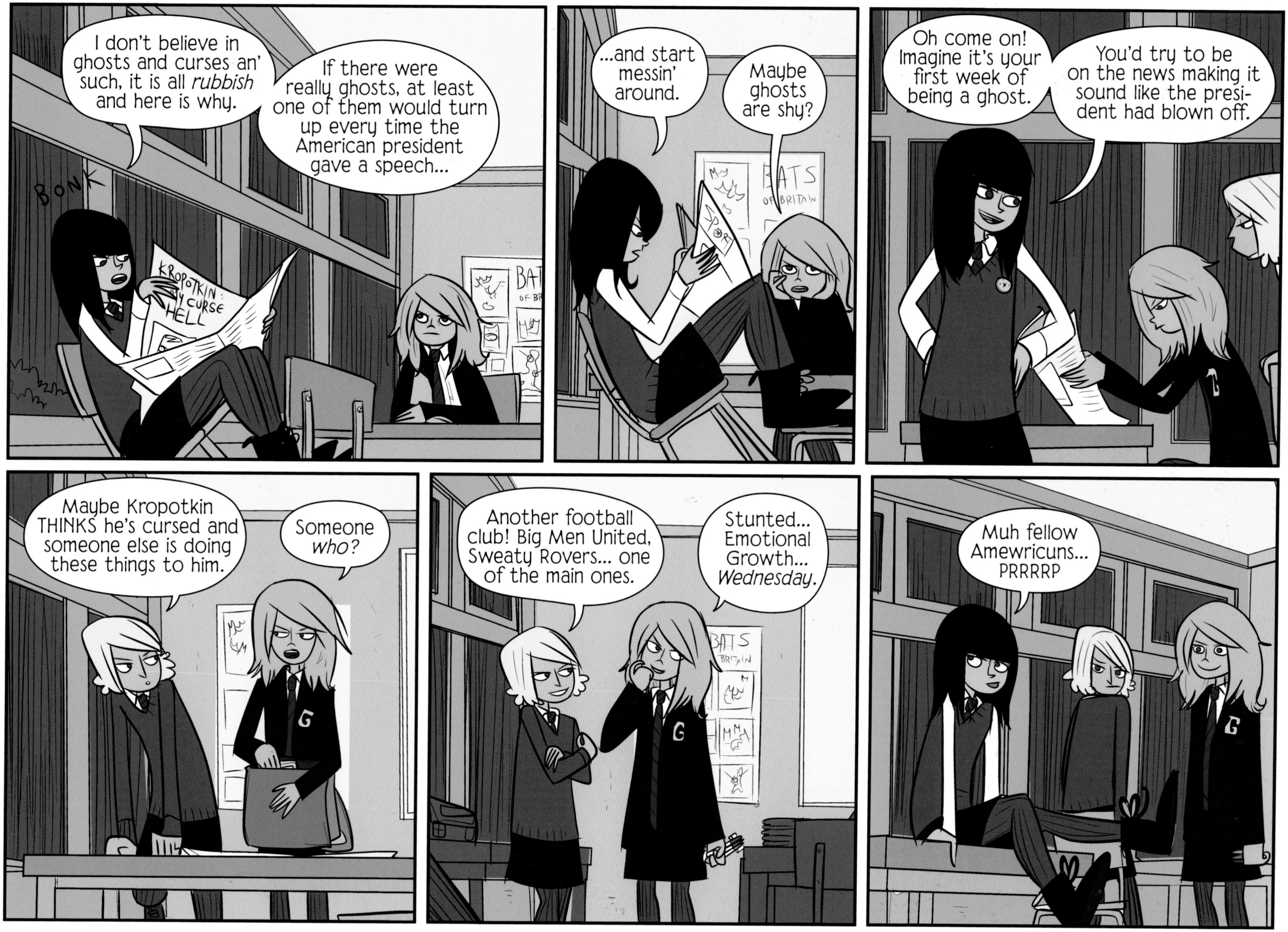
I don't believe in ghosts and curses an' such, it is all *rubbish* and here is why.
If there were really ghosts, at least one of them would turn up every time the American president gave a speech...
BONK
...and start messin' around.
Maybe ghosts are shy?
BATS OF BRITAIN
Oh come on! Imagine it's your first week of being a ghost.
You'd try to be on the news making it sound like the president had blown off.
Maybe Kropotkin THINKS he's cursed and someone else is doing these things to him.
Someone *who?*
Another football club! Big Men United, Sweaty Rovers... one of the main ones.
Stunted... Emotional Growth... *Wednesday*.
Muh fellow Amewricuns... PRRRRP

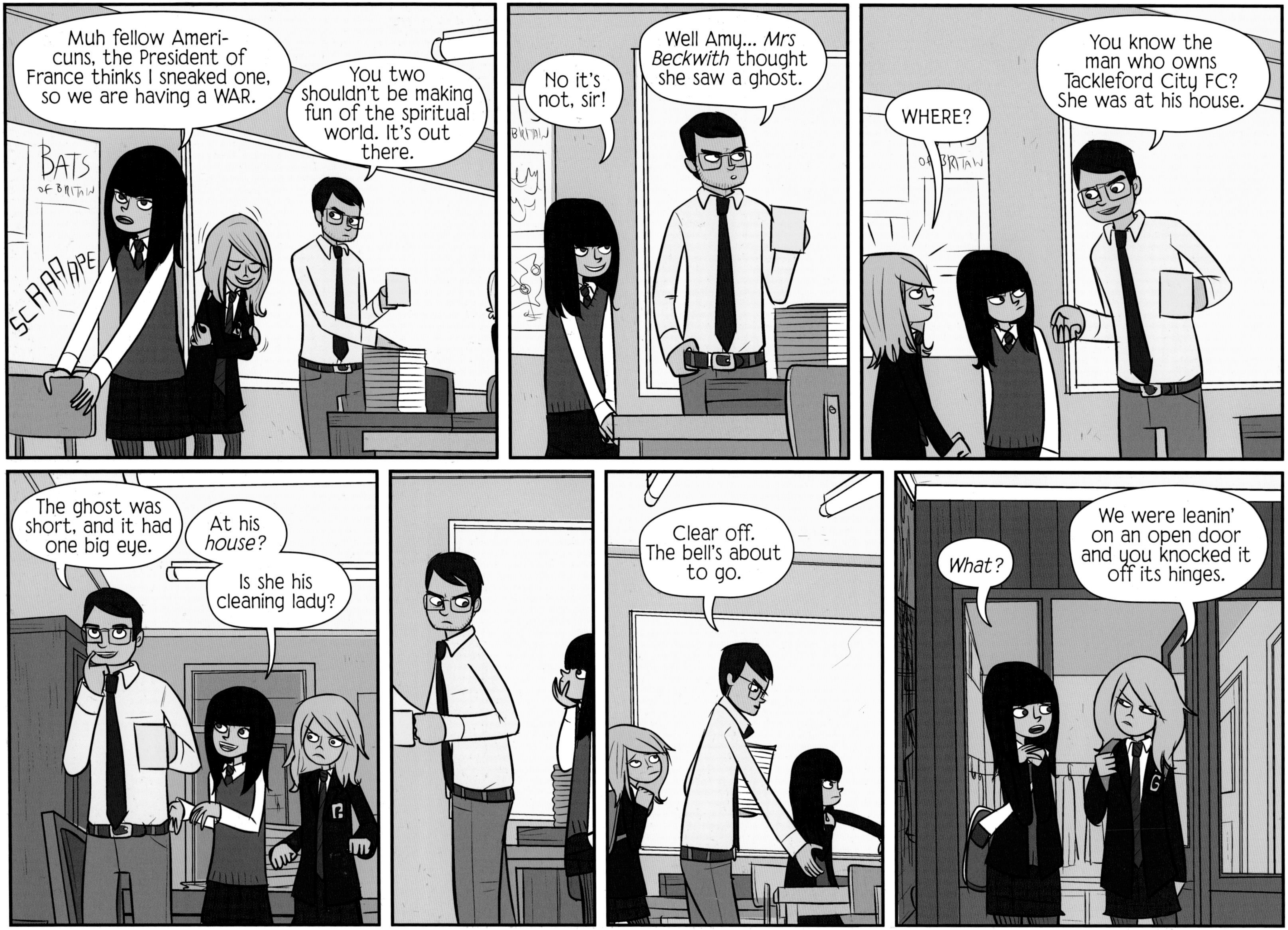
Muh fellow Ameri-cuns, the President of France thinks I sneaked one, so we are having a WAR.
You two shouldn't be making fun of the spiritual world. It's out there.
BATS OF BRITAIN
SCRAAAPE
No it's not, sir!
Well Amy... *Mrs Beckwith* thought she saw a ghost.
WHERE?
You know the man who owns Tackleford City FC? She was at his house.
The ghost was short, and it had one big eye.
At his *house?*
Is she his cleaning lady?
Clear off. The bell's about to go.
What?
We were leanin' on an open door and you knocked it off its hinges.

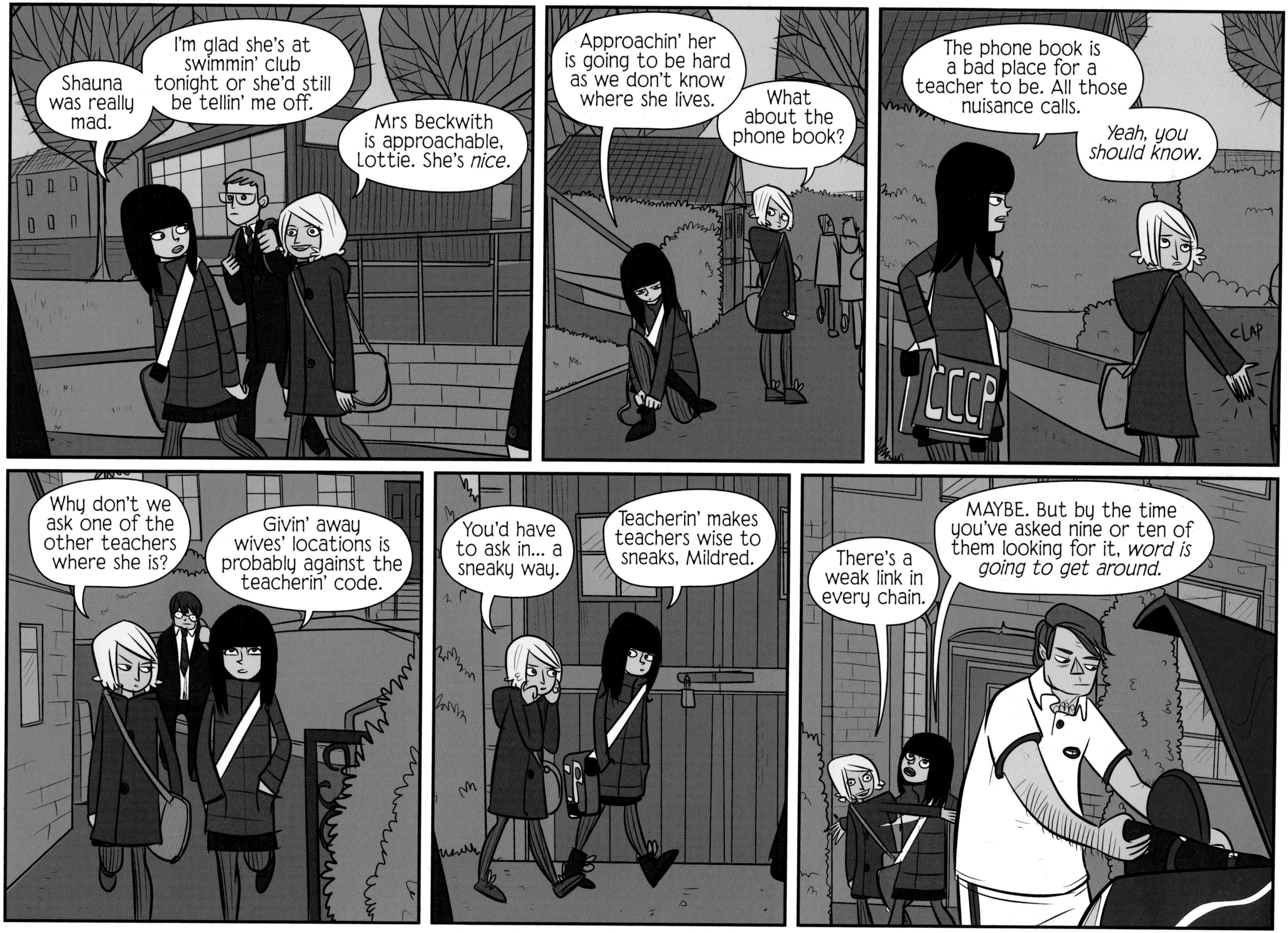
Shauna was really mad.
I'm glad she's at swimmin' club tonight or she'd still be tellin' me off.
Mrs Beckwith is approachable, Lottie. She's *nice.*
Approachin' her is going to be hard as we don't know where she lives.
What about the phone book?
The phone book is a bad place for a teacher to be. All those nuisance calls.
Yeah, you should know.
CLAP
CCCP
Why don't we ask one of the other teachers where she is?
Givin' away wives' locations is probably against the teacherin' code.
You'd have to ask in... a sneaky way.
Teacherin' makes teachers wise to sneaks, Mildred.
There's a weak link in every chain.
MAYBE. But by the time you've asked nine or ten of them looking for it, *word is going to get around.*

Bad Machinery, Volume One

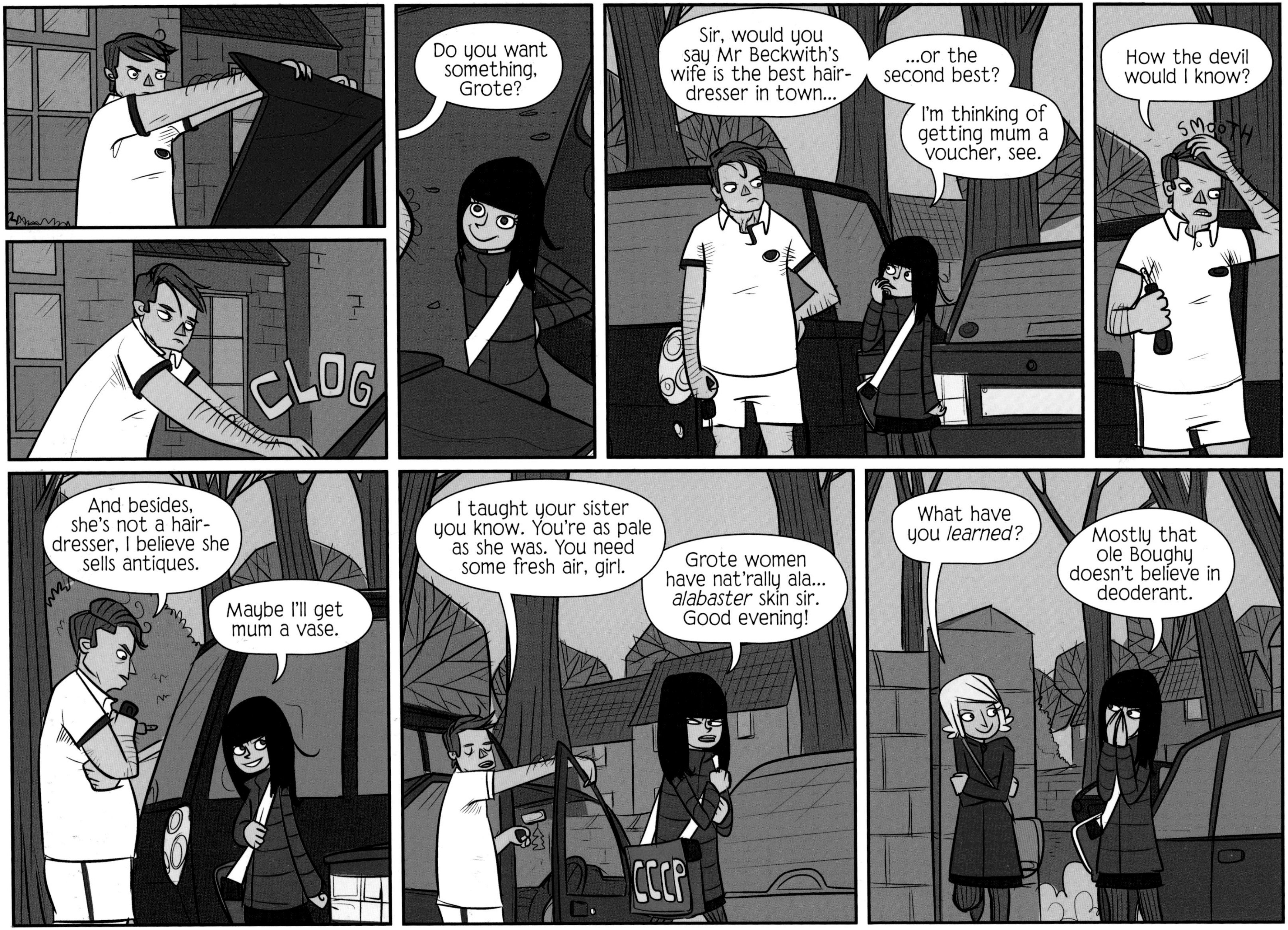
Do you want something, Grote?
CLOG
Sir, would you say Mr Beckwith's wife is the best hair-dresser in town...
...or the second best?
I'm thinking of getting mum a voucher, see.
How the devil would I know?
SMOOTH
And besides, she's not a hair-dresser, I believe she sells antiques.
Maybe I'll get mum a vase.
I taught your sister you know. You're as pale as she was. You need some fresh air, girl.
Grote women have nat'rally ala... *alabaster* skin sir. Good evening!
CCCP
What have you *learned?*
Mostly that ole Boughy doesn't believe in deoderant.

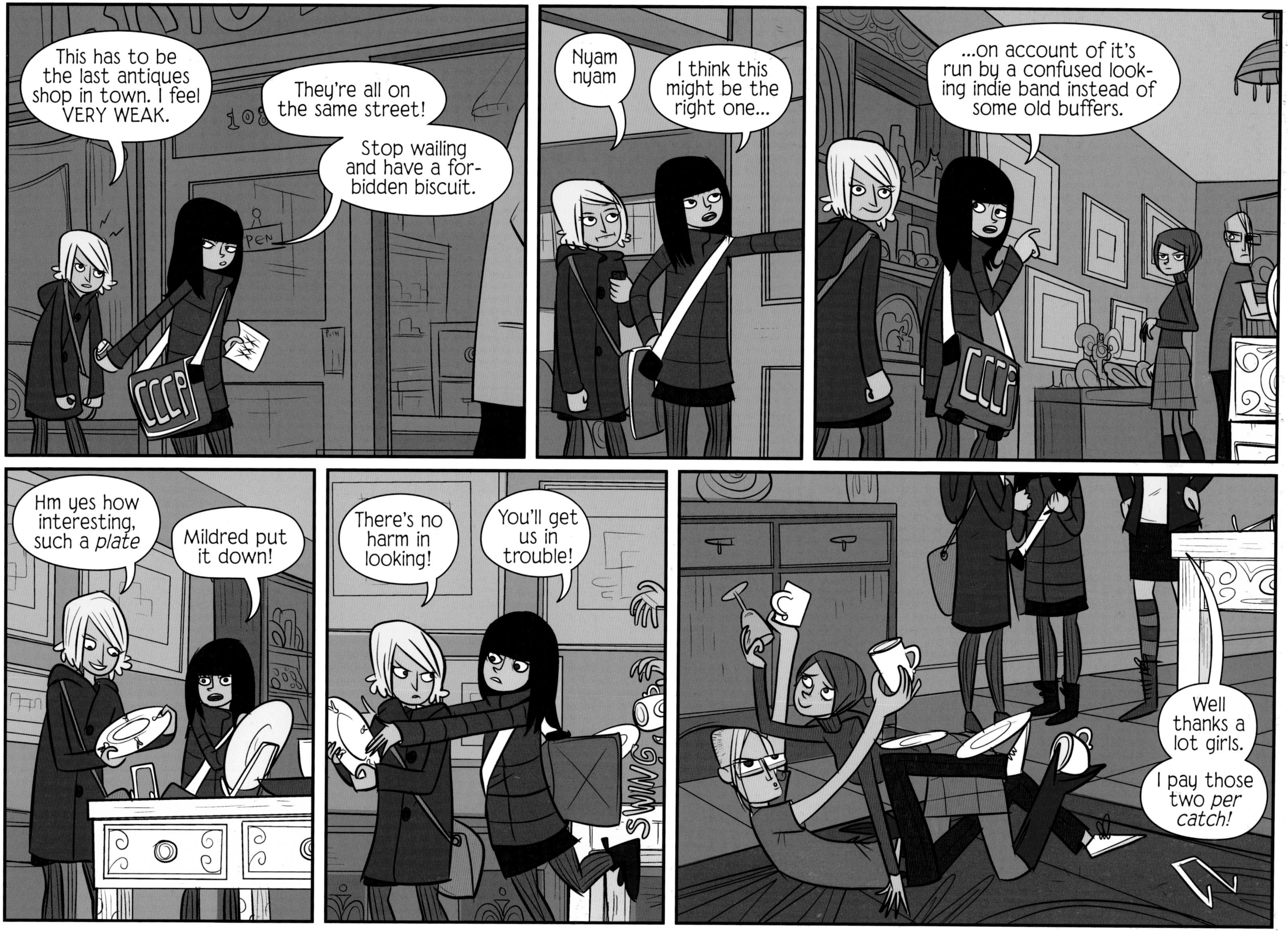
This has to be the last antiques shop in town. I feel VERY WEAK.
They're all on the same street!
Stop wailing and have a forbidden biscuit.
Nyam nyam
I think this might be the right one...
...on account of it's run by a confused looking indie band instead of some old buffers.
Hm yes how interesting, such a *plate*
Mildred put it down!
There's no harm in looking!
You'll get us in trouble!
SWING
Well thanks a lot girls.
I pay those two *per catch!*

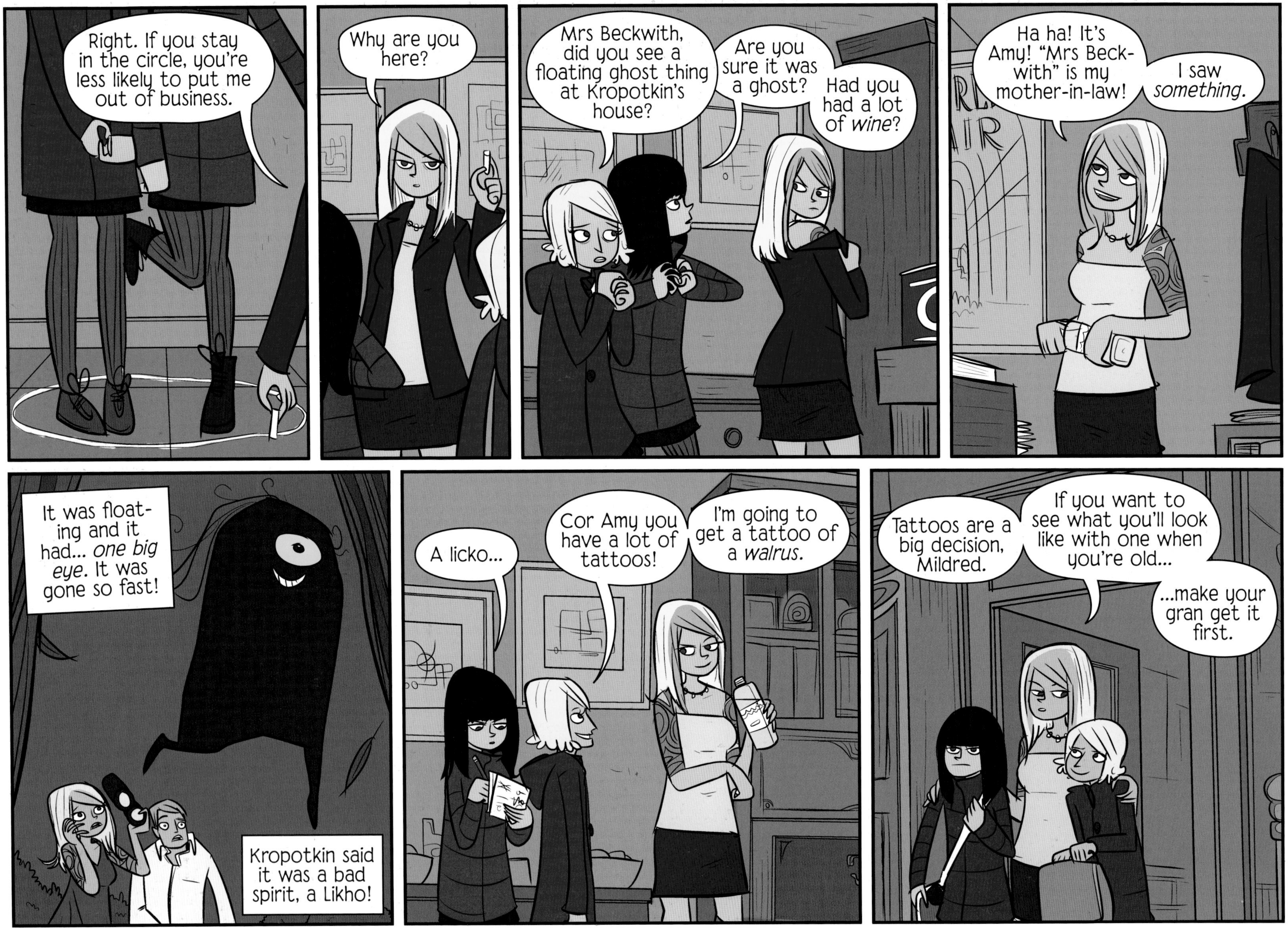
Right. If you stay in the circle, you're less likely to put me out of business.
Why are you here?
Mrs Beckwith, did you see a floating ghost thing at Kropotkin's house?
Are you sure it was a ghost?
Had you had a lot of *wine*?
Ha ha! It's Amy! "Mrs Beck-with" is my mother-in-law!
I saw *something*.
It was float-ing and it had... *one big eye*. It was gone so fast!
Kropotkin said it was a bad spirit, a Likho!
A licko...
Cor Amy you have a lot of tattoos!
I'm going to get a tattoo of a *walrus*.
Tattoos are a big decision, Mildred.
If you want to see what you'll look like with one when you're old...
...make your gran get it first.

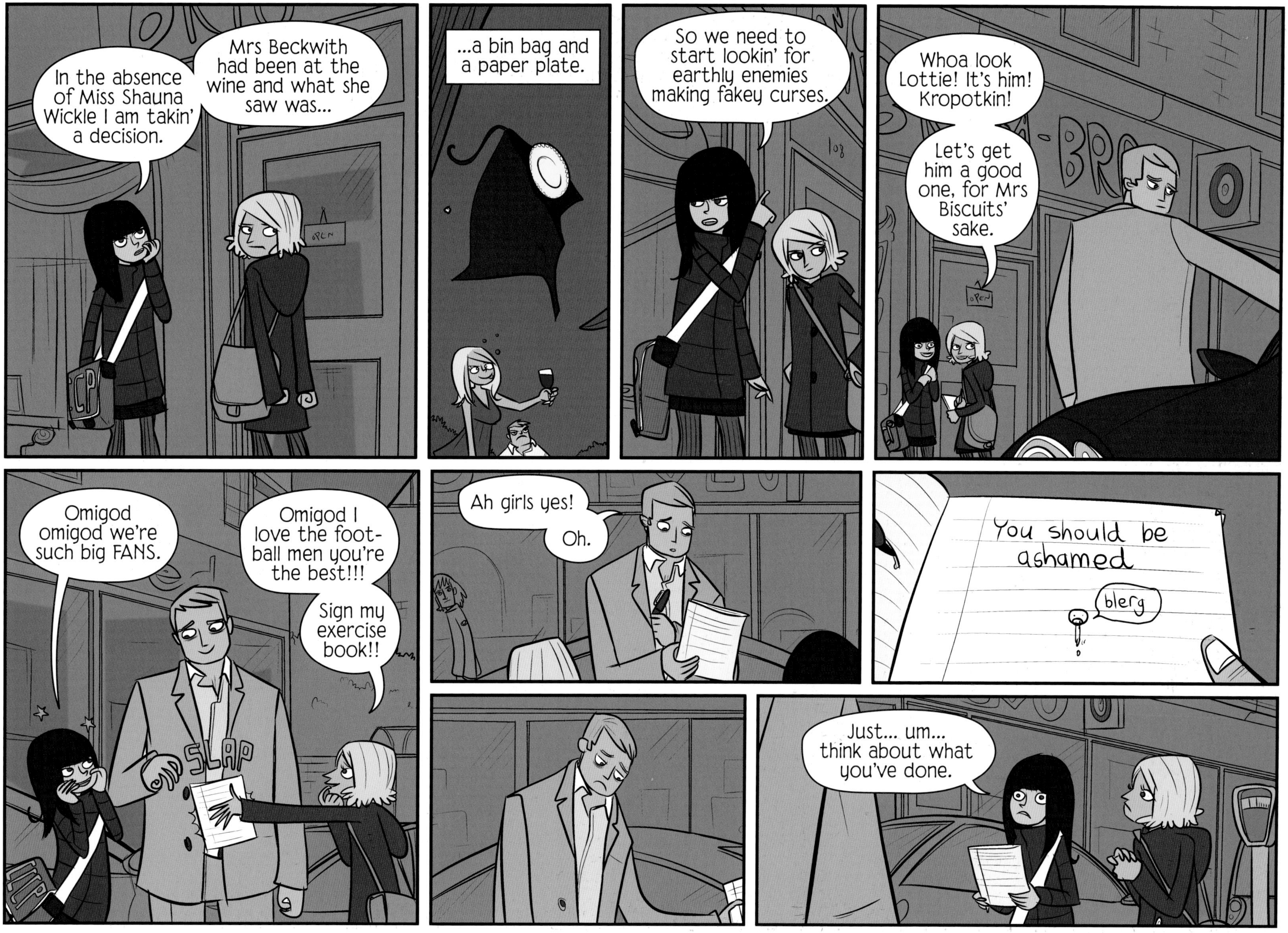
In the absence of Miss Shauna Wickle I am takin' a decision.
Mrs Beckwith had been at the wine and what she saw was...
...a bin bag and a paper plate.
So we need to start lookin' for earthly enemies making fakey curses.
Whoa look Lottie! It's him! Kropotkin!
Let's get him a good one, for Mrs Biscuits' sake.
Omigod omigod we're such big FANS.
Omigod I love the foot-ball men you're the best!!!
Sign my exercise book!!
SLAP
Ah girls yes!
Oh.
You should be ashamed
blerg
Just... um... think about what you've done.

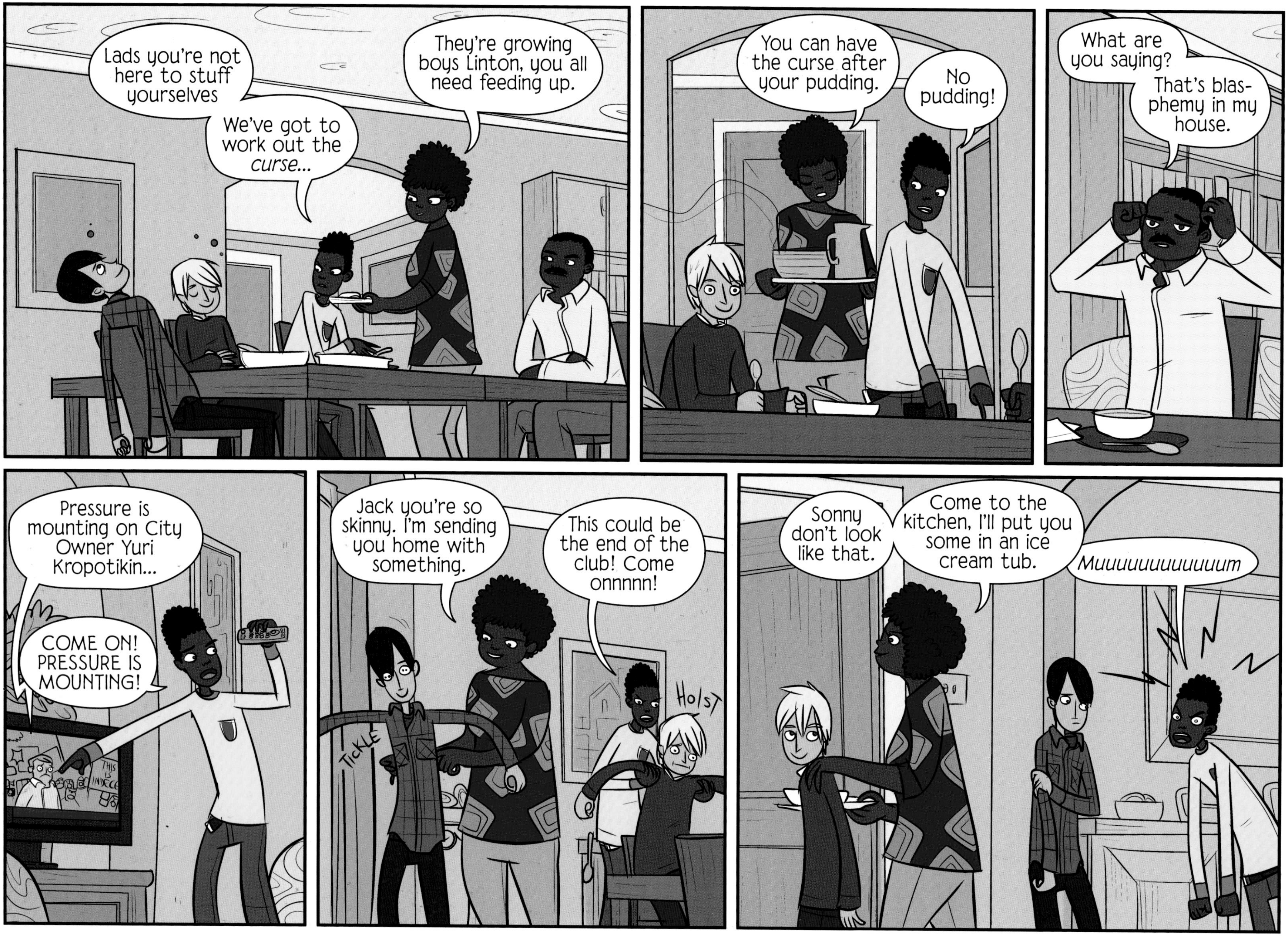
Lads you're not here to stuff yourselves
We've got to work out the *curse*...
They're growing boys Linton, you all need feeding up.
You can have the curse after your pudding.
No pudding!
What are you saying?
That's blas-phemy in my house.
Pressure is mounting on City Owner Yuri Kropotikin...
COME ON! PRESSURE IS MOUNTING!
THIS IS INDECE
Jack you're so skinny. I'm sending you home with something.
TICKLE
This could be the end of the club! Come onnnnn!
HOIST
Sonny don't look like that.
Come to the kitchen, I'll put you some in an ice cream tub.
Muuuuuuuuuuuum

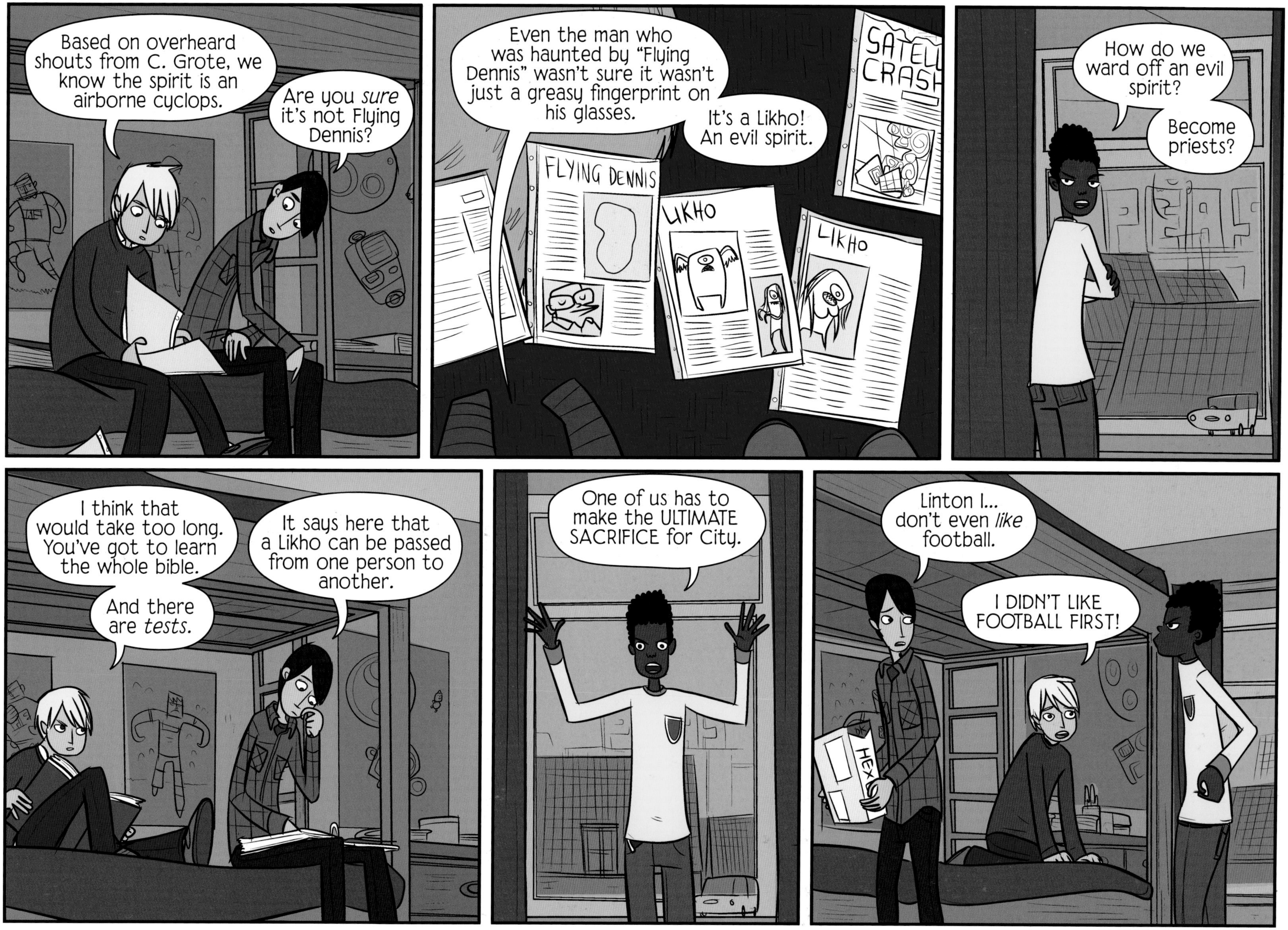
Based on overheard shouts from C. Grote, we know the spirit is an airborne cyclops.
Are you *sure* it's not Flying Dennis?
Even the man who was haunted by "Flying Dennis" wasn't sure it wasn't just a greasy fingerprint on his glasses.
It's a Likho! An evil spirit.
FLYING DENNIS
LIKHO
LIKHO
How do we ward off an evil spirit?
Become priests?
I think that would take too long. You've got to learn the whole bible.
And there are *tests*.
It says here that a Likho can be passed from one person to another.
One of us has to make the ULTIMATE SACRIFICE for City.
Linton I... don't even *like* football.
I DIDN'T LIKE FOOTBALL FIRST!

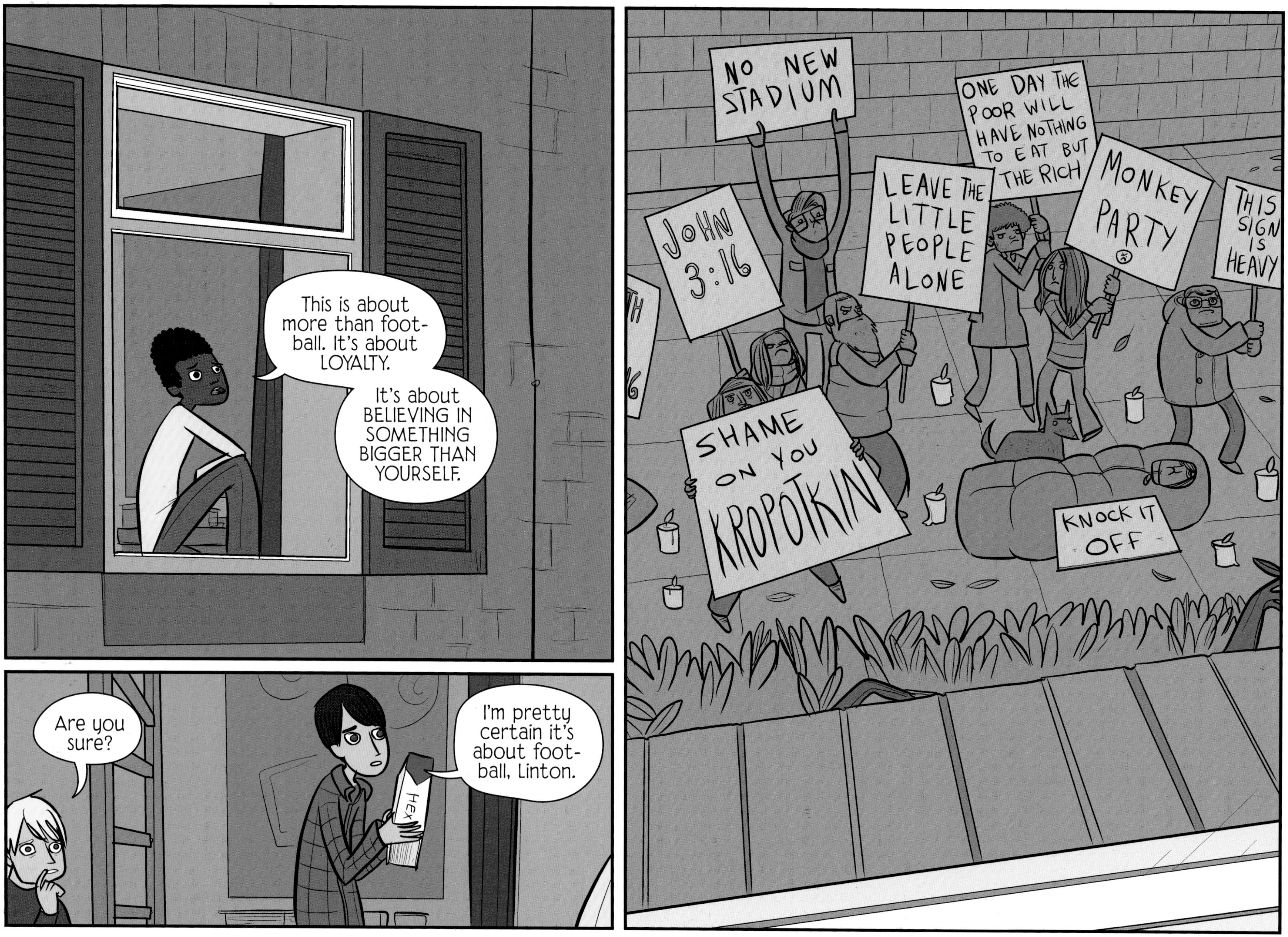
This is about more than foot-ball. It's about LOYALTY.
It's about BELIEVING IN SOMETHING BIGGER THAN YOURSELF.
Are you sure?
I'm pretty certain it's about foot-ball, Linton.
HEX
NO NEW STADIUM
ONE DAY THE POOR WILL HAVE NOTHING TO EAT BUT THE RICH
JOHN 3:16
LEAVE THE LITTLE PEOPLE ALONE
MONKEY PARTY
THIS SIGN IS HEAVY
SHAME ON YOU KROPOTKIN
KNOCK IT OFF

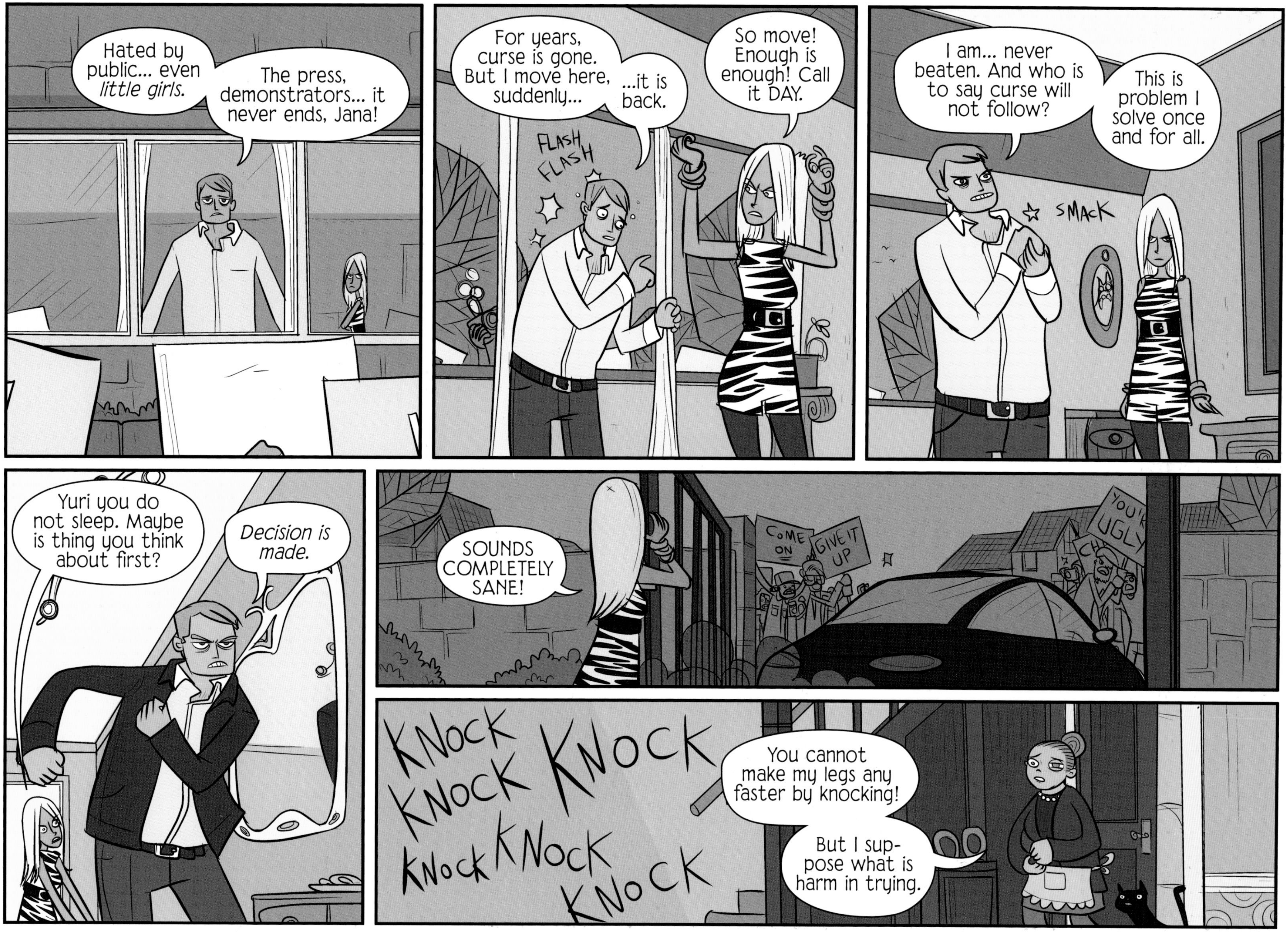
Hated by public... even *little girls.*
The press, demonstrators... it never ends, Jana!
For years, curse is gone. But I move here, suddenly...
...it is back.
FLASH FLASH
So move! Enough is enough! Call it DAY.
I am... never beaten. And who is to say curse will not follow?
This is problem I solve once and for all.
SMACK
Yuri you do not sleep. Maybe is thing you think about first?
Decision is made.
SOUNDS COMPLETELY SANE!
COME ON
GIVE IT UP
KNOCK KNOCK KNOCK KNOCK KNOCK KNOCK
You cannot make my legs any faster by knocking!
But I sup-pose what is harm in trying.

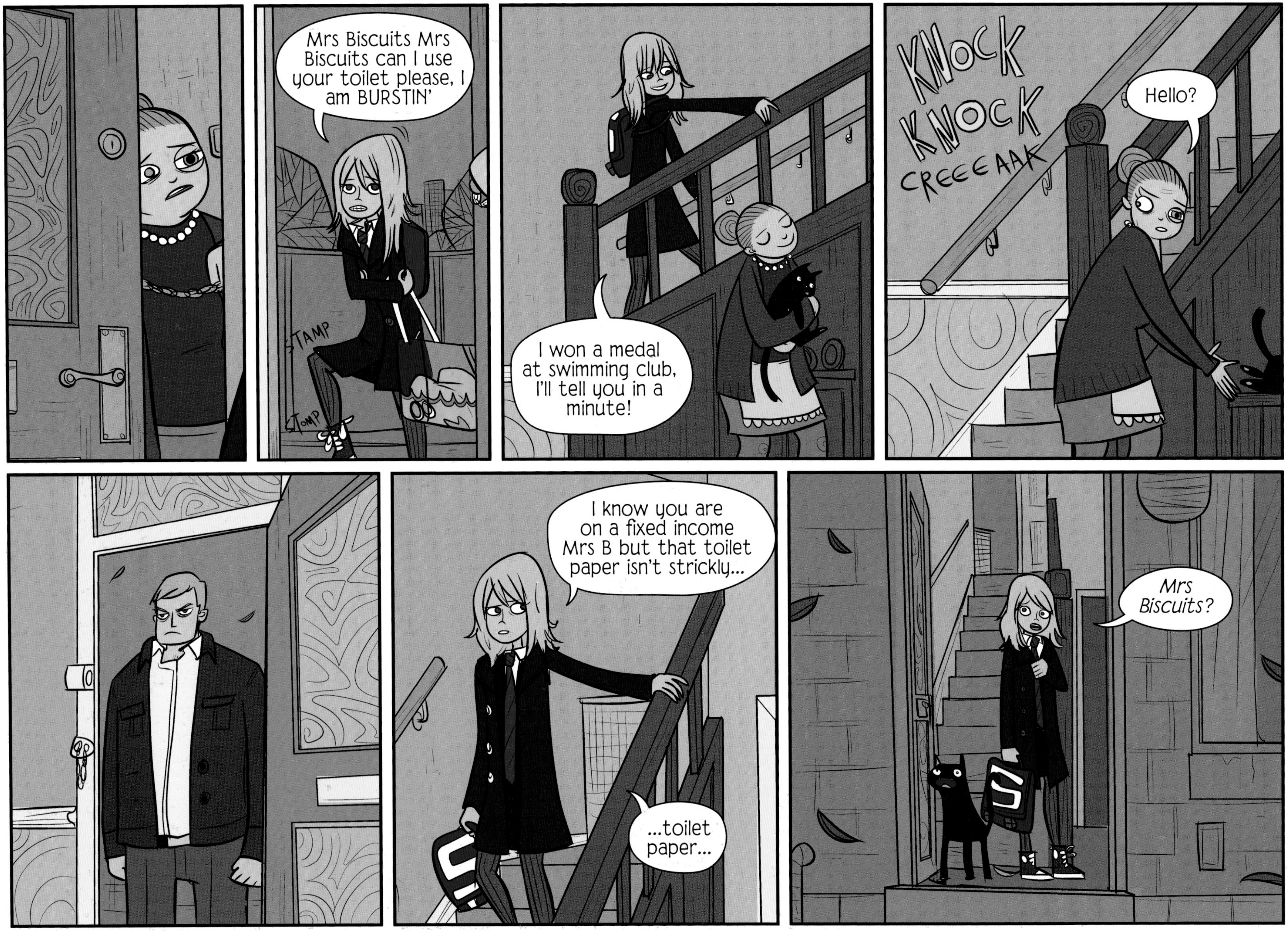
Mrs Biscuits Mrs Biscuits can I use your toilet please, I am BURSTIN'
STAMP
STOMP
I won a medal at swimming club, I'll tell you in a minute!
KNOCK KNOCK
CREEEAAK
Hello?
I know you are on a fixed income Mrs B but that toilet paper isn't strickly...
...toilet paper...
Mrs Biscuits?

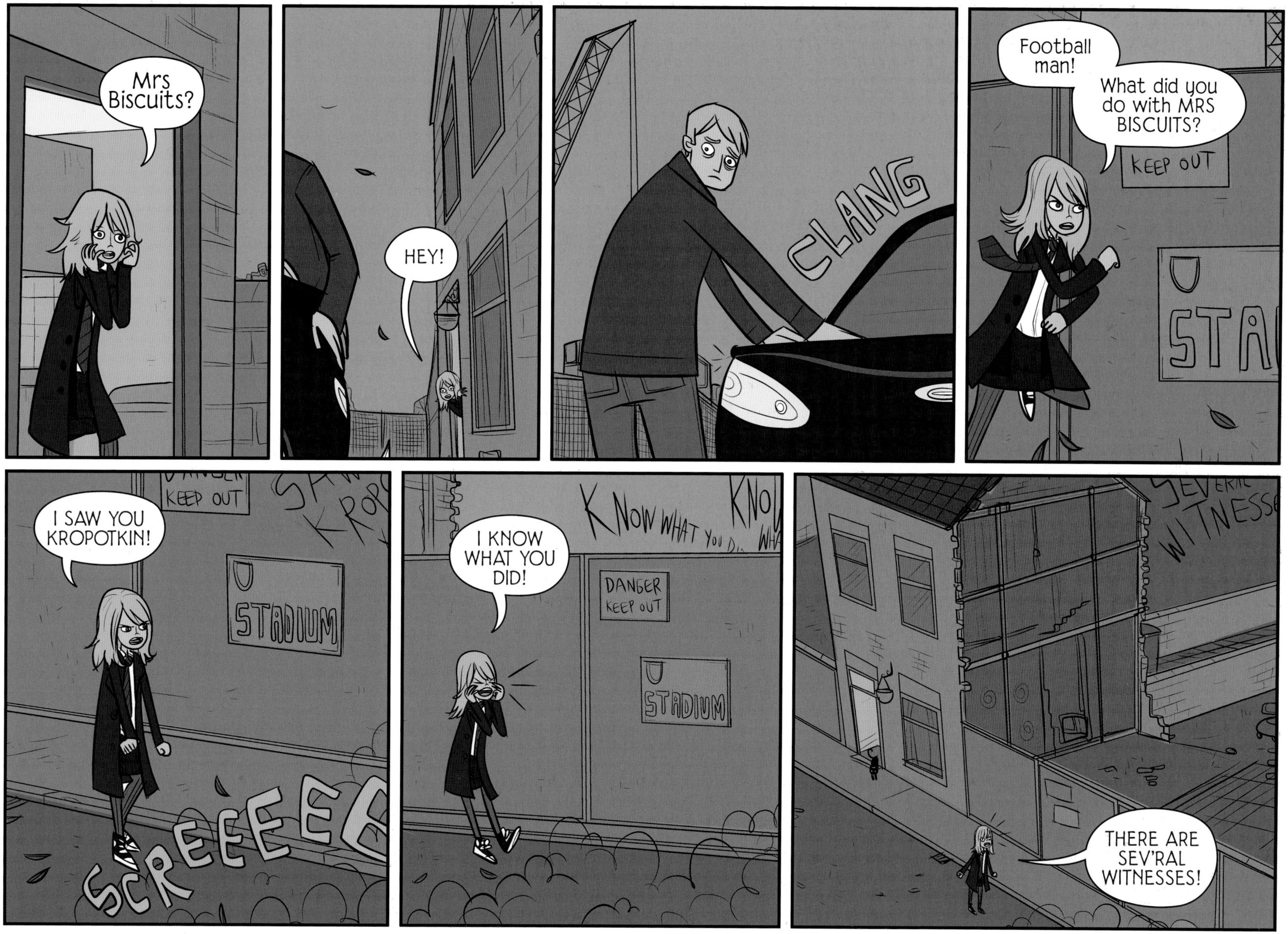
Mrs Biscuits?
HEY!
CLANG
Football man!
What did you do with MRS BISCUITS?
KEEP OUT
I SAW YOU KROPOTKIN!
KEEP OUT
STADIUM
SCREEEEEE
I KNOW WHAT YOU DID!
DANGER KEEP OUT
STADIUM
THERE ARE SEV'RAL WITNESSES!

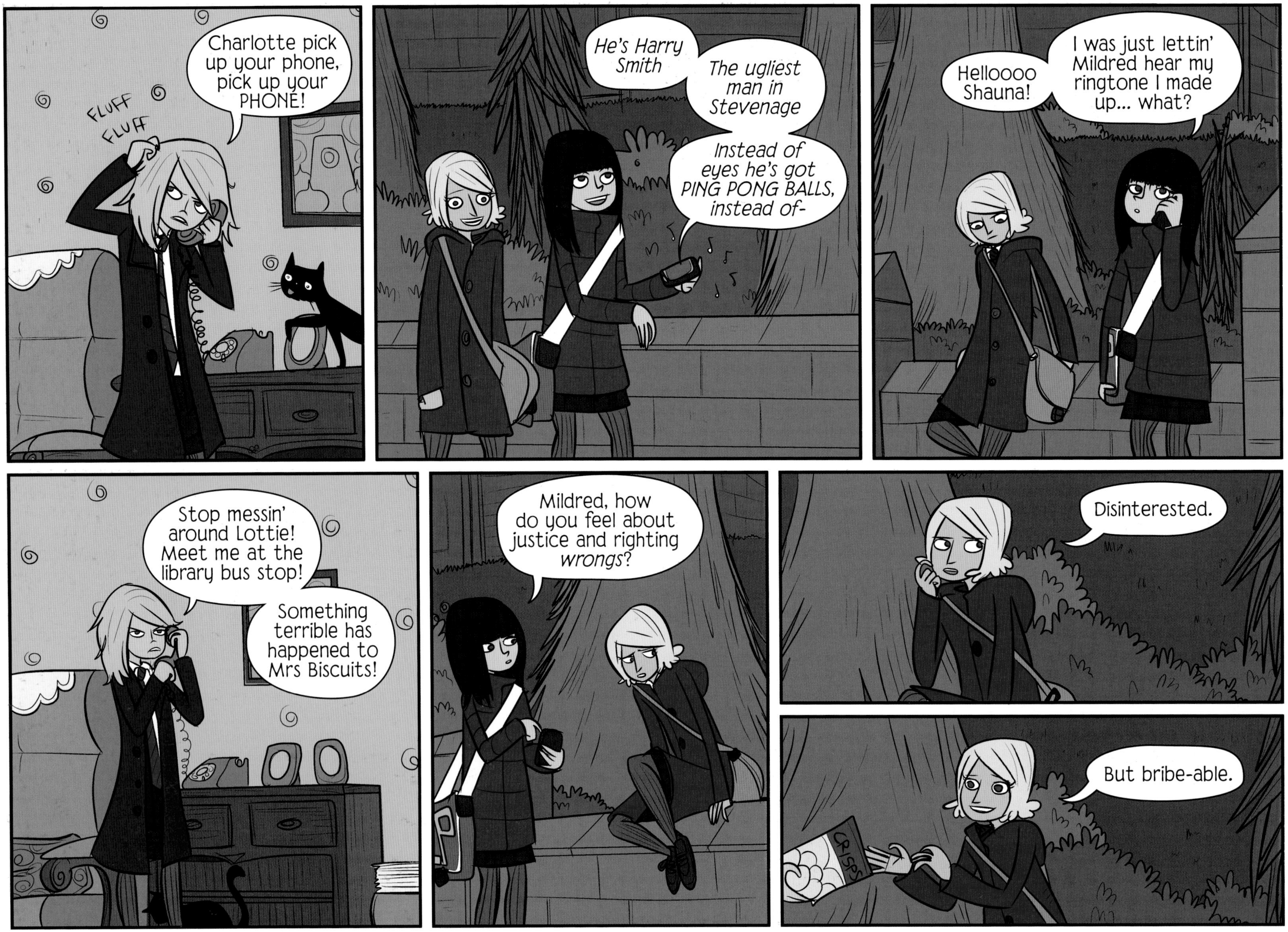
Charlotte pick up your phone, pick up your PHONE!
FLUFF FLUFF
He's Harry Smith
The ugliest man in Stevenage
Instead of eyes he's got PING PONG BALLS, instead of-
Helloooo Shauna!
I was just lettin' Mildred hear my ringtone I made up... what?
Stop messin' around Lottie! Meet me at the library bus stop!
Something terrible has happened to Mrs Biscuits!
Mildred, how do you feel about justice and righting *wrongs*?
Disinterested.
But bribe-able.
CRISPS

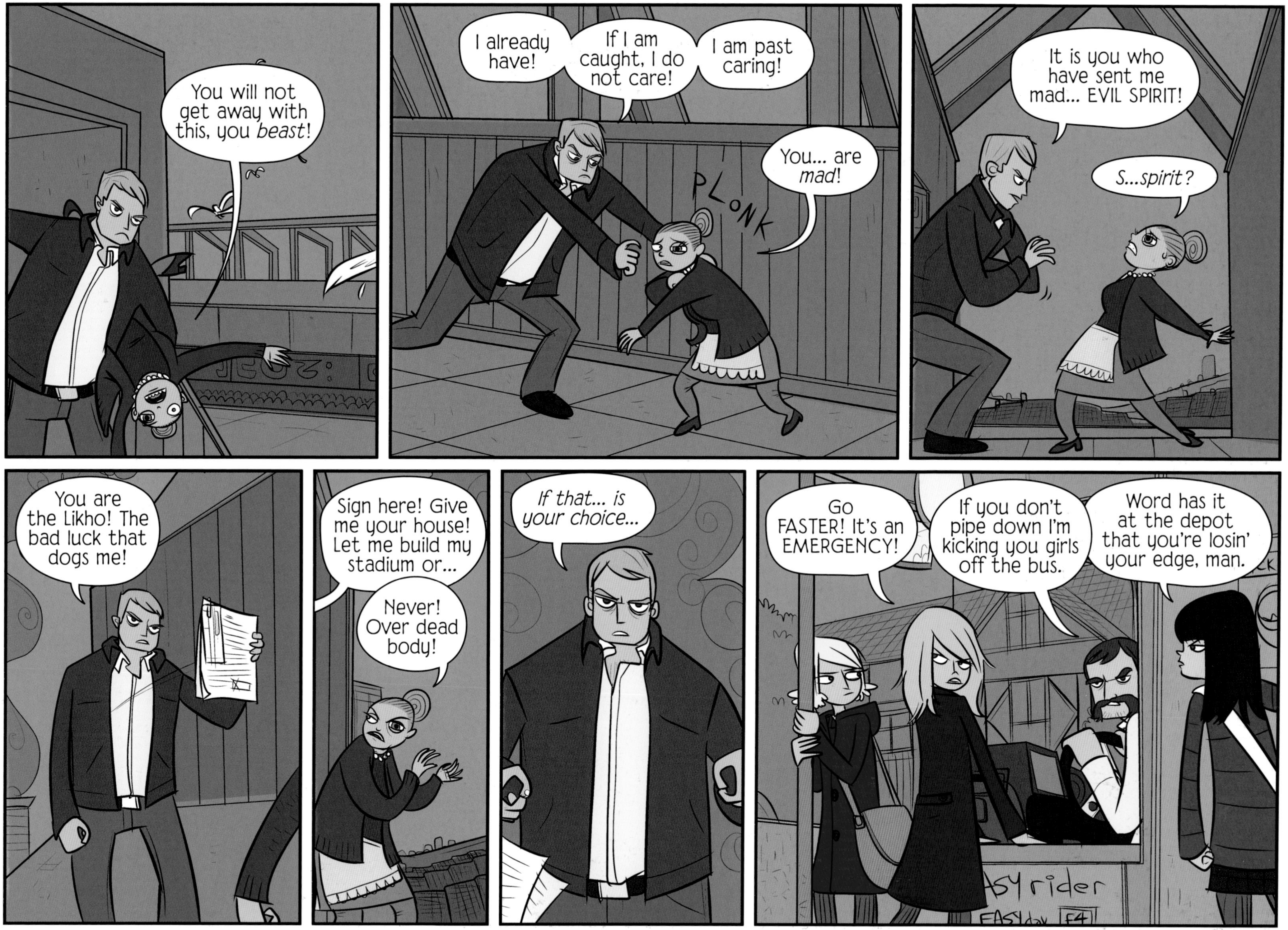
You will not get away with this, you *beast*!
I already have!
If I am caught, I do not care!
I am past caring!
PLONK
You... are *mad*!
It is you who have sent me mad... EVIL SPIRIT!
S...spirit?
You are the Likho! The bad luck that dogs me!
Sign here! Give me your house! Let me build my stadium or...
Never! Over dead body!
If that... is your choice...
Go FASTER! It's an EMERGENCY!
If you don't pipe down I'm kicking you girls off the bus.
Word has it at the depot that you're losin' your edge, man.

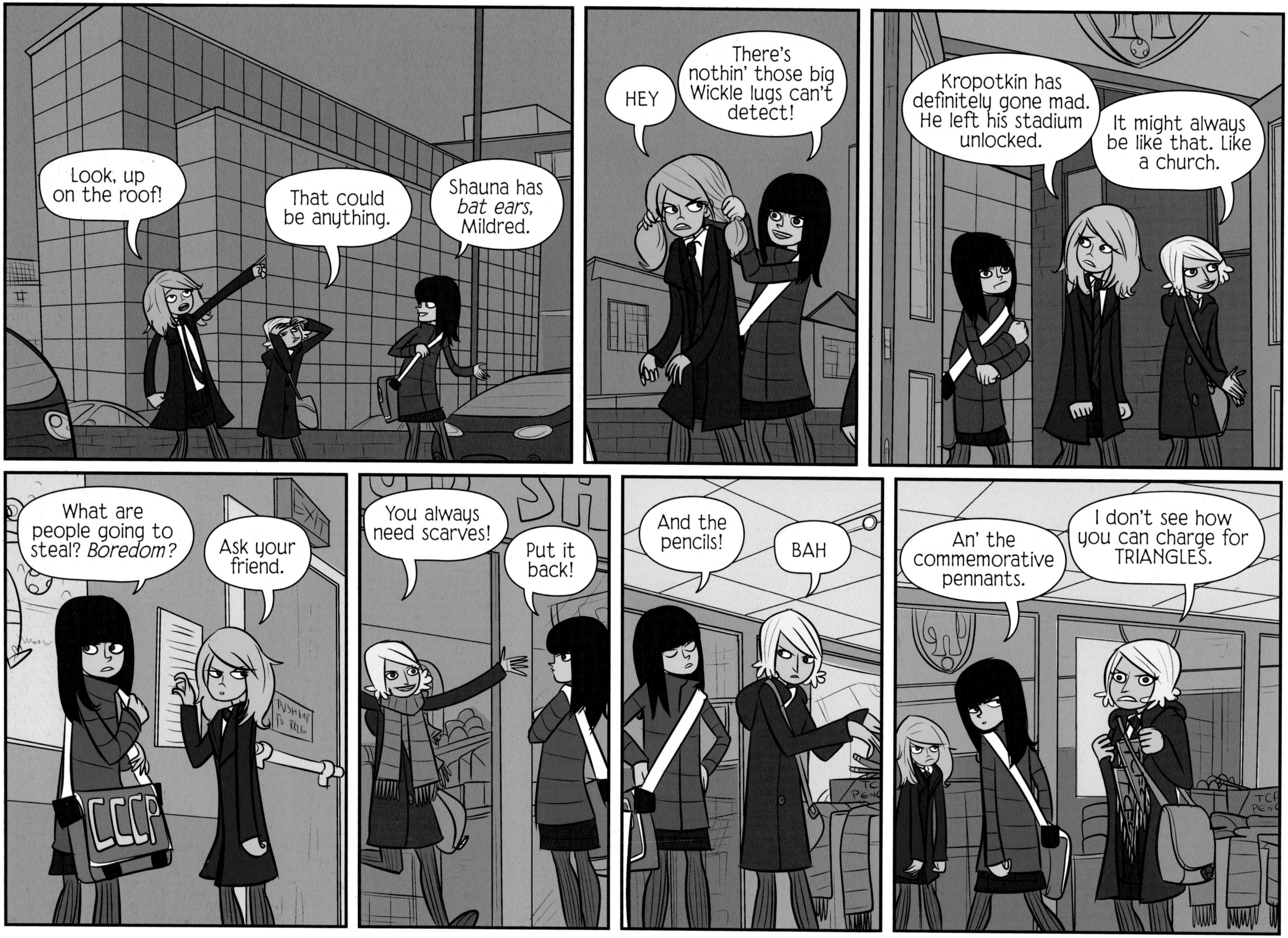
Look, up on the roof!
That could be anything.
Shauna has *bat ears,* Mildred.
HEY
There's nothin' those big Wickle lugs can't detect!
Kropotkin has definitely gone mad. He left his stadium unlocked.
It might always be like that. Like a church.
What are people going to steal? *Boredom?*
Ask your friend.
CCCP
You always need scarves!
Put it back!
And the pencils!
BAH
An' the commemorative pennants.
I don't see how you can charge for TRIANGLES.

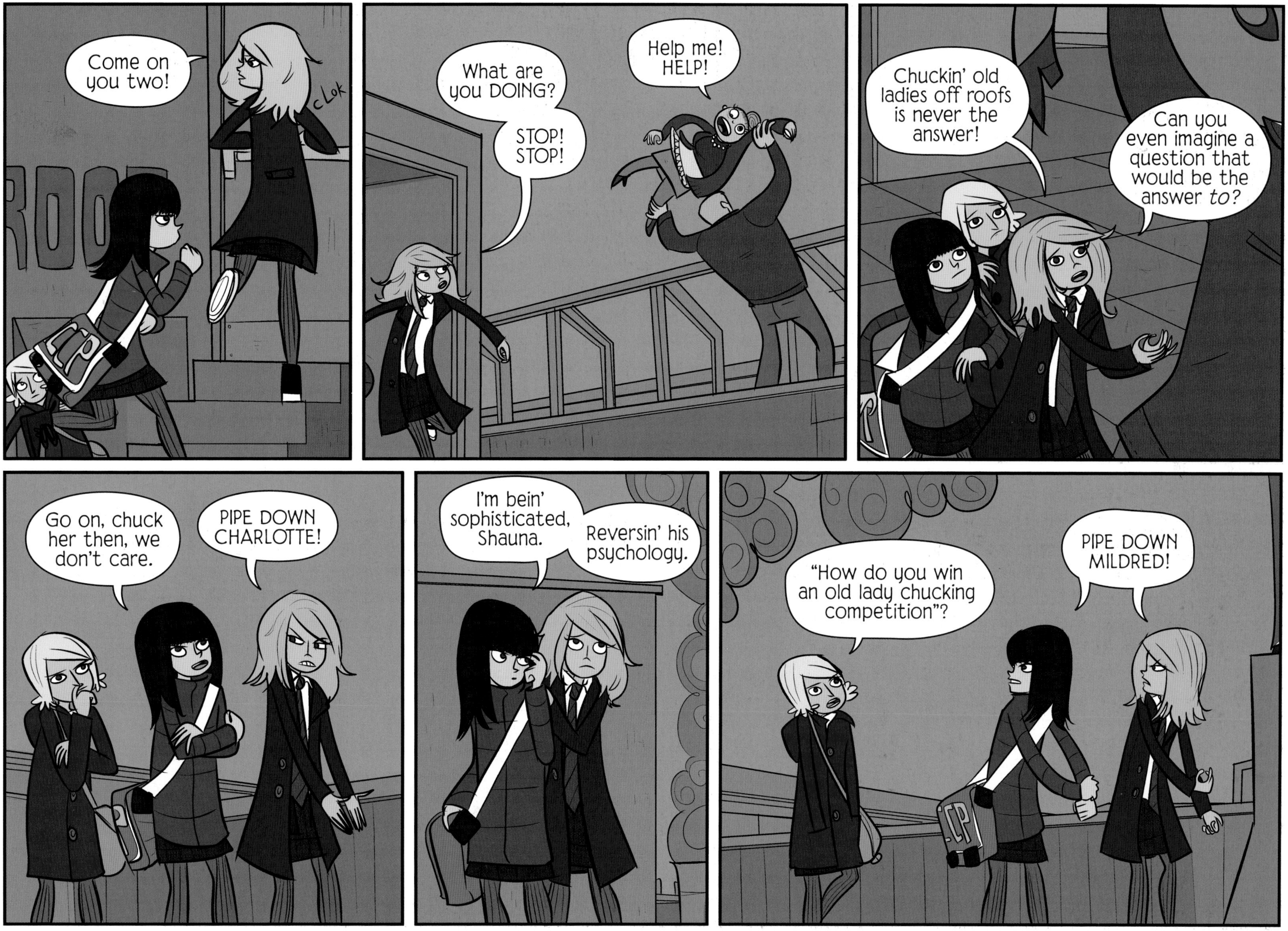
Come on you two!
cLok
What are you DOING?
STOP! STOP!
Help me! HELP!
Chuckin' old ladies off roofs is never the answer!
Can you even imagine a question that would be the answer *to?*
Go on, chuck her then, we don't care.
PIPE DOWN CHARLOTTE!
I'm bein' sophisticated, Shauna.
Reversin' his psychology.
"How do you win an old lady chucking competition"?
PIPE DOWN MILDRED!

Bad Machinery, Volume One

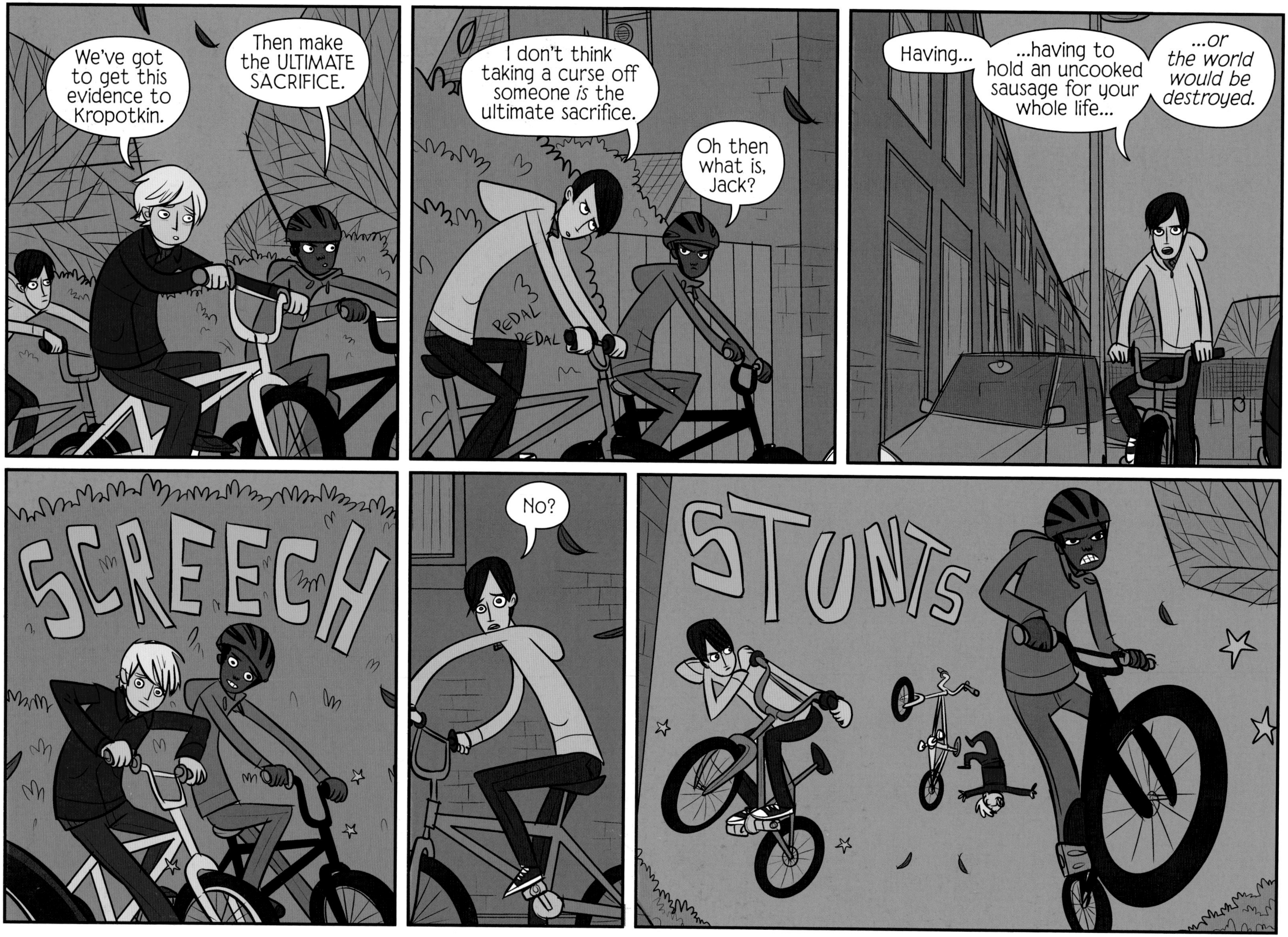
We've got to get this evidence to Kropotkin.
Then make the ULTIMATE SACRIFICE.
I don't think taking a curse off someone *is* the ultimate sacrifice.
PEDAL
PEDAL
Oh then what is, Jack?
Having...
...having to hold an uncooked sausage for your whole life...
...*or the world would be destroyed.*
SCREECH
No?
STUNTS

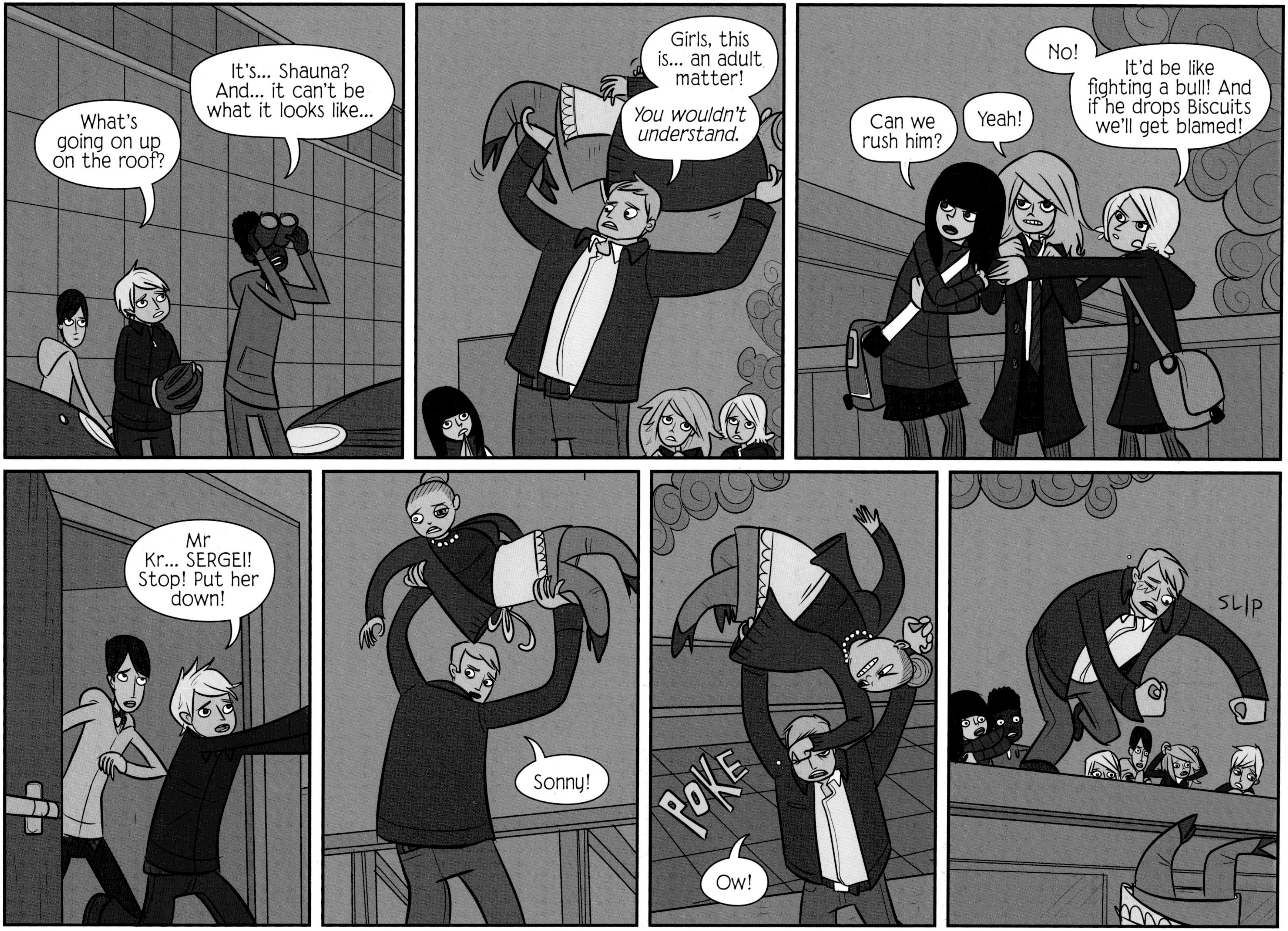

What's going on up on the roof?
It's... Shauna? And... it can't be what it looks like...
Girls, this is... an adult matter!
You wouldn't understand.
Can we rush him?
Yeah!
No!
It'd be like fighting a bull! And if he drops Biscuits we'll get blamed!
Mr Kr... SERGEI! Stop! Put her down!
Sonny!
POKE
Ow!
SLIP

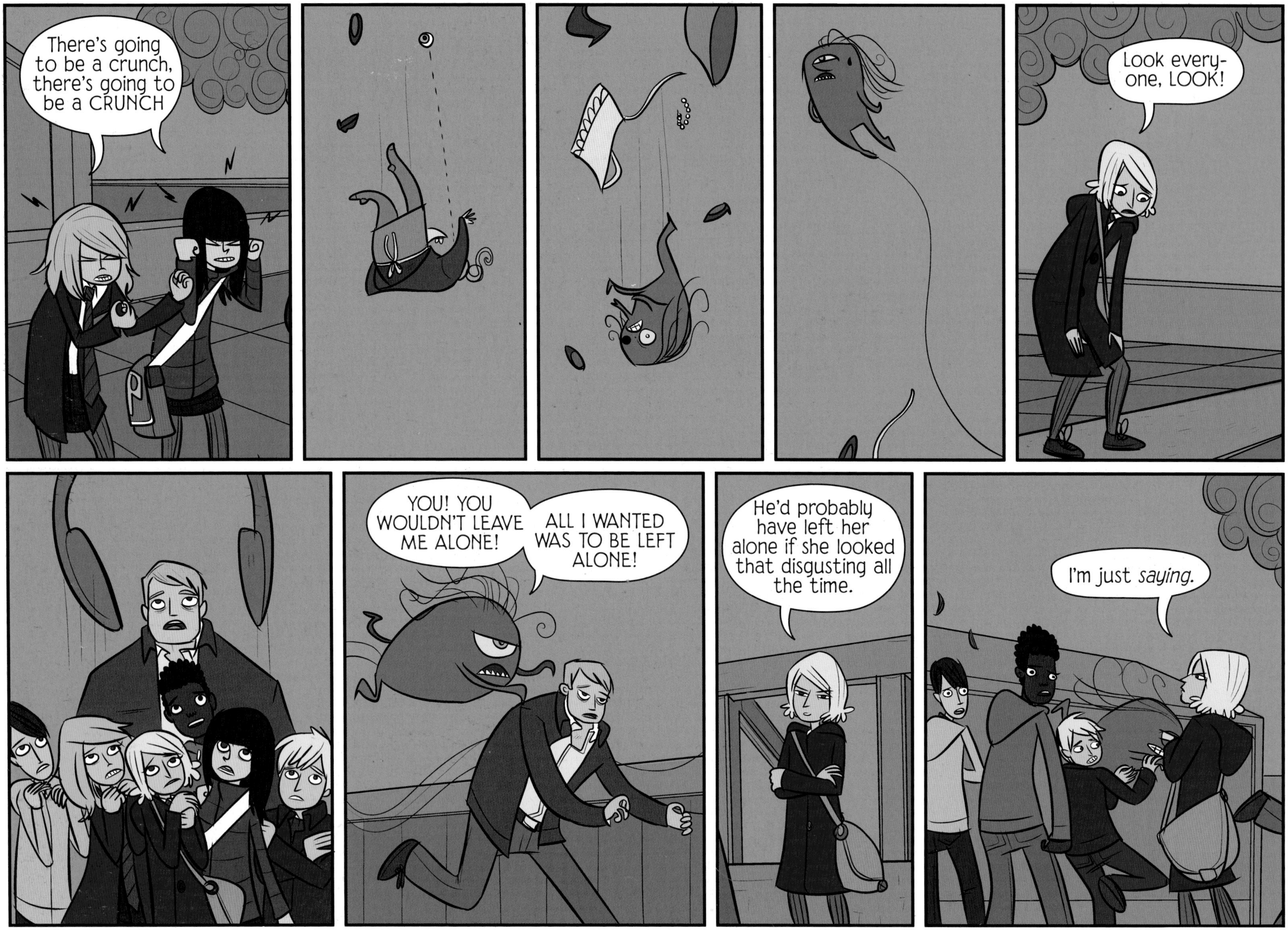
There's going to be a crunch, there's going to be a CRUNCH
Look every-one, LOOK!
YOU! YOU WOULDN'T LEAVE ME ALONE!
ALL I WANTED WAS TO BE LEFT ALONE!
He'd probably have left her alone if she looked that disgusting all the time.
I'm just *saying.*

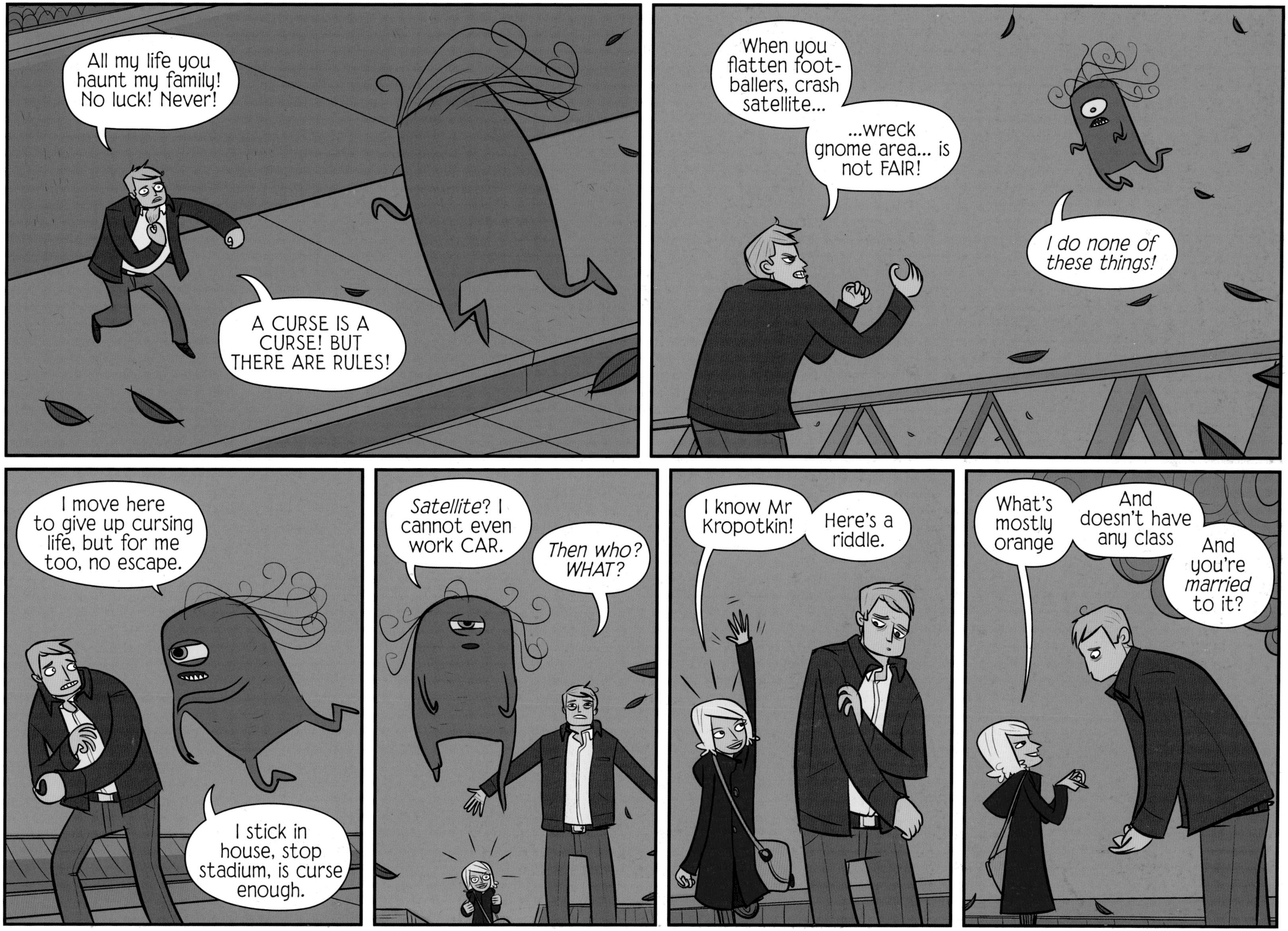
All my life you haunt my family! No luck! Never!
A CURSE IS A CURSE! BUT THERE ARE RULES!
When you flatten foot-ballers, crash satellite...
...wreck gnome area... is not FAIR!
I do none of these things!
I move here to give up cursing life, but for me too, no escape.
I stick in house, stop stadium, is curse enough.
Satellite? I cannot even work CAR.
Then who? WHAT?
I know Mr Kropotkin!
Here's a riddle.
What's mostly orange
And doesn't have any class
And you're *married* to it?

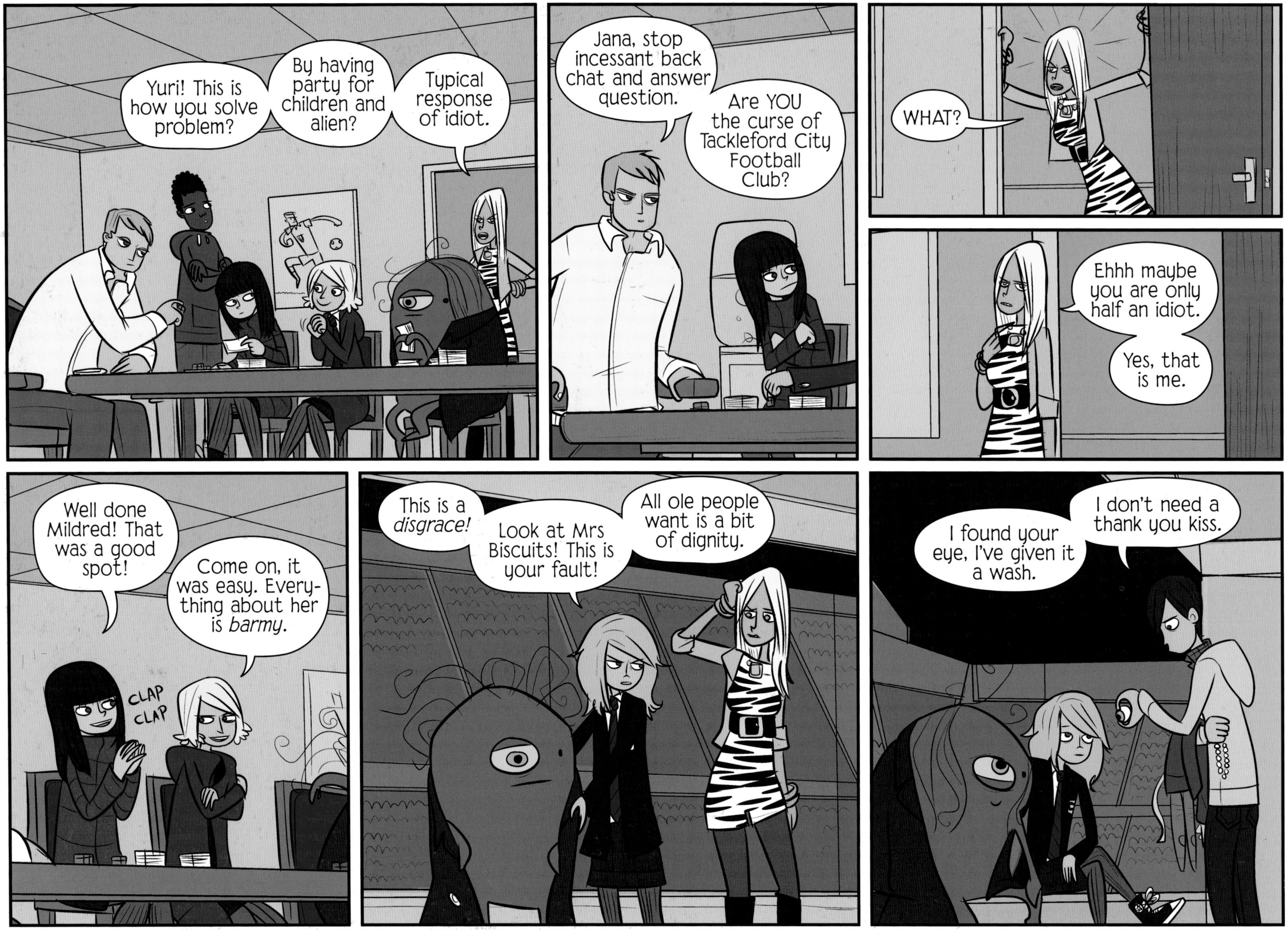
Yuri! This is how you solve problem?
By having party for children and alien?
Typical response of idiot.
Jana, stop incessant back chat and answer question.
Are YOU the curse of Tackleford City Football Club?
WHAT?
Ehhh maybe you are only half an idiot.
Yes, that is me.
Well done Mildred! That was a good spot!
CLAP CLAP
Come on, it was easy. Everything about her is *barmy*.
This is a *disgrace!*
Look at Mrs Biscuits! This is your fault!
All ole people want is a bit of dignity.
I found your eye, I've given it a wash.
I don't need a thank you kiss.

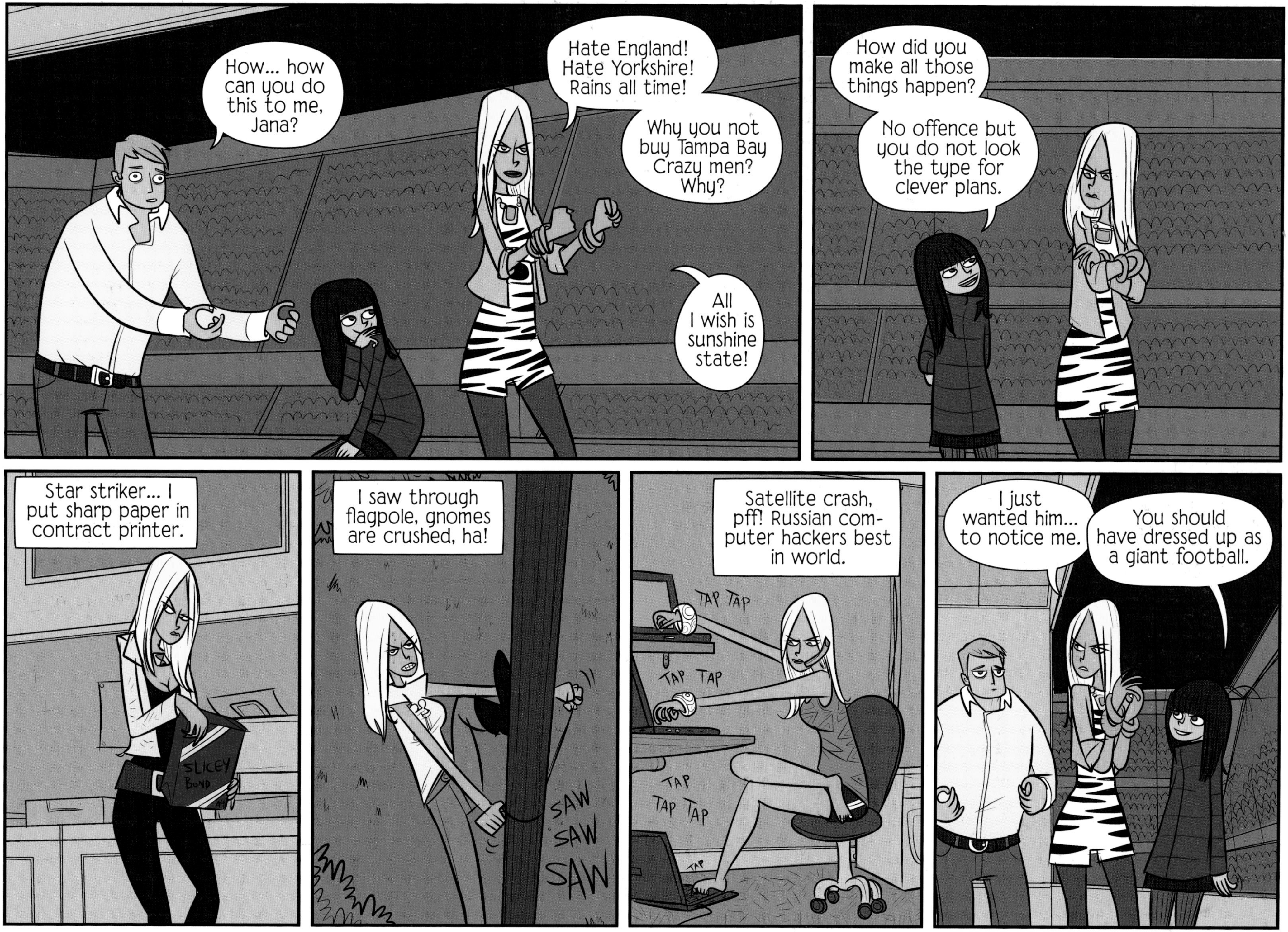
How... how can you do this to me, Jana?
Hate England! Hate Yorkshire! Rains all time!
Why you not buy Tampa Bay Crazy men? Why?
All I wish is sunshine state!
How did you make all those things happen?
No offence but you do not look the type for clever plans.
Star striker... I put sharp paper in contract printer.
SLICEY BOND
I saw through flagpole, gnomes are crushed, ha!
SAW SAW SAW
Satellite crash, pff! Russian computer hackers best in world.
TAP TAP
TAP TAP
TAP TAP TAP
TAP
I just wanted him... to notice me.
You should have dressed up as a giant football.

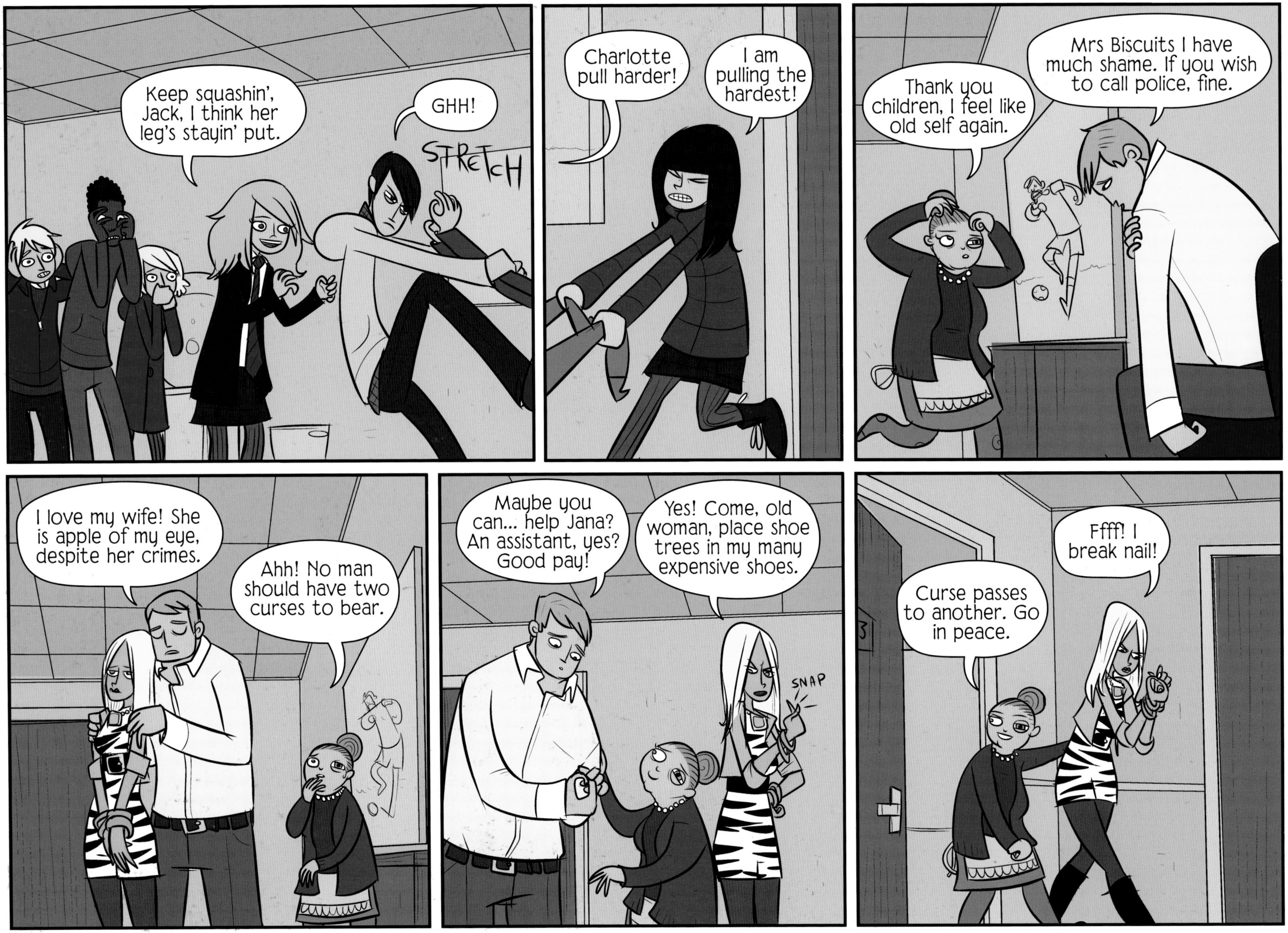
Keep squashin', Jack, I think her leg's stayin' put.
GHH!
STRETCH
Charlotte pull harder!
I am pulling the hardest!
Thank you children, I feel like old self again.
Mrs Biscuits I have much shame. If you wish to call police, fine.
I love my wife! She is apple of my eye, despite her crimes.
Ahh! No man should have two curses to bear.
Maybe you can... help Jana? An assistant, yes? Good pay!
Yes! Come, old woman, place shoe trees in my many expensive shoes.
SNAP
Curse passes to another. Go in peace.
Ffff! I break nail!

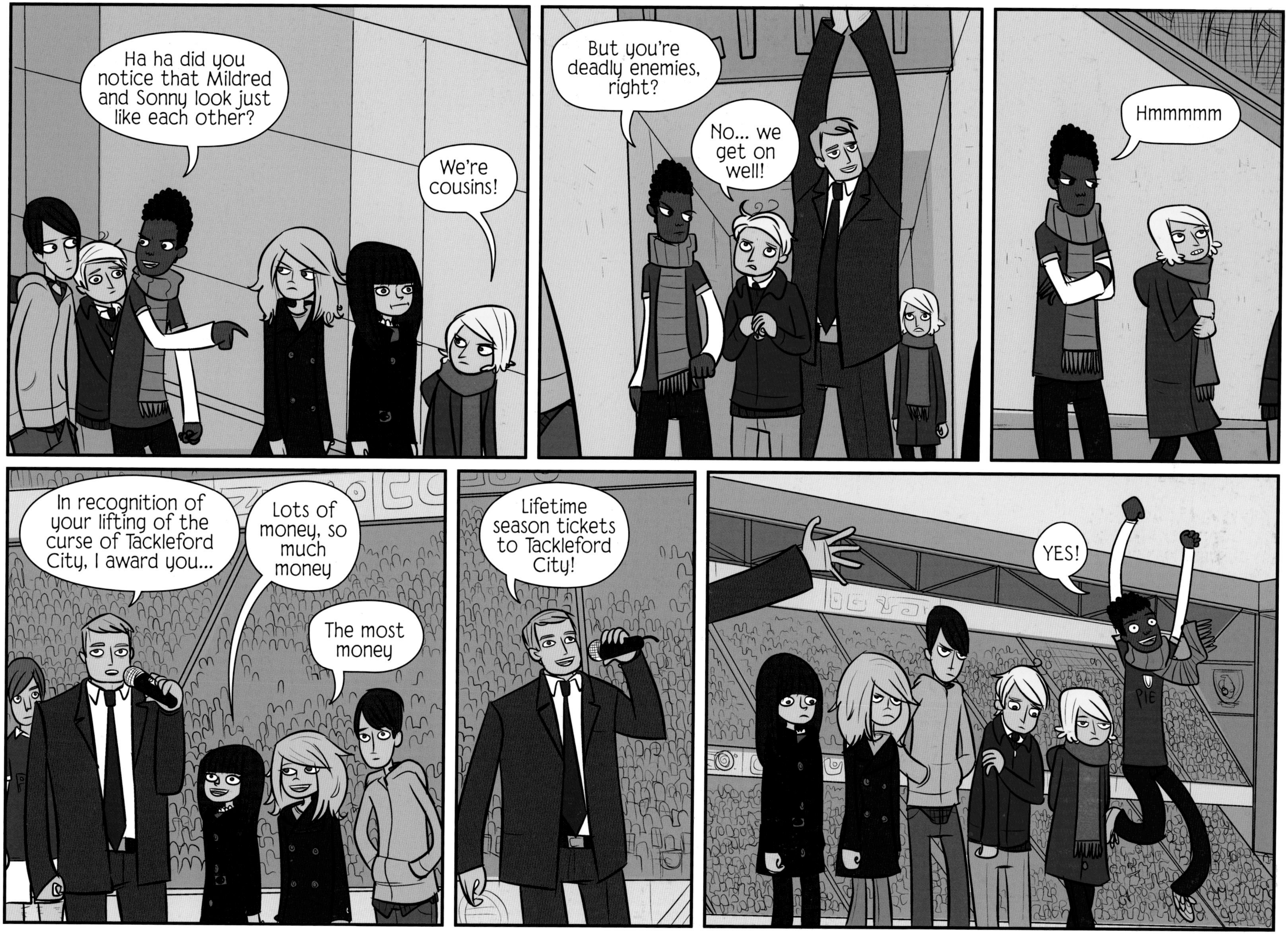
Ha ha did you notice that Mildred and Sonny look just like each other?
We're cousins!
But you're deadly enemies, right?
No... we get on well!
Hmmmmm
In recognition of your lifting of the curse of Tackleford City, I award you...
Lots of money, so much money
The most money
Lifetime season tickets to Tackleford City!
YES!

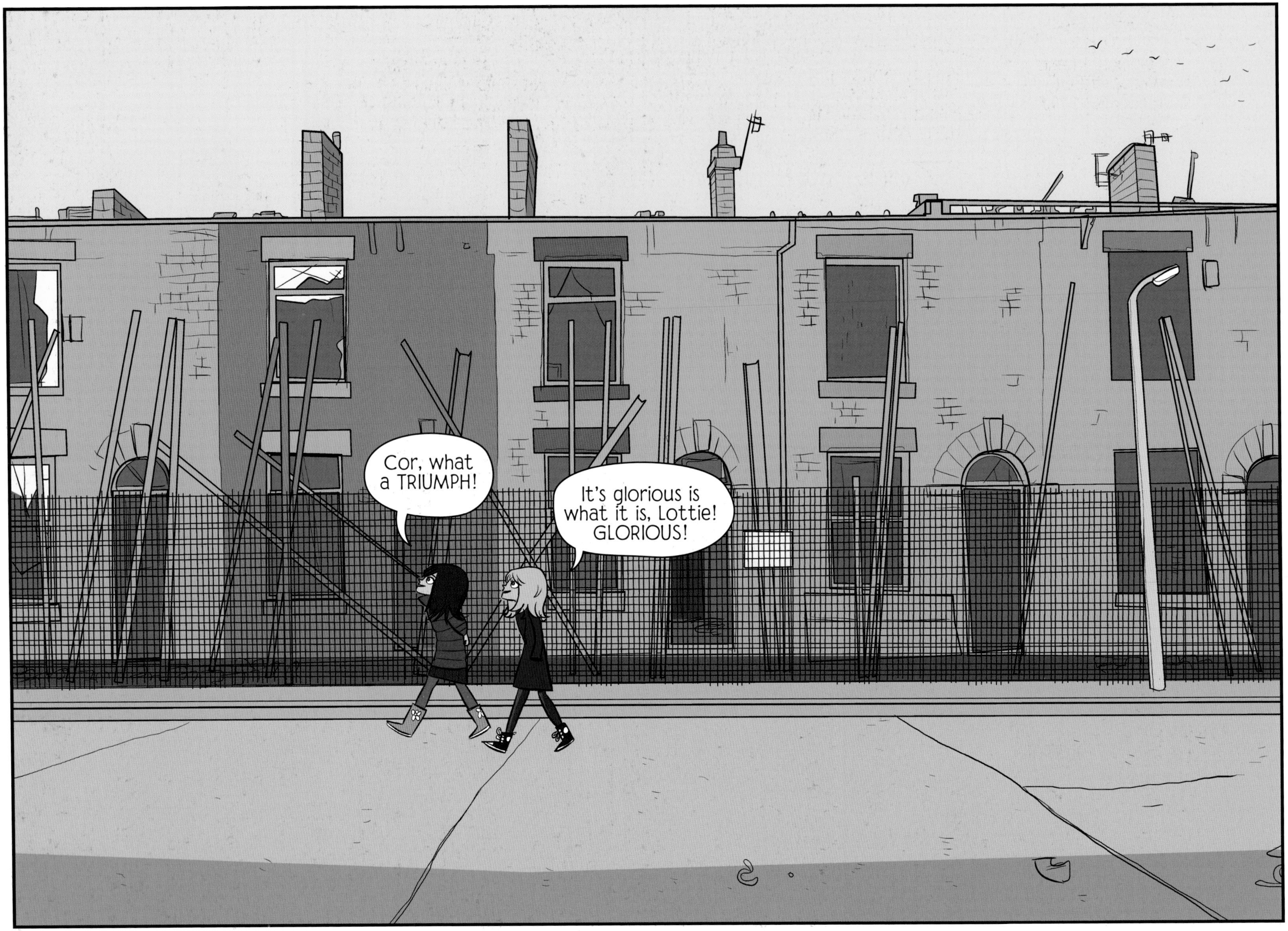
Cor, what a TRIUMPH!
It's glorious is what it is, Lottie! GLORIOUS!

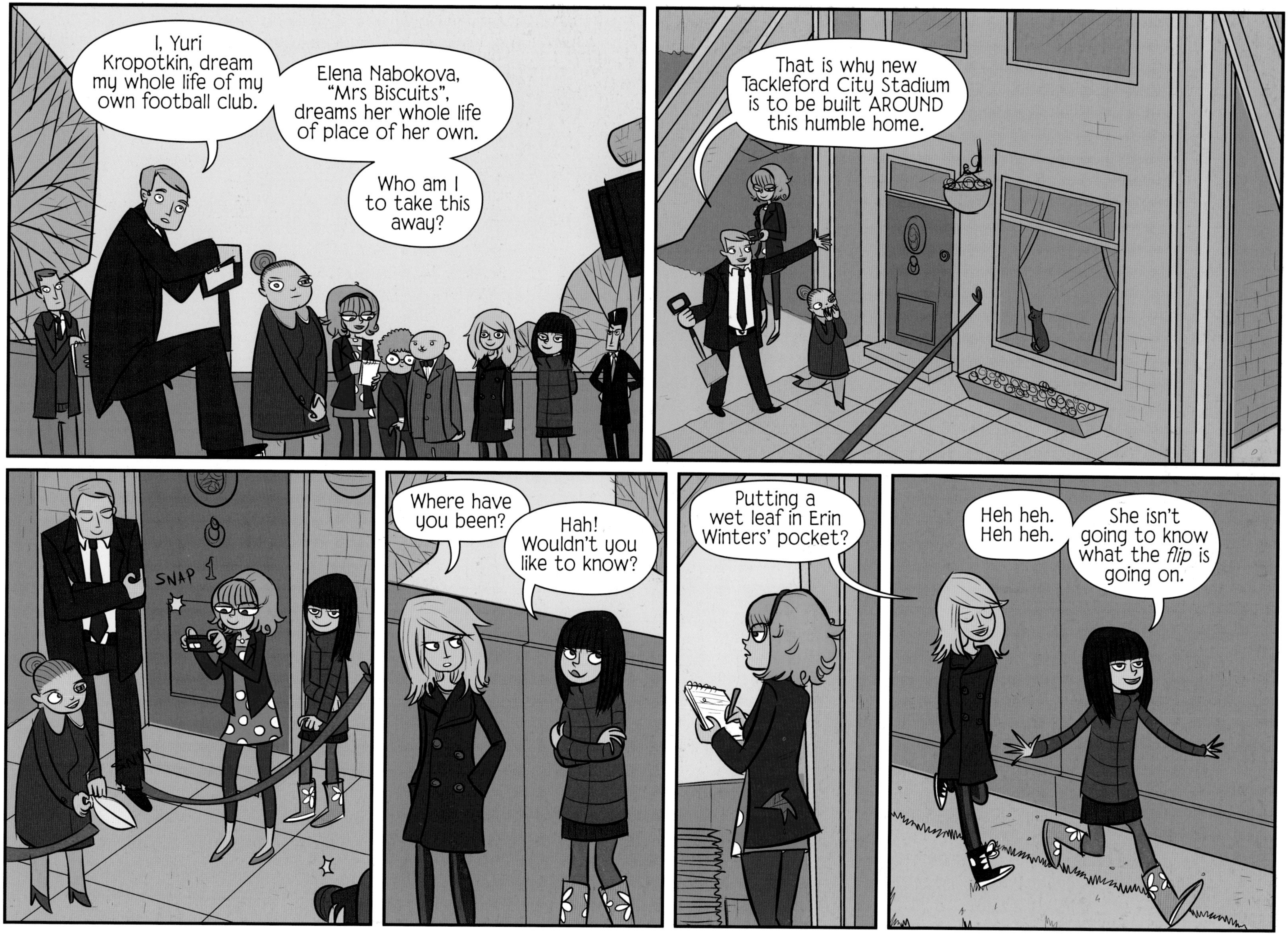
I, Yuri Kropotkin, dream my whole life of my own football club.
Elena Nabokova, "Mrs Biscuits", dreams her whole life of place of her own.
Who am I to take this away?
That is why new Tackleford City Stadium is to be built AROUND this humble home.
SNAP
Where have you been?
Hah! Wouldn't you like to know?
Putting a wet leaf in Erin Winters' pocket?
Heh heh. Heh heh.
She isn't going to know what the *flip* is going on.

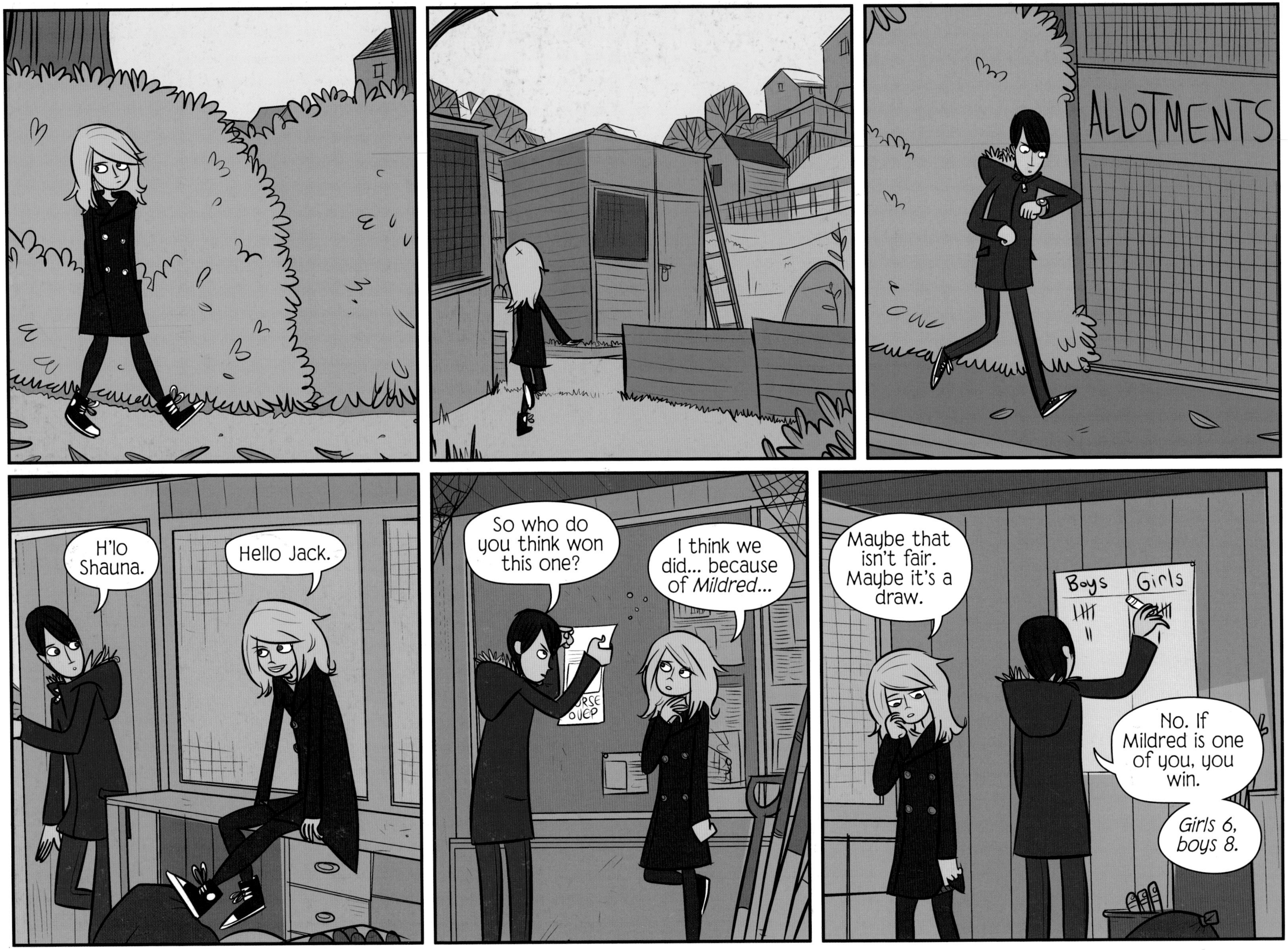
ALLOTMENTS
H'lo Shauna.
Hello Jack.
So who do you think won this one?
I think we did... because of *Mildred*...
Maybe that isn't fair. Maybe it's a draw.
Boys Girls
No. If Mildred is one of you, you win.
Girls 6, boys 8.

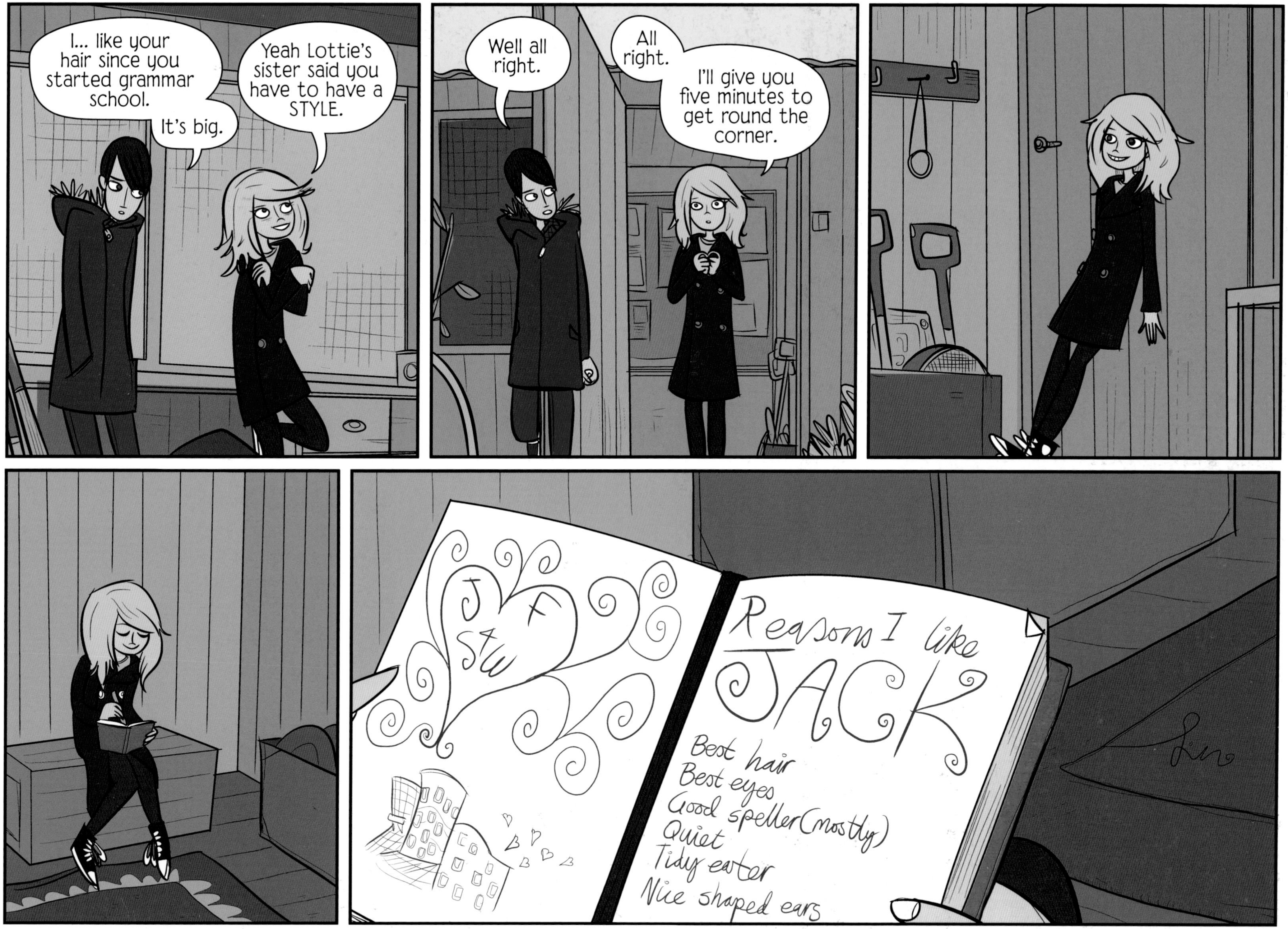
I... like your hair since you started grammar school.
It's big.
Yeah Lottie's sister said you have to have a STYLE.
Well all right.
All right.
I'll give you five minutes to get round the corner.
J F
Stu
Reasons I like JACK
Best hair
Best eyes
Good speller (mostly)
Quiet
Tidy eater
Nice shaped ears

GRISWALDS GRAMMAR SCHOOL

ESTABLISHED 1701

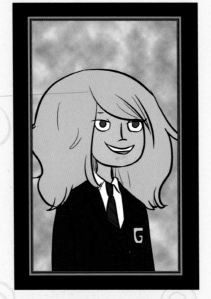

Shauna Wickle

"Today might be the first day of a troubled adolescence."

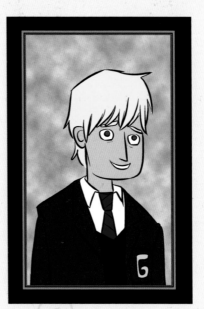

Sonny Craven

"Mr. Bough has 'surprise picnic' written all over him."

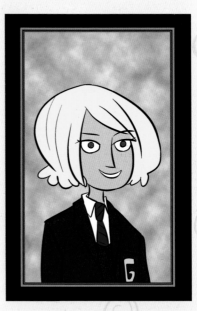

Mildred Haversham

"Fight them like you do when you see something in a bin that looks tasty."

GRISWALDS
EX VENTO SCIENTIA
EST. 1701

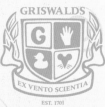

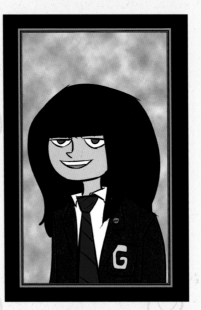

Charlotte Grote

"Messin' with people's reality is my special skill."

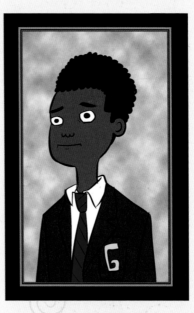

Linton Baxter

"At times like this you have to get behind the team."

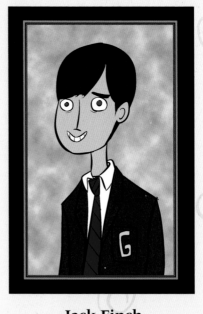

Jack Finch

"If she's not running after you with a mop handle, you aren't trying."

GLOSSARY

IDIOMS
MISCELLANEOUS JIBBER JABBER

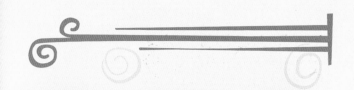

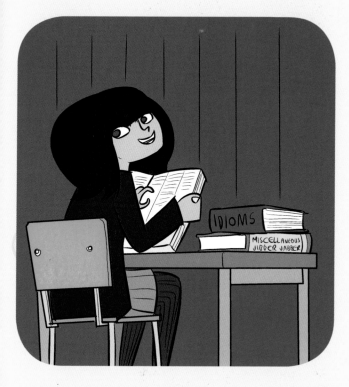

I am given to understand (hem hem) that this book may be read around the world. To assist my new, international friends, here is a list of the words, phrases and concepts used in the book what you might find well alien and weird. I've explained them pretty well, I think you will find.

LOVE,
Charlotte
XXX

Big School: There are two "tiers" to the UK education system, 4-11 and 11-16 or 18 if you hang around. Really it should be tears not tiers because you are gonna know terror at how much bigger kids can be than you. Middle schools were tried but considered "too nice" and "weakening to the mind."

Plops: "manure" is the polite way to say it maybe?

Rugby School: A school where they play rugby not soccer-style football. Schools what put on airs and graces. Flipping heck it is just running around with balls, get over yourselves.

Cricket: Mystifying game where even fans do not understand most rules and games can last five days. More polite than other sports?

V. U.

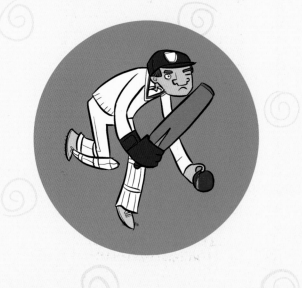

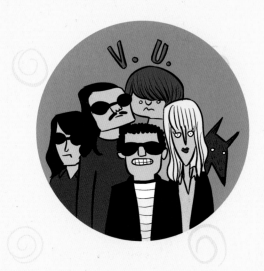

The Velvet Underground: The most frightening group of musical people ever assembled. Recruited from prison or so I heard.

Nuffink: The way you say "nothing" if you were dragged up rather than brought up.

WORR: Just a sound you make when something is pretty good. Very versatile I would say. (Also "worrrrr" or "wor.")

Lithium: A sort of metal that cheers you up I think? You probably shouldn't eat it raw.

Zine: A magazine that under normal circumstances would not be considered good enough to a. read or b. buy but people persist anyway because it is fun.

Pie: In Great Britain pies are usually savoury, it is just our way, we eat the other kind but only on special occasions e.g. Queen's birthday, national whipped cream surplus.

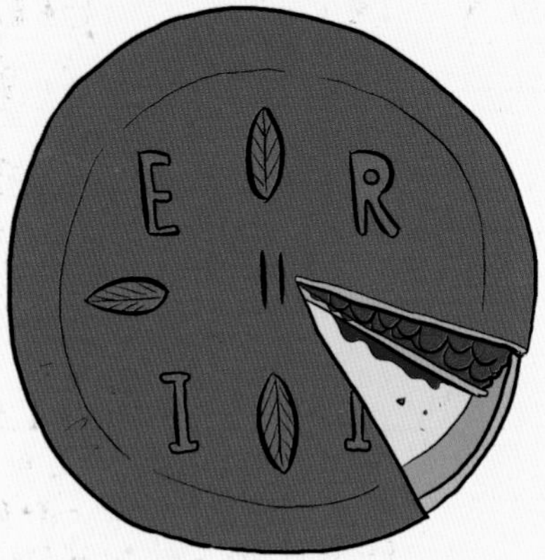

Diggers: Those yellow trucks with an arm that digs deep holes in the living earth, what are you, two years old? Keep up.

Football Ground: The stadium. A big old waste of seats and grass if you ask me but I suppose that you aren't (asking) so never mind.

Mutually Assured Mutual Conference Division 2: The football league tables in England are named and numbered in such a way as to keep newcomers to the game guessing. The selection of a cryptic sponsor really helps the process. The top league should be called something like "the Premierity", then the second one is "the Deluxe Parade" and then the third is "Division One" and the fourth perhaps "Stage Two (North)." Remember, they are just kicking an old ball about. They have to dress it up or no one would show up to watch.

Dribble: Drool. Also, kick an old ball about.

Local Newspaper: newspaper about your town, telling you how a local man stole four bags of charcoal from a supermarket.

Brass Monkeys: The full phrase is that it is "cold enough to freeze the balls off a brass monkey," but that is pretty rude you will agree. The vicar would not like it.

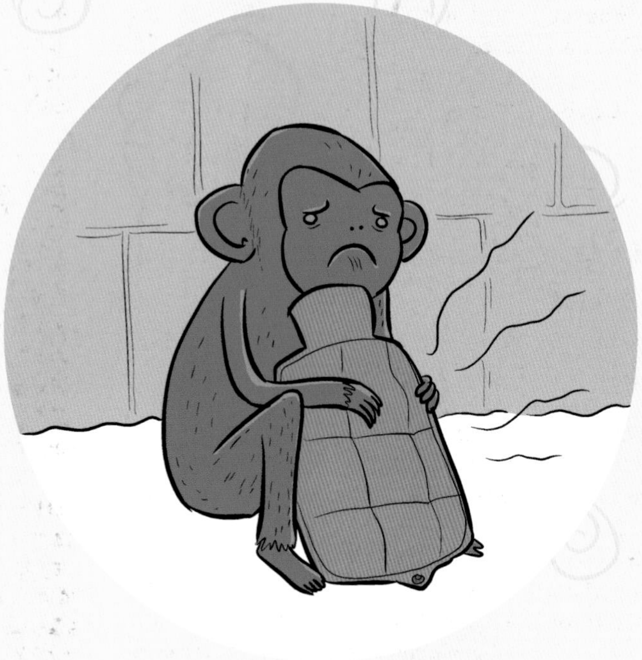

Sorreh: The way you say "sorry" if you were dragged up rather than brought up.

The Milk Cup: Apparently people in the 1980s were so bored of football that it had to be sponsored by the second least interesting drink (after water.) This really happened.

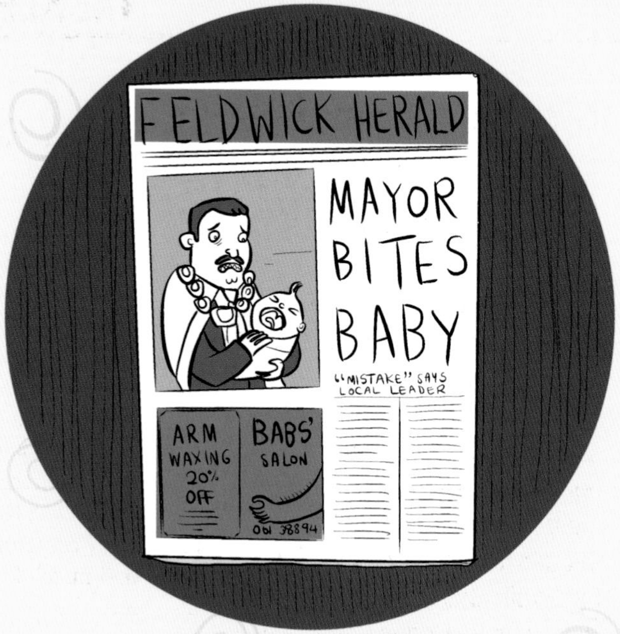
FELDWICK HERALD
MAYOR BITES BABY
"MISTAKE" SAYS LOCAL LEADER
ARM WAXING 20% OFF
BABS' SALON

The lads played their hearts out: Football men have special phrases they are taught to say on television because they didn't pay any attention in school. This is the best one. If they really played their hearts out, they would all be in hospital.

Biscuit: What you have at four o'clock with your tea slash coffee drink. Like a cookie invented in a world without luxury. Different from the American biscuit which is a savoury scone that has been drowned in gravy for its crimes.

Buffers: The very old.

Pudding: Dessert. The most important meal of the day.

Bursting: Piddle crisis point.

Tackleford City is a club with a history reaching back more than 100 years. For the last century, City have prided themselves on "football played the right way."

Many players have passed through the club, not to mention managers, coaches, team doctors, bus drivers, ball boys, groundskeepers, board members and kit-men. But the most important people to pass through the great gates of the Fig Roll Stadium (previously Wasp's Nest Cottage) are you, the fans.

In this brief guide, it was necessary to miss out many moments that fans will remember fondly. But in the space allowed, we've tried to bring you the pivotal events that have made this football club famous and beloved world-wide.

Written in the news clippings collected here are the foundation stones of "a gilded history". I certainly enjoyed my trip down "memory lane", and I hope you do too! I'm proud to have played for, managed, and eventually provided janitorial services for, the greatest club on earth.

Brian Nuttall
October 2009

October 4, 1912

Association football finally comes to Tackleford

FOLLOWING A RELAXATION of the strict town by-laws, the newly formed Tackleford City Association Football Club played their first ever home game this afternoon, an exhibition match against Pendlebury & Rasmond Colliery.

The match was a 5-5 tie, with Reggie Dimmock bagging all five for the visitors and Jimmy Brett, Walpole McGinty (2) and Edgar Storch (2) replying for Tackleford.

This first match for the city's newly-formed football club was cause for great celebration in the pubs and cafés of Tackleford. Men and women, boys and girls poured out onto the streets, keen to see the game played at last by local lads. Due to the enthusiastic haste with which the game had been arranged, no "pitch" had been secured, so the match was played in the ancient style, with stone goalmouths erected at the city's most northerly and southerly points.

While the initial passages of the game were chaotic, and goals looked unlikely, the locals (and a large travelling contingent from Pendlebury) aligned themselves with the teams, swelling each to around 75 men, and the match was played along the two miles of Main Street for four and three-quarter hours.

Pendlebury & Rasmond coach Ted Bentham declared the game "the stuff of great human endeavour," over meat pies and gravy served at St Austwick's church that evening.

July 18, 1915

First match at Wasp's Nest

HAVING PLAYED THEIR first season in the Second Division on marshland, Tackleford City finally have a purpose-built stadium from which to launch their aspirations to top-flight association football.

But the move to the luxurious new Wasp's Nest Cottage ground, paid for by the City Trust, has not proved popular with the players, many of whom preferred the club's previous home on the marshes.

"Teams didn't like playing us on the marshes," said centre-back Humbert Jones. "While it was difficult to play on that surface, we were used to it. Once you'd learned where the quagmires and water pits were, you could play around them."

"We could usually rely on the opposition losing at least a couple of players to broken legs or trench foot."

It was the disappearance of Wanderers and England outside-right Walter Hayes during a particularly foggy night game that lead Tackleford City to abandon their home on Hamble Moor. The new ground will provide terraced standing for 30,000 and offer top-line health and training facilities to the team.

"We're leading the way in cleanliness," said City Trust chairman Alan Gough. "Dirt is the number one cause of goals conceded. If a player is caked in filth, how can his team-mates tell who they're playing to?"

To that end, a 13-man bath, the first of its kind, has been installed in a purpose-built hut behind the stands. Bars of soap have been provided by local disinfectant manufacturer Wallis Hornbeam & Sons, and the local Women's Institute have supplied monogrammed towels for all first team players.

IN THE NEWS

• Lord Sunderland's Sunderland FC dominated English football throughout the 1910s and '20s. Only the death of Lord Sunderland himself, trampled by the King's horse during a tragic game of polo, ended their run. Without his guiding genius, they faded from view.

• In the early days of the professional game, many players "doubled up", playing different sports on other nights of the week. It was not uncommon for a footballer to represent his local area in cricket, lacrosse, or kabaddi.

• The most notorious game of the 1920s was the 'Horrible Final' between Leyton Orient and Bognor FC, where the King's horse broke loose onto the pitch mid-game, carrying the powerless-to-resist monarch with it. The two teams' players, feeling unable to run away without the King's permission, allowed themselves to be trampled into the soggy earth by the mad beast.

April 26, 1924

"Fabulous Swami" proves too much for Sunderland

VISITORS SUNDERLAND were put to the sword on Saturday after a virtuoso performance by Tackleford City in the FA Cup Final.

Sunderland, unbeaten in 21 games, started the game well, but proved no match for Empire signing Sanjay Rhamaswami, whose unconventional playing style helped City secure a 4-0 win.

"Swami", hailed by City manager Bert Best as "a decent enough fellow once you spend time with him," astonished the opposing team by floating over the pitch, shooting an eerie green ray from an emerald on his turban, vanishing only to appear on a completely different part of the pitch moments later, and scoring a penalty in the 54th minute following a goalmouth foul on City full-back Paul Barrington.

City's other goals came from Don Hardwyck, Dennis Andrews and Mr Watson. Sunderland's best chance came when their star forward Bob Kelly broke through City's defence, but he was distracted by Swami's suddenly red, glowing eyes, and failed to convert the opportunity.

Sunderland chairman Lord Sunderland is understood to be asking for a replay. "These foreign footballers are spoiling the game. Sooner or later the rules of association football must be written down somewhere."

TACKLEFORD CITY FOOTBALL CLUB - "A GILDED HISTORY"

March 19, 1942

Makeshift player makes fine debut

AS THE WAR IN Europe and beyond drags on, Tackleford City's participation in the Northern League has been continually hampered by lack of manpower, with most able-bodied men stationed abroad fighting the Axis powers.

However, Bulldog Bobby spirit and good old British innovation were to the fore as City introduced their newest recruit, "Rufus X-15", an entirely mechanical player constructed from reclaimed crashed aeroplane parts.

"Rufus may represent the future of the game," said interim City coach Don Dickens. "He only needs a quart of petrol and a squeeze of oil and he'll run for 90 minutes."

Dickens, whose dropped arches and fancy ways made him unsuitable for service in battle, has made his name with a series of innovations on and off the pitch. Wasp's Nest Cottage is the only stadium in the country with radar, ground-to-air munitions, and a cannon generating thick fog should enemies strike from the air.

Rufus X-15 put an astonishing eight goals past Hardwycke FC keeper Ken Best in an 8-0 thrashing that saw City go second in the league, with a game in hand. "He moved so fast," said Best, "his legs were like pistons. In that they were actually driven by pistons. He really kept me on my toes."

A visiting Mr Churchill described the mechanical man as "queer, but oddly exciting."

April 30, 1953

Nuttall's men are champions

A LAST MINUTE header by Ken Toblowsky secured the Division One championship for Tackleford City on the final day of the season, taking them ahead of defending champions Rye Athletic on goal difference.

Player-manager Brian Nuttall, who replaced the late Austin Mansfield as team boss mid-season, put the late run down to "grit and heart." The team's victory may also be due to the return of Rufus X-15, discovered in a caretaker's cupboard below the Whittaker Stand, covered in rust and cobwebs.

"There's no discounting Rufus X-15's 61 goals in nine games," said Nuttall, "but this is the story of eleven men, not one man who isn't actually a man, technically speaking."

Nuttall was reluctant to discuss the tin player's fortunes, adding that the wartime hero had "seen better days," and would probably "be sent to the knacker's yard or sold for scrap."

February 1, 1964

Alpine disaster claims keeper

RELIEF AT THE recovery from an avalanche of the train carrying the Tackleford City team in the Alps was tinged with heartbreak, when it was discovered that goalkeeper Lawrence "Fatty" Vickers had died during the week that the locomotive was lost.

"After supplies in the buffet car were exhausted, starvation drove us half-mad," said striker Neil Bosson. "We came together and made a decision. There was more eating on Fatty than on the rest of us put together."

"The choice was simple. Either we ate Fatty, or we ate four other people."

Vickers, who had played for City since 1961/62 and had 8 caps for England, was known for his cat-like agility, far greater than that of other men of his size. He is survived by his wife and six children. Fatty will be replaced in goal on Saturday by reserve keeper "Tiny" Tom Lane.

IN THE NEWS

• Following the war, where regional leagues replaced the usual programme, football got back into its swing with the 1946/7 season. After nearly six years of national unity, many men found it difficult to engage each other in competition. 91% of games in the first post-war season ended in goalless draws.

• There were many innovations in the game during the fifties, and few were more controversial than the "kit wars" of 1958/59. Exploiting lax regulations, teams turned out in ever more outrageous couture, often inspired by the fashions of Paris and Milan. The Football Association stepped in after Leeds Utd took to the pitch for a league cup tie in tin foil dungarees and berets.

• Mechanical player Rufus X-15 was one of the most intriguing figures of the era. He escaped to Switzerland in May 1953 where he managed Neuchâtel Xamax for six successful seasons.

May 1, 1975

Sir Ron steers City to their historic "quadruple" in Milan

AFTER NEARLY TWO decades in the doldrums, few could have predicted that, following a win in the league championship and triumphs in both League and FA Cups, Tackleford City would cap their season with a 4-2 victory over Paris St Germain in the Fairs Cup.

The night was marred in places by City's "tactics", which involved a kind of fierce physicality rarely exercised by teams on the continent.

PSG were unable to play their usual skilful passing game under a volley of sliding tackles, hard-headed jostling, robust language and energetic two-man challenges. After creating an early two-goal lead through Michel Dugarry and Jean le Coq, they wilted under City's relentless pressure and capitulated to quick-fire goals by Smith, Smith, Smith and Susan. The French side struggled after their goalkeeper Leon Potiche fell down a set of stairs at half-time.

Manager Ron Ramsay made no apology after the match for his team's uncompromising style.

"We're not here to play like a bunch of fairies at a tea party," he said. "We're here to win games. If the French don't like it, they're welcome to complain. I doubt anyone will be listening to them carping on."

An open-top bus parade of Tackleford city centre is planned for Friday.

The most feared team of the mid-seventies, in their pomp

TACKLEFORD CITY FOOTBALL CLUB - "A GILDED HISTORY"

October 4, 1978

Ramsay's rein ends after 30 "awful" days

JUST A MONTH after departing Tackleford to become England manager, Ron Ramsey has quit to take up a role as national coach of oil-rich football newcomers Saudi Arabia.

"The move has nothing to do with money," said Ramsay, rumoured to be receiving a golden palace and an obsidian limousine alongside a £1 million-per-year salary. "England are an unmanageable team."

Ramsay, who lead City to nine trophies in four years, declared the England players "an utter shambles" to reporters from all over the world at a press conference in Jeddah.

"Modern players are more interested in combing their hair than they are winning games," he blasted, "they'd rather be appearing on tea-time television than mastering performing a roundhouse kick while the referee's back is turned."

"Kenny Jones might be the most talented dribbler of the ball since the days of Arthur Clackett, but he's no idea how to snap another man's cruciate ligament during a mid-air fight for the ball. Modern players just don't have it. I've had an awful time."

"The Saudis are going to change football overnight," he declared.

Dismissing the cream of English talent as "a shower, a pathetic shower," Ramsay departed the press conference throwing gold coins at the assembled reporters, before being sped away by two sheiks wearing sunglasses.

March 28, 1985

Plucky Tackleford steal Milk Cup from Totley Town

A DECADE AFTER they won four trophies in the famous "quadruple season", Tackleford City finally have a new piece of silverware on the shelf.

An extra-time goal from Norman Cresswell secured a 3-2 League Cup Sponsored By Milk win for a side whose fortunes have greatly diminished since their days as the powerhouse of English football in the mid-seventies.

The board's refusal to replace Ron Ramsay lead to three successive relegations from 1979 to 1981, with a new manager only being sought as the team faced ejection from the league in the spring of 1982. Then-chairman Ted Spofforth notoriously turned up for work in pyjamas and slippers for months at a time, becoming renowned for crying during board meetings.

Fans, bereft at the loss of their iconic manager, took to wearing black and refused to celebrate the scoring of goals, often turning their backs on the pitch and sobbing.

It was only a new generation of players, all of whom were drawn from outside the club's grief-stricken youth team, who managed to save the club from vanishing altogether.

"There's a new spirit at the club," said Cresswell. "If the gaffer sees anyone weeping uncontrollably in the dressing room, we whips them with a wet towel. Things are looking up."

August 16, 1994

"Team of the nineties" powers back into top flight

AFTER COMING CLOSE to promotion over the last three years, Tackleford City begin their first Thompson's Menswear Premiership campaign at Finsbury Park FC today.

City will be the last team promoted using the controversial "montessori system", which was abandoned at the end of the last season.

The complicated formula combining matches won and drawn, goal difference, charitable work, player politeness and a written examination was introduced in 1992 by European football chiefs, but produced some very unreliable results.

Clubs complained that the ability to factor in the chart position of pop recordings made by first team players encouraged sides to spend too long in the recording studio. City midfielder Carl Patterson's "Baby, I Think I'm In Love With You" spent two months in the singles top ten in March, easing Tackleford back into football's elite.

"Carl's disappointed that his golden throat can't help the lads any more," said manager Brian Bassett. "But he's going to keep working on his songs. He's excited about making music."

July 11, 2007

Chastened City face bankruptcy

AFTER EIGHT YEARS of wild, profligate spending, Tackleford City were declared bankrupt today.

Citing ever-rising wage bills, the failure of expensive £20 million transfers Luciano Bosma from FC Dubrovnik and Terry Timms from Grimethorpe, City were issued with a winding-up order by administrators at 10am today.

Investors heard how a culture of lavish parties, with caviar, dwarves on horseback, witch doctors, high-kicking chorus girls and moustachio'd sharpshooters, had drained the northern club's cash reserves.

"We've made mistakes," said outgoing chairman Rod Wainwright. "But we had a good time. Good lord, we had one hell of a good time."

IN THE NEWS

• After the hooliganism and violence of the 1980s, football got back on its feet in the nineties. Billionaire team owners like Sir Ledley Egg (Peckham Forest), Dame Lucille le Havre (Cheshunt Rangers) and Henry Fox (FC Yorkshire Force) pushed player prices - and attendances - ever higher with their deep pockets. le Havre was frowned upon for "buying the title" in 1994, but the league championship has now not been held by a traditional "pauper" team since Wrexham Rovers triumphed in 1996/7.

• The influx of cash into football meant that many foreign superstars were lured to England's shores by the promise of gold. Not all of them proved successful. Signed by league-leaders Harrogate West FC, Spanish striker Juan Costas ended his debut season living in a caravan in his club's car park.

• In 1999, the Queen's horse was allowed into Wembley for the FA Cup Final. This proved to be a very costly and dangerous mistake.

August 9, 2007

New owner: "trophies or else" for City

NEW OWNER YURI Kropotkin, who bought Tackleford City for £1 this morning, has set his sights on "trophies or else" in the new season.

"This is a family club, but the team must play well. If they do not, I fire them, get new team. Manager fails, I fire him, get new manager. No one is safe. We must win all the cups."

However, despite City's slide into financial ruin, billionaire Kropotkin sees no reason to rein in the organisation's more flamboyant side.

"Caviar, dwarves on horseback, witch doctors, high-kicking chorus girls and moustachio'd sharpshooters are all welcome here. Man is on earth for only short time. It must be a good time. Otherwise why live at all?"

"Our lads will win on the pitch by day and spend their nights in luxurious ecstacy. It is only right."

OTHER BOOKS FROM ONI PRESS!

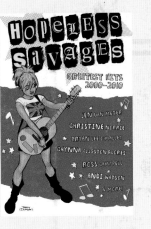

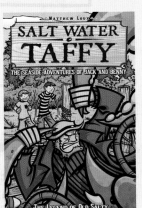

COURTNEY CRUMRIN, VOLUME 1:
THE NIGHT THINGS
By Ted Naifeh
136 pages, hardcover, full color
ISBN 978-1-934964-77-4

CROGAN'S VENGEANCE
By Chris Schweizer
192 pages, hardcover, black and white
ISBN 978-1-934964-06-4

HOPELESS SAVAGES:
GREATEST HITS 2000-2010
By Jen Van Meter, Christine Norrie,
Bryan Lee O'Malley, Andi Watson,
Chynna Clugston Flores,
Ross Campbell, & More
392 pages, digest, black and white
ISBN 978-1-934964-48-4

GLITTER KISS
By Adrianne Ambrose &
Monica Gallagher
176 pages, 6x9, black and white
ISBN 978-1-62010-082-0

MERMIN, BOOK 1:
A FISH OUT OF WATER
By Joey Weiser
152 pages, 6x9 hardcover, full color
ISBN 978-1-934964-98-9

PLAY BALL
By Nunzio DeFilippis, Christina Weir, &
Jackie Lewis
152 pages, 6x9 hardcover, black and white
ISBN 978-1-934964-79-8

POSSESSIONS, BOOK 1:
UNCLEAN GETAWAY
By Ray Fawkes
88 pages, 6x9, two-color
ISBN 978-1-934964-36-1

SALT WATER TAFFY, VOLUME 1:
THE LEGEND OF OLD SALTY
By Matthew Loux
96 pages, digest, black and white
ISBN 978-1-932664-94-2

SCOTT PILGRIM, VOLUME 1:
PRECIOUS LITTLE LIFE
By Bryan Lee O'Malley
192 pages, 6x9 hardcover, full color
ISBN 978-1-62010-000-4

BAD MACHINERY™

THE CASE OF THE GOOD BOY

Coming Soon!